The Command Decisions Series

• VOLUME 6 •
Human Factors

The Command Decisions Series • Volume 6

Human Factors
The Forces Within

Richard L. Taylor

Belvoir Publications, Inc.
Greenwich, Connecticut

Also by Richard L. Taylor

IFR for VFR Pilots: An Exercise in Survival
Understanding Flying
Instrument Flying
Fair-Weather Flying
Recreational Flying
Positive Flying (with William Guinther)
The First Flight
Pilot's Audio Update (Editor)

ISBN: 1-879620-09-X

Printed and bound in the United States of America by Arcata Graphics, Fairfield, Pennsylvania.

Contents

Preface 6

Part 1. Pilot Judgment and Attitude 8

Part 2. The Pilot's Age 42

Part 3. The Pilot's Vision 48

Part 4. The Pilot's Hearing 78

Part 5. The Stress Factor 104

Part 6. The Fatigue Factor 122

Part 7. Hypoxia and Hyperventilation 142

Part 8. Illusions and Spatial Disorientation 154

Part 9. Alcohol, Drugs, and Medications 172

Part 10. Pilot Error 198

Index 219

Preface

Homo sapiens, the most highly developed earth-dweller, got that way through a complex arrangement of senses, intelligence, emotions and personality. Unlike machines—predictable, precise, replicable—human beings possess a unique capability to alter circumstances, to take actions that may be totally illogical and fly in the face of convention.

The combination of factors that make us human provides a wide range of responses to situations that show up in everyday life...and particularly to those we encounter in aviation. "Human factors"—sights, sounds, physical and mental condition, age, fatigue, personal habits, the list goes on and on—leave their mark on virtually every aircraft accident. If we intend to understand mishaps with a view toward preventing repetition in our own experience, we need to have a good handle on the human factors involved; that's the objective of this volume of the *Command Decisions Series*.

An accident several years ago in the Southwest illustrates how human factors can complicate an otherwise routine flight operation.

A pilot young in aeronautical experience (total time less than 300 hours, private pilot certification just a few months before, no instrument rating) arrived at the factory in Texas to pick up a brand-new single-engine airplane for his flying club. The planned itinerary included a visit to Las Vegas as part of the return trip to New Jersey.

The pilot's day began with a 5:30 a.m. airline flight from Newark to San Antonio, where he was picked up in the new airplane for the short trip to the factory. Although he had never flown this make and model before, the pilot turned down the customary checkout and headed for Las Vegas, five hours away.

It was now almost 10 p.m. MST, and the pilot had been up for at least 19 hours...the most sleep he could have gotten would have been a few hours on the airliner. Nevertheless, he refueled and departed Sky Harbor Airport, but got only seven miles away...the airplane crashed in a residential area and killed the pilot, having fallen out of the sky in a spin, according to eyewitnesses.

Post-accident investigation revealed no evidence of failure or malfunction of the airplane or its systems, leaving only the pilot as the primary suspect in causing the accident.

This situation fairly screams "human factors!" Fatigue—perhaps even profound fatigue—must have been at work to cloud this pilot's normal thought processes and derogate his motor skills; visual illusions may have been present as the result of flying from a brightly lighted urban environment toward a pitch-black background of desert and mountains; the sights, sounds and feels of an unfamiliar airplane may have had a hand in the outcome, and certainly, a strong case can be made for the insidious effects of "get-home-itis"—the sometimes uncontrollable urge to complete a flight, no matter what. It's difficult to imagine a pilot in his right mind accepting such a high-risk operation; remember that this was a night VFR flight in a strange single-engine airplane over some pretty inhospitable country, with no flight plan.

Some, one, or all of the factors we just mentioned must have blinded him to everything but "getting there," and you could speculate until the cows come home with no completely satisfactory answer to the question "why?"

There are so many possible combinations of human factors that we can only make you aware of some facts and knowledgeable theories concerning the major areas of concern; we leave the application of this information to, well, your best judgment.

We hope that when (not "if" but when) you are confronted with a situation in which that small voice is trying to tell you something about the flight operation upcoming, you will recall something you've read here, and make a good decision accordingly.

We have arranged this volume of the *Command Decisions Series* toward that end, with sections on each of the prominent, identifiable human factors; whenever possible, we've included reports of mishaps that point out where *homo sapiens*—that's all of us, none are immune—might have come up short.

Richard Taylor
Dublin, Ohio
October 1, 1991

1 Pilot Judgment and Attitude

The aviation community is no doubt going to be inundated with studies and training theories as the researchers continue their attempts to figure out exactly why pilots do some of the things they do, and why they don't do some of the things they should.

In addition to the obvious concern about flying safety, this interest in judgment and attitude seems to have grown from a reluctance to continue blaming the pilot—unconditionally—for virtually every accident. It's no longer good enough to attribute mishaps to "pilot error" without digging a lot deeper to find out why pilots behave as they do.

Most pilots recognize that along with the freewheeling nature of general aviation comes the responsibility to exercise good judgment, and to maintain a positive attitude toward flying safety. They conduct themselves with a prudence born of respect for the challenges of flying. They choose not to fly when the weather is beyond their abilities, when the airplane is not up to the task, or the pilot is not at his peak of competence and fitness.

But some pilots, whether due to lack of proper training, a fundamental naivete concerning the dangers of aviation, or perhaps a momentary submission to peer pressure or self-image, undertake to fly when all good judgment augurs against it.

It often seems that once this first misjudgment is made, others follow from it in an inevitable stream. In many years of accident reporting, we have encountered countless cases where the investigator commented, "There are times when you just wish you could have tapped the pilot on the shoulder and said, 'Think for a moment about what you intend to do. Isn't it a little foolish? Can I convince you to stay on the ground?' But if he's a licensed pilot, he's free to make the mistake; we can't stop him. We can't legislate common sense."

Nowhere is the problem of undeveloped aeronautical judgment more critical than in the case of the newly licensed pilot. Prior to gaining his license, he was not free; his instructor made nearly every decision for him. The day after gaining his license, he is free to fly from New York to San Francisco if he chooses. If he wanted to set out on that trip in marginal VFR weather, he legally could. And if he had the required three hours of night experience and stayed out of Special VFR situations, he could make the trip at night. Only the pilot's own "little birdie" perched on his shoulder can dissuade him from making the attempt.

Perhaps a coast-to-coast marginal VFR trip at night is an outlandish extreme, but a new private pilot's domain of freedom lies somewhere between this and not flying at all.

These issues come to mind in reviewing the crash of a Piper Archer in the early hours of an April morning at Lakeland, Florida. Two of the three persons aboard died from injuries sustained when the plane struck powerlines in the fog not far from Lakeland Airport. The pilot survived, but with serious injuries. Had someone tapped him on the shoulder, he now tells us, he might not have gone flying that night.

'PIPER CLUB'

Lakeland was, at the time of the accident, the home of a division of Piper Aircraft Corporation. As part of a program to encourage employees to learn to fly, Piper made available certain of its aircraft in a kind of "company airplane club," run in a manner similar to many other clubs throughout the country. Employee-members of the club instruct the novitiates, and in due course when they earn their licenses, they are at liberty to sign out aircraft from the "club" fleet.

Timothy A. Boyd had such privileges. As an employee of Piper who had earned his private ticket a week and a half earlier, the 21-year-old production line assistant foreman was the proud owner of a Piper "airman card" showing he was qualified to fly Tomahawks and Archers. His logbook showed a total of 69 hours, including 5.3 hours of night time, 2.1 hours of simulated instruments, and 5.2 hours in the Archer. After

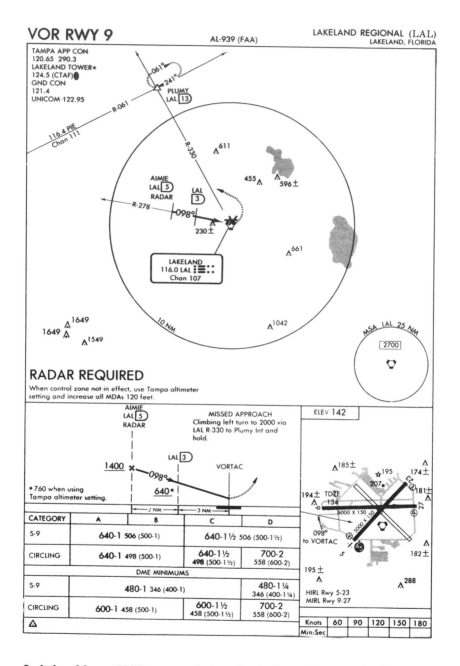

Lakeland has a VOR approach, but the Archer pilot never bothered to ask Tampa approach for assistance in flying it. Instead, he flew his own version of the approach, eventually crashing into powerlines.

4.2 hours of dual in the Archer, he had flown it 1.0 hour solo prior to the night of the crash.

Donald J. Hebert was a 25-year-old student pilot and also a Piper assistant foreman. Hebert, flying mainly in Tomahawks, had logged 25 total hours, 2.0 of them solo, all in the past three months. He had logged no night or instrument time. Steven L. Asbury, 23, also a Piper employee, was said to be a student pilot, but NTSB records do not show his flight time (he occupied a rear seat in the Archer).

LET'S GO FLYING AFTER WORK

The three worked an evening shift at Piper, which resulted in them getting off work at 1 a.m. on April 2. It should be noted that a person on an evening shift typically adapts to a schedule of waking up in mid-afternoon, going to work after dinner, leaving the job at quitting time and being awake for several more hours thereafter. It is a rare individual who can go home and go directly to sleep just after work; most need time to "wind down" from their labors. What a "day person" might feel like doing at 5 p.m., a "night person" feels like doing at 2 or 3 a.m.

So the three friends planned to go flying after work. Boyd, as the licensed pilot, would act as pilot in command. And since Boyd was aware of a Piper "club" rule that barred members from leaving the Lakeland pattern at night unless they had instrument ratings, Boyd said all the three planned to do was shoot touch-and-goes for an hour or so.

Normally, a pilot might have to schedule a club airplane in advance to prevent conflicts with other club members, but Boyd knew at night there wouldn't be any need. He could just arrive at the field and sign out the Archer.

TEMPTATION

There was no rush, and Boyd's companions suggested they stop off at a local tavern before flying. This they did. Boyd said he went with them but had nothing alcoholic to drink. In support of this, a Piper employee who had been in the tavern submitted a written statement, and NTSB's investigators said other witnesses present agreed that no one had seen Boyd drinking alcohol. Boyd said his two friends "were trying to get me to have a drink, but I never did go ahead and take one." According to Boyd, the two companions consumed about three beers each. Boyd also said at no time did the two show signs of intoxication, such as slurring their words or having trouble walking.

WEATHER

It had been a calm, clear Florida spring evening, but Lakeland is not far from the state's west coast, and it often occurs that low fog develops along the coast and creeps inland, getting thickest just before dawn and "burning off" after sunrise. This was to be such an evening.

It was a dark, moonless night, but just after 1 a.m. before entering the tavern, Boyd could see that it was clear and the stars were out. For this reason, he told us, he had no reason to call the local FSS or file a flight plan.

At 2 a.m., the three friends headed for the airport. At about 2:15 a.m., Boyd signed out Archer N8235H. It only took a moment to show the night security guard his card, and Boyd had an airplane. The guard, of course, had no grounds to question whether Boyd was competent to fly that night. In his own report, the guard did remark that conditions appeared to be VFR at the time the aircraft was signed out.

Now, Boyd noticed some cloudiness, but reckoned it was above 1,500 feet, so it would not be a problem. And besides, he could always complete a circuit of the pattern and land if the weather was worse, he figured.

However, the three did not immediately take off. The airplane was low on fuel. So they got the local fuel truck and put some 100LL aboard. Boyd said because the truck pumped so slowly, they did not top off the tanks, but filled each within about five gallons of the top. (Investigators therefore surmise the Archer had about 37 gallons aboard at takeoff, or enough for nearly four hours of flying.)

Boyd and Hebert conducted a thorough preflight, too, he told investigators. All this took time. In addition, Boyd told us, the plane's windows were covered with dew when they set out from the tie-down area, and so he did not get a good look at the sky. It was thus 2:45 a.m. before Boyd got into takeoff position, and there had been enough time for the weather picture to change dramatically.

Boyd was in the left front seat, Hebert in the right (Boyd

would refer to him as the "copilot"), and Asbury in the aft seat when the plane started down Lakeland's runway 5. The Archer had climbed to about 600 feet when it entered fog.

ON THE GAUGES

Boyd immediately went on instruments, as his training dictated. He kept the airplane climbing straight ahead, well under control, and was rewarded when the Archer broke out on top at about 2,000 feet. At this point, he said, "We stabilized there for a while," thinking about what next to do.

It is quite common for people under stress to have a compressed notion of elapsed time. It also is common after an airplane accident for a pilot to have no memory of events just prior to impact. These two factors combined in Boyd, so that the ensuing period can only be related in general terms, with inherent contradictions.

For instance, Boyd would later tell investigators that they had only been above the fog a short time when Hebert contacted Tampa Approach for weather information. Boyd estimated this occurred at about 3:15 a.m. In actual fact, Tampa Approach logged the call at 4:25 a.m.

So the events of the two hours from takeoff to crash cannot be related precisely, except to say that Boyd and Hebert proceeded to make perhaps seven or eight attempts to execute what amounts to a homemade VOR approach to Lakeland. From the first of these tries shortly before 3 a.m., until the moment of impact at 4:48 a.m., the Archer made pass after pass over Lakeland. Ground witnesses recall hearing an airplane make at least five passes over the general vicinity of the airport.

To paraphrase what Boyd told investigators, they dialed in a likely radial, flew it until the VOR indicator flipped, passed outbound and took note of the time, then turned and flew inbound, descending for the airport when they estimated they were back near the VOR.

During each attempt, Boyd would fly the instruments and Hebert would watch for runway lights or other ground contact. Boyd would descend to 500 feet (or later, 400 to 350 feet) each time, he told investigators, then level off and then climb back up. He found he didn't need to go back to 2,000 feet. "I was roughly staying around 1,500 after I got used to it," he said. And he said he was careful to keep his climbs and descents straight ahead, performing turns only after levelling at altitude.

This activity essentially proceeded until at last the Archer contacted powerlines and crashed. Boyd to this day cannot recall the last approach, or the impact, or post-crash events until he woke up in the hospital.

Investigators pieced together wreckage evidence to show that the Archer was probably at full power (suggestive of a go-around) in approximately straight and level flight when its left wing struck a powerline pole at about 40 feet AGL.

The plane continued through three seven-eighths inch high-tension wires attached to the pole. It carried on through the air about 250 feet and then hit a fence on the far side of a road, impacting on the left side of the fuselage and the nose. The plane now cartwheeled and shed pieces, the major part of the fuselage ultimately coming to rest another 100 feet farther away. Propeller and engine damage, a small brush fire after impact and similar evidence indicate that the airplane probably still had ample fuel aboard. No pre-impact malfunction of the airplane was discovered.

Boyd was found alive in the wreckage, Hebert was dead and Asbury, critically injured, died four days after the crash without regaining consciousness.

Airport Environment

Lakeland is a large, well-maintained municipal airport with reasonably good facilities. It has three runways, none of which is less than 5,000 feet long. It lies in generally flat country. It has a VOR on the field, situated a few hundred yards to the right of runway 5. Lakeland has a control tower, but it closes at 6 p.m. Thereafter, the field is uncontrolled, but instrument approaches can be conducted through Tampa Approach Control.

Runway 5 is also the lighted runway, and the lights are left on all night. And besides the two VOR approaches serving the field, there is an ILS system for runway 5, which is also left on. Published field elevation is 142 feet MSL. Piper's facilities lie on the southern side of the airport, and a large lighted sign faces the runways.

Some of this information was beyond Boyd's ken. He was

only vaguely aware of what an ILS was, and did not realize there was a system serving runway 5, nor would he have known how to tune it in, he told us. He had neither approach plates nor charts in the airplane.

He did know where the VOR was in relation to the runway. He had what might be described as a rudimentary knowledge of VOR navigation. Interviews with investigators were taped. Here is an excerpt from the interviews:

Question: Did you have the OBS—do you know what the OBS is?

Answer: The OBS? What's the OBS?

Question: Some places it's called the CDI—course deviation indicator—where you set in a radial, you know, and your needle will swing either to the right or to the left?

Answer: Well, we had this in the field, whatever it is. You've got a round compass, right? And all we've got is a round compass which we turn around and it shows us what radial we're on and it shows the TO and FROM, the radial extending from the field, or for going to the field on this radial, and that's all we had in the aircraft.

Question: You were following the inbound radial to runway 5?

Answer: I was, to a certain extent, but then once I knew that I was getting close, I knew that the radial that I was following would be off a little bit from the radial....now that I'm thinking about it, I was having it set up with runway 5, so I was setting it to radial 5, so I should be coming in parallel with the runway. But like I said, whenever I got close to the field, I just knew that I was there and I had to look around for visual effects—I mean, like the runway, the lights."

Although Boyd believed it was the 050-degree radial he was following, he couldn't remember precisely. In the wreckage, investigators found the OBS on the 040-degree radial. The radio was tuned to 116.0 MHz on the nav and 120.65 on the comm. The transponder was set to 1200 and operational at the time of the crash.

Boyd also said he had adjusted his altimeter to the

*After striking powerlines, the Archer cartwheeled before coming to
rest. The pilot survived, but one of the two passengers was killed on
impact; the second died later.*

Lakeland field elevation before takeoff. This he stated was
144 feet; published field elevation is 142. This was not
considered to be a major discrepancy. Investigators found the
altimeter adjusted to 30.10 inches of mercury, which was
consistent with area barometric observations at the time of
the crash, and the altimeter was therefore believed to have
been reading close to the correct altitude.

Boyd said he was aware of a large water tower south of the
field, and he was making sure he didn't hit that. He would
normally only go down to 500 feet on his approaches, but on
perhaps two occasions he went to 400 or 350 feet, he said. This
would have kept him at about 200 feet AGL; he now concedes
he could not have hit the powerline if this were so.

But investigators noted that, despite what may seem an
imprecise piece of navigating, Boyd did arrive at a point only
a mile short and slightly to the right of the runway 5
threshold, on a course that would have taken him approximately down the 050-degree radial to the VOR. The powerline and fence struck by the Archer are along a road which
forms the airport boundary. The crash area was within sight
of the Piper plant, had anyone been able to see that far.

Investigators estimate the weather at the time of impact was an indefinite ceiling 200 feet obscured, visibility one-half mile in fog.

One more piece from the record is the transcript of the 4:25 a.m. call to Tampa Approach. Here is the total conversation:

Pilot: Tampa Approach, this is Archer 8235H. Can you give us a weather report, please? We're over Lakeland.

ATC: Archer 35H, affirmative. Where are you landing?

Pilot: Lakeland.

ATC: I have no weather reported from the Lakeland area, sir. The weather in the Tampa area...Tampa, St. Petersburg, MacDill is IFR.

Pilot: Three five hotel.

As had been forecast, low fog was covering the area. Observations at Tampa and the other fields included indefinite 300-foot ceilings. On the other hand, fields some distance away to the east, airports such as Ft. Lauderdale, were reporting clear skies.

Haunting Question

The facts speak adequately to the first and foremost analytical question about this accident: Why did Boyd undertake to fly that night? He believed the weather was good (good enough that he didn't need to call Flight Service); he had the license and experience to fly at night; he would only be flying the Lakeland pattern. He was mistaken in his judgment of conditions.

But a much more enigmatic question arises to haunt Boyd and investigators alike: Why didn't he choose an alternative course? Why didn't he go east to a clear airport? Why didn't he actively seek help; why didn't he initiate emergency procedures? What kept him doggedly trying to get into Lakeland? We believe the answer is probably unattainable, but if it could be found, it would surely be the sum of many parts.

Boyd told us he had gone on a flight with one of his three primary instructors in rain and scud to expose him to the hazards of bad weather. But that flight was conducted in the daytime, and conditions were not strictly IFR. He also had practiced some "under the hood" flying and had been given training on recovery from unusual attitudes. These pieces of experience may have had both positive and negative influences when it came to the accident flight, he told us.

On the one hand, when he entered the fog, he immediately went on instruments and maintained good control of the aircraft. He had come away from training with the realization that, were the airplane to "get away" from him due to distractions while on instruments, he might never recover. So he kept his eyes on the horizon and DG, fearing even to look over to tune the radio; he had Hebert perform this task. So far as he can recall, his control of the aircraft was excellent.

But on the other hand, it left him with little ability to pay attention to anything else. And as time wore on, flying the gauges was becoming a severe strain.

"It's one thing to be under the hood for a few minutes with an instructor and you can see a little bit of the horizon out of the corner of your eye and you can always take the hood off. It's a whole different feeling when you can't see anything outside the windows and you turn on the landing light and it reflects back at you. And you just have to concentrate on the instruments. I could control the aircraft, but it took a lot of concentration," Boyd told us.

A second factor might be fear. Boyd agreed he was frightened upon entering the fog, and from then on. "But it was a kind of controlled-scared," he said.

Another factor might be peer pressure. Boyd told us he feels he was the pilot in command and he made decisions based on his own judgment, but he agreed that Hebert had at least an influence. Indeed, it should be noted that Don Hebert had fueled the airplane and filled out the fuel ticket, had helped in the preflight, and had made the flight's only radio call. After the crash, the first person on the scene heard a voice from the wreckage (presumably Boyd's) saying, "Don, get me out of here. Keep calling. Somebody get on the radio."

Boyd said shortly after going into the clouds, he suggested diverting to Tampa. But he said Hebert disagreed with that idea, pointing out that Hebert's wife would have to drive the 30-odd miles to that airport to pick them up.

Later, Boyd said, he did instruct Hebert to call Tampa Approach on the radio. Upon learning that Tampa and vicinity airports were IFR, he did consider going elsewhere. Boyd told us he felt he could capably have gone to Ft. Lauderdale if he had chosen to. He did at least consider declaring an emergency, and he told us he knew how to use emergency frequencies and tune the emergency code on the transponder. But since there was plenty of fuel, this wasn't yet necessary. "When my fuel was getting low, I was going to be left to the factor of doing it, 'cause there was no other way out," he told investigators.

But yet another influence was what we'd call the "just one more try" factor, and this may have been the overriding one. Boyd conceded that on several of the approaches, "you could see lights, but you couldn't tell what they were." However, on several other passes, he recognized when the big Piper plant sign went by. And on the last approach before the crash, he said he sighted the lights at the departure end of runway 5 just as they slid under the nose. This tempted him to try for the runway one more time—with disastrous results.

Prevention

Beyond his injuries, the memory of the accident is something Boyd will have to live with. Moreover, the FAA suspended his license for a year, and he would have to take a flight check with an FAA inspector to regain it. Boyd said he still loves to fly and has done so with other friends, but can't afford the expense to resume his own flying.

Lessons to be Learned

What is the lesson for other pilots? How could this accident have been prevented? In our interview with Boyd, we discerned three possible answers.

First, Boyd suggests that the club ought to have had a rule requiring a certain minimum number of hours—perhaps 100 to 150— before a pilot could take an airplane up at night, even around the pattern, and another rule requiring pilots with less than the minimum to check with an FSS and file a flight plan before every flight.

These are interesting notions, and some clubs have rules along these lines. Others do not, nor is there any federal requirement or even an over-all consensus of what pilots ought to have for experience, beyond the minimums specified in the FARs. And it should be stressed that Piper's club was not unlike many thousands of others, where access to the airplane is relatively easy (in other clubs, members often are handed keys upon joining) and there is no feasible way to enforce any rules which might be made.

Second, Boyd believes that part of the private pilot training experience should include a healthy dose of actual, solid-IFR flying. He said the real thing is so totally unlike the simulation that "I have to agree I was not competent to be doing what I was doing."

Finally, when we asked how Boyd might have reacted to an experienced pilot tapping him on the shoulder that night before the flight, he breathed an empathic sigh. "If anybody had said one word to me about what I was getting into, I sure would have thought twice about doing it," he said.

Whether something in the new pilot's own psyche can be relied on to provide that tap on the shoulder, whether it can be instilled during training, or whether it should come from a rule or regulation is not easy to decide, especially in view of the tradition of American flying freedom. But perhaps someday another pilot will have the opportunity to pass another Tim Boyd at the tie-down, and recognize, and reach out a hand.

Sharing the Risks

Aviation is an on-going study in risk management behavior. Every go/no-go decision involves the explicit recognition of possible risk factors, and an assessment as to whether the risks are manageable and reasonable.

The passengers, unless they're pilots, are rarely consulted. If they were, according to a recent study, they'd vote in favor of sharing the risks equitably rather than exposing any one person to a greater chance of harm—unless, that is, the risk was caused by one person's voluntary exposure to high risk.

The results emerged from a study by two University of California professors who presented volunteers with several scenarios in which they were asked to choose the fairer of two possible actions. One action called for sacrificing an individual's life or safety to save the group; the second action spared the individual but at the cost of increased risk to the group.

In one example, 100 people living on an island were susceptible to a fatal disease. If one of them was given the disease artificially, antibodies from his blood could be used to make serum which would prevent the other 99 from getting sick. Asked to vote, 92 percent of those tested said that all 100 should share the risk.

However, in another scenario where a person chose to live in a flood plain and was subsequently trapped by a flood, only 53 percent of the people thought it would be fair to risk the lives of others to save that person who had knowingly exposed himself to the risk.

"Our research shows that in forming equity judgments, people not only consider the consequences (such as number of deaths) but also the distribution of these consequences and the underlying causes that resulted in the risk situation," say the researchers. "Therefore, *it is impossible to determine how people will act in a given situation based on potential consequences alone.*" (Emphasis added—ed.)

Such research casts light on how the non-flying public might perceive the risk to itself from general aviation, and why blame gets apportioned as it does when there is an incident involving loss of property or life on the part of those who don't voluntarily assume the risk of flying.

Macho in Extremis

Some aviators are almost mystic in their capacity to "fly to the edge" of their abilities or "push the envelope" of the airplane. They often gain local fame (or notoriety) and even some admiration. But more often than not, their exploits hold little instructional value and raise more questions than they answer when it comes to safety.

As a case in point, a 1949 Cessna 170A with three people aboard crashed while attempting to recover from a hammerhead stall over Lopez Island, a remote community in Washington's Puget Sound. The 39-year-old private pilot, his son, and a friend and fellow pilot were killed. The NTSB investigator's report and statements taken from several witnesses not only illustrate a classic aviation mistake, but also yield a profile of almost nihilistic behavior which would have been alarming even in a non-pilot.

After a Sunday morning card game, the two men, accompanied by the pilot's son, departed the home of a friend for the Lopez Island Airport around 11 a.m. They commented that they intended to fly over to Center Island, a private strip on the opposite shore of the small island. Weather included a 2,000-foot overcast with visibility six miles and light winds.

The men were described as alert and in good spirits, although the pilot had commented about feeling somewhat fatigued due to poor sleep the previous night. The NTSB later found no indication of alcohol or drug consumption by either of the front-seat pilots.

The pilot was considered by a friend to be very competent, especially in taildraggers. His logbook indicated 591 total

A stock Cessna 170 is capable of good all-around performance but low-level aerobatics aren't in its repertoire.

hours with 118 in the Cessna 170, all of which were logged within the last 90 days. He was the owner of the airplane. No flight records were available on the other front-seat pilot.

The Cessna departed the Lopez Island Airport at 11:15 a.m. and the pilot quickly encountered a friend who had just departed in his Super Cub from a grass strip northeast of the airport. Witnesses indicated that the men recognized each other immediately and decided to indulge in a little formation flying. It is worth noting that witnesses on the ground, familiar with both the pilots and airplanes, promptly spotted the Cessna 170 and took the time to observe its progress.

The flight lasted five minutes. The planes flew in formation at an altitude of approximately 250 feet for a short time. Witnesses reported the Cessna was to the right and slightly ahead of the Cub. The pilots banked their planes to cross headings, the Cessna into a sharp ascending turn to the left, the Cub descending to the right. When clear, the Cub resumed its original heading.

The Cessna, however, continued into a near-vertical climb to what was variously described as a wingover or hammerhead stall, reaching an estimated altitude at the top of the stall of no more than 350 feet AGL. The Cessna then accelerated rapidly in a vertical dive. The pilot's attempt to recover was not successful and barely into its pullout the Cessna impacted the ground with what one witness called a "dull whoomp."

As both men in the front seats were certified pilots, it should be emphasized that there can be no way of knowing who had the yoke during the final moments of flight.

There was a rather eerie consensus which emerged from the statements given by friends and acquaintances of the pilot. The witnesses expressed no sense of wonder or disbelief, either about the wingover attempt or the result. Instead, what becomes clear is that the pilot had a "reputation." From the statements, it appeared everyone knew the pilot on a first-name basis, and expected to see him taking risks.

One witness, himself a pilot, knew the deceased pilot very well. He gave investigators a very illuminating statement: "I have known him for a long time; I worked with him 40 hours a week up until this accident. I have also flown with him. He has always insisted on showing off and impressing people. In the past he has landed in fields he couldn't get out of, ran out of fuel, etc. On the morning of the accident, he pulled up and went into one of his favorite maneuvers, a hammerhead wingover. It was 100% intentional. What it amounts to is that he was showing off and was too close to the ground. I know this for a fact . He told me last week that if he ever crashed, he hoped he wouldn't take anyone with him."

"It Won't Happen to Me"

Everyone knows there are dangers in flying, just as there are in any activity. But lots of pilots think the dangers somehow don't affect *them*. It's *other people* who run out of fuel, bust minimums, buzz houses or cheerfully fly themselves into bad weather. The "It won't happen to me" mentality is what makes safety hard to sell.

Numerous studies show that in many contexts people tend to underestimate their risks of something happening to them, though they may accurately perceive the risk for their peers. This is called the optimistic bias. To try to understand a bit more about how people arrive at the seemingly inconsistent conclusion that the group of which they're a part is more at risk than they themselves are, Rutgers researcher Neil Weinstein surveyed a group of people about their health risks.

He first asked them to imagine there were seven groups of people the same age and sex, arranged from lowest risk to highest risk of having a variety of health problems. For each problem, the person was asked which risk group he or she would fall into. For each risk judgment, those being studied were asked to provide a brief explanation of why they had placed themselves in the group they chose. These explanations were grouped into five categories: behavior patterns ("I try to stay in shape"), heredity ("My father has diabetes"), physiology ("I get lots of colds"), environment ("My roommates all smoke a lot"), and psychological attributes ("I don't believe in suicide").

Of 23 items on the list, the optimistic bias turned up 17 times, and in 10 of the 17 there was a tendency to offer action explanations for why people felt it wouldn't happen to them. The data showed people have a much greater tendency to see controllable factors (their own actions, and psychological leanings) as working in their favor rather than against them.

Further research turned up an even more interesting finding. As the investigator put it, "In a surprising number of cases, there was no relationship between a person's reported actions and his or her perception of vulnerability to harm. The lack of correspondence between seat belt use and auto safety, between sugar consumption and tooth decay, and between walking alone at night and the risk of mugging are just a few examples."

It seems to be the case, he concludes, that while people are willing to incorporate a number of other factors into their risk judgments "they seem much poorer at recognizing the relationships between their own actions and their risk of harm."

BUT I *THOUGHT* IT WAS THE RUNWAY

Each of the two private pilots aboard suffered minor injuries when their Cessna landed about 150 feet parallel to the runway. The pilots were attempting to return to Bakersfield even though they couldn't turn on the radio-activated runway lights.

The pilot in command was a 62-year-old airman with some 2,500 total hours, occupying the right seat. Accompanying him was a 48-year-old pilot with some 379 total hours, who was operating the airplane during the landing attempt.

Investigators said the pilots regularly flew a weather data-gathering mission in which they would take temperature measurements at various altitudes. They had launched from Bakersfield at about 4:35 a.m. and were returning to the airport when the 5 a.m. accident occurred.

The pilot in command told investigators he was unable to activate the runway lights after repeated attempts, and therefore elected to attempt a landing on what was thought to be runway 31. In the flare, the plane hit a three-foot-high dirt berm about 150 feet to the left of the runway, causing the aircraft to nose into the ground. The two pilots managed to exit the airplane as a fire broke out in the engine area and the plane burned to destruction.

Bakersfield officials reported to investigators that nothing could be found wrong with the runway light system. NTSB's investigator noted that a plane's radio transmitter and antenna condition may affect the ability to activate the runway lights, but due to the fire, an assessment of the radio in the C-152 could not be made.

In a telephone interview, the pilot remarked to NTSB's investigator that he ought to have considered landing at a nearby, lighted airport rather than Bakersfield.

OR, HOW ABOUT THIS ONE?

Neither the 38-year-old ATP pilot nor the 23-year-old instructor pilot giving him a checkout ride in the Seneca was injured when their twin lost power and was forced to land in a high school football field short of Runway 19 at El Monte Airport. The crash came after the two airmen had performed some airwork maneuvers for about half an hour and were returning to El Monte for landing practice.

The instructor pilot had a total of 1,020 hours, including 45 in multi-engine aircraft, of which 44 were in the Seneca. Undergoing the checkout was a 9,360-hour ATP with 3,317 multi-engine hours. According to the ATP pilot, he informed the checkout instructor that he had not flown a Seneca in about 11 years, and had not flown a reciprocating-engine airplane in about a year.

After what the CFI termed a thorough preflight, the two departed El Monte and performed some airwork. During the preflight, the ATP pilot removed the caps on both wings to look at the fuel level. But, he said, the CFI informed him that he would not be able to see the fuel, since the tanks were only partially full. The gauges read 30 gallons on the left side and

When the pilot applied power for the go-around, neither engine responded and the Seneca landed short of the runway. One fuel tank was nearly empty, another had 42 gallons. Investigators found that the instructor pilot was unfamiliar with the Seneca fuel system.

25 on the right side, the ATP told investigators. He asked whether the gauges were reliable and whether there was sufficient fuel for the flight. The CFI replied that the gauges were indeed reliable, and that the plane would burn 25 gallons per hour, giving two hours worth of fuel on board.

The airwork included a demonstration of Vmc followed by a simulated engine failure. For the ATP, most of the flight was "under the hood." As the ATP related it, the instructor commenced the engine failure exercise by turning the left engine fuel selector off. After power was restored, the CFI called on the ATP to perform a VOR approach to El Monte.

After removing the hood, the ATP recalled finding that the instructor had put the right fuel selector in the crossfeed position for what he said was an attempt to "balance the fuel load." It was returned to the "on" position. When the Seneca was on final and added power was needed, the engines failed to respond. The pilots confirmed that both selectors were on, and that throttle, propeller and other controls were in the proper position. The ATP maneuvered the plane to an emergency landing when it became apparent that the Seneca could not reach the runway. According to the CFI's account, since the plane was under control and he deemed no one in danger, he did not assume control of the airplane. About 150 feet after touchdown, the aircraft was "arrested by a chain link fence," the CFI said.

FAA inspectors said they interviewed the instructor and found he was not knowledgeable of emergency procedures regarding use of the "Hi" position of the auxiliary fuel pump when attempting to restore power.

Inspectors also found that the Seneca's left fuel tank contained a total of about 1.5 gallons of fuel, while the right had approximately 42 gallons.

Warning: Hazardous Thought Patterns at Work

To pilots they're nothing much, really, just the way things are. To psychologists who specialize in studying aviation psychology, they're "Hazardous Thought Patterns," or HTPs. They're nothing to pilots because they are pilots, or at least they are pilot behavior.

Over the years the concept of HTPs has been honed and certain types have been pretty well defined. Types widely recognized include anti-authority, impulsivity, invulnerability, macho and resignation. It's these types which form the basis for almost all attempts to teach the topic of judgment to pilots.

The notion involved is that certain clusters of attitudes constitute HTPs, and that such HTPs lead to the faulty decision making which shows up on FAA reports as "continued VFR flight into IFR" or "ran out of gas." In other words, what usually becomes the two bleak words representing the ultimate system failure: pilot error.

In pursuit of more information about HTPs, two researchers administered questionnaires to 152 students in a university aeronautical sciences program who had between 75 and 600 hours of flight time (average was 190 hours). Each person completed a battery of standard psychological tests, and one of two forms of a Pilot Decision Making Questionnaire (PDMQ). Form A presented some standard scenarios worded in the second person and asked pilots to rate on a six-point scale whether the decisions of the pilot were "very much like me" or "not at all like me."

Form P of the PDMQ described the irrational decisions in the third person and asked pilots to make an attribution about why the pilot in the scenario acted as he or she did. Each scenario was followed by a series of reasons, each represented one type of HTP, and pilots were asked to say on a five point scale (highly likely to not at all likely) what they thought the contribution of that factor was to the outcome.

All pilots in the study were judged for their predominant type of HTP. Of those completing Form P, about 13 percent fell into no clear classification. Few were anti-authority and none showed the resignation HTP. That left 39 percent as invulnerables, 24 percent as impulsives and 19 percent machos. These numbers conformed closely to those found in similar studies, and lead the researchers to conclude that irrational pilot decision making "can be accounted for by reference to the invulnerable, macho and impulsive patterns alone."

Using Form A, the researchers divided the pilots into groups deemed to have either "better" or "poorer" judgment. Those with better judgment had a significantly more internal locus of control, a psychological measure of the degree to which a person feels he controls his own destiny. Internals feel they largely arrange their own fate; externals feel the world mostly does things to them which are beyond their control. This was the only personality trait on which the two groups of pilots differed significantly.

"The study," the researchers conclude, "provides evidence of a connection between pilot judgment and pilot personality." The results, they say, "strongly suggest that the HTPs, as well as the global measure of irrational pilot judgment, are related to pilot personality and to the risk of involvement in dangerous aviation events."

What Do *You* Think About Safety?

It's pretty difficult to find a reliable answer to that question. It's well known that everybody believes in safety, but what has remained largely unknown is how many people actually do anything about it.

Now there's the beginning of an answer, in the form of a survey of pilots conducted by researchers in the Wright State University aerospace medical program. They distributed to a local flying club's 210 members a questionnaire asking about their behavior in regard to 50 safety-related items. For each item the pilot was asked to check whether his behavior was to attend to the item always, sometimes or never. Items receiving the highest rate of "optimum" (always) response were:

• checking for respiration rate and oxygen starvation (96 percent always do)

• maintaining proper VFR cruising altitudes on cross countries (95 percent)

- removing all airframe ice prior to takeoff (95 percent)
- waiting eight hours after having a drink before flying (95 percent)
- using current maps on cross country flights (93 percent)

Those were the best of times. The worst included:

- doing a weight and balance calculation when known to be under gross (only 3 percent always do)
- flying with hearing protection (7 percent)
- turning on the rotating beacon prior to engine start (10 percent)
- use of an intersection takeoff when the full length would permit a safe emergency landing (16 percent)
- carrying appropriate survival gear over sparsely occupied areas (27 percent)
- getting a weather report when the destination is less than 25 miles away (28 percent)

Dividing the questions into five categories, the order of concern for safety was: (1) aerodynamics, with 70.5 percent optimum answers; (2) weather (59.2 percent); (3) aeromedical (58.8 percent); (4) preflight (55.2 percent); and (5) operations (53.9 percent).

The researchers cite as "potentially dangerous" the combination of two or more behaviors from the bottom half of the response list. Among the areas of concern are flying on self medication with an AME's advice, flying with a cold, improper scanning, failure to identify VORs aurally, leaving passengers on board during refueling, not filing flight plans, and not knowing that freezing temperatures and visible moisture can produce structural icing.

More experienced pilots (more than 500 hours) showed a better safety attitude than those whose flying time was less, though there seems to be room for improvement for everyone.

Personal Preflight—A Look in the Mirror

You're looking forward to this flight, the first long cross-country you've taken in a long time. It'll be mild IFR part of the way and a good thing, too—you need the currency time. You haven't done a lot of flying lately, but there should be no problem. You've taken extra care with your briefing, trip planning and aircraft preflight.

It'll be good to get away from the office, too. It's been a long, hard week, and you need the release of tension that flying provides. You're ready, right? Maybe not. You've checked everything except the most important part of the system: the pilot. Are *you* ready for this flight? How can you tell?

Ready or Not

To make a flight as safe as possible, a pilot needs to look at all the variables, including his own condition, before starting the engine.

Naturally, a pilot is not always in perfect physical and mental shape, and it's important that he is aware of when he's not performing at a hundred percent (which for most of us is much of the time) and exercises greater caution at these times. If things really aren't going well, the pilot should seriously consider staying on the ground.

The decision on whether or not you're fit to fly is a tough one to make, and there are a lot of factors to be weighed. There's proficiency and its close cousin, currency. There's also physical condition. Did you eat well today? Are you tired? Have you been sick recently? All of these can affect your performance.

The real kicker, though, is mental state. A pilot's overall attitude towards the flight can have a powerful influence not only on the decision to launch but also on every decision made thereafter during the flight.

The pilot's mental state, his ability to adapt and react to a changing, demanding situation, is strongly affected by what psychologists call stressors. Broadly defined, a stressor is anything that upsets one's equilibrium, including recent experiences (both good and bad), physical events (such as lack of sleep) and environmental factors (noise, heat and so forth).

Stressed Out

Many stressors, such as frustration from being stuck in traffic, are mild by themselves, but their effects can be cumulative. An extreme example might be that of a pilot who's running late, has had a lousy day, hasn't slept or eaten well in the last 24 hours and is getting a runaround from ATC. The result is likely to be an individual who isn't really fit to fly and, worse, probably doesn't even realize it.

For example, consider an accident that occurred several years ago. The pilot and his wife were returning to their home in Alabama from a hunting trip in Arkansas. They made one stop along the way to see the people who had sold them their Cessna Skymaster and to pick up a nav radio that had been left behind for repairs.

During the stop, the pilot got into an argument with the former owners and was very upset when he took off again early in the evening. No flight plan was filed, but the pilot received flight following until the Skymaster was 18 miles from the destination. There were no further communications with the aircraft. The wreckage was located seven days later in a wooded area about 400 yards short of the runway threshold.

Investigators found that although the pilot had a prescription for medication to control hypertension, there was no trace of the drug in his system. The pilot had over 3,500 hours but not a great deal of experience in the Skymaster. He had performed four night landings in the 49 hours he flew the airplane during his two and a half months of ownership.

GETTING RATED

The pilot had had to acquire a multi-engine rating to fly the centerline-thrust twin. During a familiarization flight prior to purchase, an FAA designated examiner noted he was "completely unfamiliar with the Cessna 337 and his flight proficiency was very low." The pilot agreed to get some dual instruction.

The next day, he flew for an hour with a part-time instructor, who endorsed him for his multi-engine check ride. The day after that, the pilot again flew with the designated examiner, who discontinued the check ride due to the pilot's poor performance and recommended more dual. The pilot was very angry when the examiner told him that he had failed. He got the rating a month later, though, from a different examiner.

In determining what might have caused the accident, the NTSB concluded that physical impairment was a factor. As mentioned earlier, there was evidence the pilot hadn't taken his hypertension medication and had become very upset during the argument only 45 minutes before the crash. On top of this, he was unfamiliar with the aircraft, particularly for night operations.

Stacking the Odds

It is not often that a pilot gets so badly wrapped up that he can't fly the airplane. However, many pilots routinely stack the odds against themselves without consideration for the resulting effect on their ability to fly.

Often, pilots allow their flying to be driven by outside forces. For instance, if an instructor is only available on a certain day, a student might ignore the fact that he isn't feeling well or that the winds are a little brisker than he'd be comfortable with, just to accommodate the CFI's schedule.

The trouble is that the accumulated effect of stressors can easily overcome the pilot's better judgment about staying on the ground. A pilot who's distracted by other troubles may not notice the little mistakes he or she is making.

Piling Up

As mentioned earlier, the effects of individual stressors can be cumulative. In an extreme case, the pilot will get so keyed up that any semblance of flying ability will be lost. More typically, a pilot who has too much to think about will make mistakes, like forgetting to switch tanks or lower landing gear.

A pilot will likely arrive at the airport having already experienced several stressors. Once there, the input continues as the pilot has to get the airplane properly loaded, deal with the front desk and line service, flight service, clearance delivery and ground control. Not to mention getting a properly thorough preflight done in time to get airborne on schedule. All this time his stress level can slowly be rising.

Once airborne, there are more stressors to deal with. ATC, congested traffic, noise, vibration, turbulence, unfamiliar airports, nighttime operations and deteriorating weather all can take their toll on the pilot's ability to make sound decisions and fly the airplane safely.

Further, studies have shown that the pilot's ability to handle all of this decreases as the flight progresses—not surprising to anyone who's made a long cross-country flight in a modern lightplane and been subjected to the high noise and low comfort levels found in most of them.

The result is that one too many stressful events might occur on a flight and cause the pilot to slip up—the demands of the situation will excced the pilot's ability to handle them correctly. In most cases such a mistake will be minor and easily corrected. Occasionally, though, the mistake can be fatal.

The pilot should keep in mind that much can happen while airborne and consider how he or she will feel at the end of the flight, not just at the beginning.

Bad Attitudes

Another important factor in pilot decision making is the effect of attitude on judgment. Psychologists have come up with five clearly defined attitudes that can have a negative effect on the pilot's approach to the problems of flight:

• **Anti-Authority.** "Don't tell *me* what to do!" Pilots with this attitude tend to believe that most of the rules are unnecessary or that the person in the cockpit knows better than the person in the tower.

• **Impulsivity.** There's often an overwhelming urge to do something—anything—quickly if there's a problem. This attitude keeps pilots from stopping to consider all the alternatives and choose the best one.

• **Invulnerability.** This is the feeling that an accident will only happen to the other guy, never to oneself. It can lead to pilots taking unnecessary risks or getting lax about following procedures. Many pilots who land airplanes gear-up for the first time believe they'd never make such a mistake—until they did.

• **Macho.** This attitude leads pilots into risky behavior to prove that they're better than everyone else. It's commonly manifested as showing off.

• **Resignation.** "What's the use?" Pilots with this attitude tend to be fatalistic, feeling that they have little to do with the outcome of a situation. They also will follow the lead of others, even if it would put them in a dangerous situation.

Shadings of each and every one of these attitudes are likely to exist in everyone—and that's not entirely bad. Though an anti-authority attitude is counterproductive, a pilot should be willing to question authority enough to override instructions or regulations when necessary for safety but not so much that the rule book is thrown out the vent window just because the pilot thinks it's silly. Likewise, while it's a good idea to consider alternative courses of action, delaying a decision too long can lead to an accident. And so on, down the list.

Part of the pilot's personal preflight might include an objective look at how he is going to approach the task of flying, with an eye towards each of these attitudes.

I'm Safe

The well-known IM-SAFE mnemonic is one tool a pilot can use to evaluate his condition during the preflight routine.

Illness? Do I have any symptoms?

Medication? Have I been taking prescription or over-the-counter drugs?

Stress? Am I under psychological pressure from the job? Worried about financial matters, health problems or family discord?

Alcohol? Have I been drinking within eight hours? Within 24 hours?

Fatigue? Am I tired and not adequately rested?

Eating? Am I adequately nourished?

Whether this mnemonic is used or not, some consideration on the part of the pilot to his own condition should be a part of every preflight. That includes thought given to the demands of the flight and the pilot's ability to deal with them.

A pilot can go to great lengths to manage the external risks in flying, but that pilot may still be making an unsafe trip if he hasn't taken a carefully considered and objective look at himself.

Poor Judgment and the Domino Effect

"Plan your flight and fly your plan" is an axiom that has served aviation well. The importance of thorough preflight planning cannot be overemphasized. But to minimize the risks of flying, a pilot must go beyond merely "flying the plan." It's rare when situations encountered en route don't require the plan to either be changed or scrapped in favor of safer alternatives.

Detecting and responding to change requires sound decision-making. A good plan followed by good headwork can do much to minimize risk. But, as the following accident scenario shows, the results of poor planning and decision-making can be tragic.

As you read along, try to pick out the points where decisions either weren't made or were not made properly. An organized method for decision-making might have prevented this accident.

FLORIDA-BOUND

It was 7 o'clock on a Friday evening in March. A non-instrument-rated private pilot, his wife and an instrument-rated flight instructor departed Zelienople, Pennsylvania, on a VFR flight to Clearwater, Florida, with a fuel stop in Raleigh, North Carolina.

The private pilot flew from the left seat, with the flight instructor next to him and his wife in the back seat of the rented Cessna 172L. The Skyhawk had 4.7 hours' endurance at 75 percent power and 5,000 feet with the mixture properly leaned. At 82 percent power, endurance was 4.2 hours. Neither figure includes the fuel needed for taxi, takeoff, descent and landing.

Remember those endurance numbers; they were critical in the events that followed.

CHANGE IN THE WEATHER

Weather was VFR along the first 100 miles of the route, but there were warning signs that it would change. Morgantown, West Virginia, was reporting 5,000 broken and 15 miles visibility, temperature 58 F/dew point 39, and "pressure falling rapidly." Martinsburg, 94 miles east, was reporting 1,000 scattered, 2,500 overcast and 7 miles' visibility, temperature 39/dew point 36, and "ridge top obscured west."

The flight instructor got the current conditions before takeoff but didn't ask for the synoptic situation, winds aloft, sigmets and airmets. As a result, the pilots had no knowledge of a sigmet for their entire route for locally severe turbulence over and west of the mountains, and moderate turbulence below 20,000 feet east of the mountains. Nor did they know about an airmet warning of occasional moderate mixed icing in clouds and precipitation above the freezing level, which was 4,000 to 6,000 feet in their area and sloped to 8,000 feet over South Carolina.

There was no evidence that either pilot had obtained an earlier briefing, and no flight plan was filed.

SLOW PROGRESS

By 8:30 p.m., over Morgantown at 5,500 feet, they realized their progress was slower than expected—a lot slower. It took 90 minutes to travel 76 nm, a groundspeed of 51 knots.

The instructor called Morgantown FSS and asked for the Raleigh weather. He was told that there was a stationary front in the area, with low ceilings and poor visibility. He told Flight Service they would stop in Richmond, instead of Raleigh, but didn't ask for the winds aloft.

From Morgantown, they planned to fly direct to Kessel Vortac, direct to Linden Vortac (43 miles southeast), then direct to Richmond. Unaware of the 60-knot crosswind, the pilot had difficulty tracking Morgantown's 121-degree radial to Linden, and the aircraft began deviating far to the north.

CONFUSION

About 50 miles southeast of Morgantown, the Skyhawk entered the clouds and the instructor took control. He soon became confused about his position and, at 9:43 p.m., called Washington Center and said, "We're not quite sure where we're at and wonder if you could help us out?"

The controller identified the aircraft on his radar display and determined that the instructor's VOR indications were correct. At this point, the instructor said they had one hour of fuel remaining. The controller replied, "Six-Eight-Quebec, you're in radar contact, 10 miles north and east of the Kessel VOR. Say your intentions." The time was 9:52 p.m. "Where can we get down, sir?" the instructor asked. "We'd like to get down."

The controller checked weather at Washington-Dulles, Martinsburg and Harrisburg, Pennsylvania. All were below minimums, but Hagerstown, Maryland, was reporting 800 overcast, with 2-1/2 miles' visibility. The instructor decided to go to Hagerstown.

TURN AROUND?

Two minutes later, the controller called, "68Q, Morgantown is carrying 4,500 broken with 10 miles, if you'd like to go back towards Morgantown."

"Maybe that'd be better yet. Let's go back there," replied the instructor. He accepted a heading of 270 degrees for vectors to Morgantown. The aircraft was handed off to Cleveland Center at 10:04 p.m., and the following conversation ensued:

ATC: 4368Q, turn left to a heading of 260.

68Q: 260, 4368Q.

ATC: I'm gonna vector you over to Garrett County Airport, which is at your 12 o'clock position, 25 miles. It's a lighted field and you may be able to make it in there.

68Q: Okay, roger, 4368Q.

ATC: And 4368Q, in about another 10 miles, I can start you down. If I start you down now, I'll lose you on radar.

68Q: Okay, we'll (unintelligible) whenever you're ready.

ATC: Roger, you say about an hour's fuel left?

68Q: (Unintelligible) probably about 45 minutes.

ATC: Roger.

NIGHT NDB APPROACH

It was 10:10 p.m. N68Q was seven miles south of Cumberland and 25 miles east of Garrett County Airport. The controller asked the instructor if he could fly the NDB approach into Cumberland if the controller read the approach procedure to him. The instructor agreed. The Cumberland weather was given as 2,500 overcast and five miles' visibility.

When the instructor reported receiving the Cumberland NDB, this conversation ensued:

ATC: You can proceed out on the 316-degree radial. Your inbound radial is 208 degrees.

ATC: 68Q, did you receive?" (No response). 4368Q, Cleveland. (No response). 4368Q, if you receive Cleveland Center, the Cumberland Airport is at 12 o'clock, two miles.

68Q: 4368Q, we have the beacon, I...the squawk turned on. I didn't...the last transmission from you.

ATC: 68Q, roger, if you have the field in sight, you are cleared to land.

68Q: We're still 8,000 feet. Can we start down now?

ATC: That is correct. I'm going to lose you on frequency. You are cleared to land. You do say you have the airport in sight?

68Q: We don't. I'm at 8,000 feet with an overcast beneath me.

ATC: 68Q, roger, you are cleared to circle to land at the Cumberland Airport.

68Q: Roger, cleared to circle to land at the Cumberland Airport.

ATC: 68Q, that is correct. Now I'm going to lose you on Center frequency here. Cancel with Martinsburg Radio. Call Martinsburg Radio with your ground time.

ATC (background conversation): He most certainly did have it in sight. He had the rotating beacon in sight.

ATC: 68Q, you receive Cleveland?

68Q: Yeah, we gotcha.

ATC: Roger, you are two miles north of the field now.

68Q: We're circling here trying to descend to get it down. I'm still coming out of 7,000 descending. We just passed the beacon.

ATC: 68Q, roger, but you do still have the field in sight? (No response). 68Q, you still hear Cleveland?

68Q: Yeah.

MISSED APPROACH

As 68Q descended slowly from 7,000 feet, the controller asked, "You will be turning south toward the field?" The instructor replied that he was still trying to lose altitude and asked the airport's position relative to the NDB. "The airport is two miles southwest of the beacon," the controller answered.

At 10:20, the controller told the pilot, "Cross the beacon inbound at 3,000 feet on heading 208." Then, radio contact was lost for awhile.

The instructor would later recall that he had crossed the NDB at 3,000 feet on a heading of 208. He was in heavy rain and couldn't see the ground. He remembered the reported ceiling and descended to 2,500 feet. He could see lights glowing through the clouds but couldn't identify anything. He then descended to 2,000 feet, where he could see the tops of houses and other objects but not the airport. He circled once in an unsuccessful attempt to find the airport, which is flanked by high ridges, then executed a missed approach.

Climbing on a southwest heading, the instructor called Cleveland Center to report that he had missed the approach due to low ceilings and heavy rain. He was cleared to 5,000 feet on a heading of 200 degrees.

At 10:36, 68Q was told to turn to 270 degrees for Morgantown and was asked to report the amount of fuel remaining. The instructor responded he had 30 minutes left.

Eight minutes later, the controller said, "The rain showers seem to have passed by the Cumberland Airport. Would you like to try another approach? With the amount of fuel you have there and the winds, it's going to be rather close to Morgantown." The instructor declined.

TIME RUNS OUT

At 10:57 p.m., the instructor said he had the rotating beacon at Garrett County Airport in sight. The controller gave him a heading to the airport and told him to stay at 5,000 feet until five miles from the airport. The following conversation took place about 15 minutes later:

ATC: 68Q, I have lost you on radar 2.5 miles northeast of the field.

68Q: Roger, 68Q. We have the (unintelligible) runway.

ATC: 68Q, roger. You can stand by with the airport personnel on 122.8 now for your down time.

68Q: 122.8, thank you very much now. We appreciate everything you've done.

The instructor recalled that he switched to 122.8 and made one transmission when his tanks ran dry and the engine lost power. He found an open field to land in, but during landing roll, the aircraft struck a line of trees and crashed two miles

from the end of the runway. The time was 11:16 p.m. The
private pilot was killed by the impact. His wife and the
instructor were seriously injured, but survived.

What Went Wrong?

A close examination of the accident reveals that inadequate preflight
planning, poor decision-making and some overly helpful controllers
played significant roles.

When asked why he hadn't prepared a flight log for the trip, the
instructor said it wasn't necessary because he had a "pretty good
idea" of what his fuel and time estimates should be. Though a
thorough weather briefing was in order, especially for such a long
trip, the instructor had checked only current conditions. Had he
known about the strong winds aloft or the airmet and sigmet, they
might have canceled the flight.

By the time the aircraft reached Morgantown, a third of its fuel
had been used up. Though the instructor realized that they could not
reach Raleigh and changed their destination to Richmond, about 174
nm from Morgantown, he wasn't fully aware of just how slowly the
trip was progressing. Had he checked his ground speed, he would
have known that even Richmond wasn't feasible.

When the instructor had difficulty tracking the VOR radial, he
didn't believe the CDI indications. "I could not get back to the right
and get on course," he said. At no time did he consider that he had a
60-knot direct right crosswind.

His circling only worsened the fuel situation. He also pressed on
into the clouds without an IFR clearance. At this point, the aircraft
had been airborne for 2 hours and 25 minutes and had traveled only
140 nautical miles.

After contacting ATC and learning that the weather at nearby
airports was below minimums, the instructor decided to return to
Morgantown—a good decision. But after that, like too many pilots in
a sticky situation, he put all of his eggs into ATC's basket.

He told Cleveland Center he had one hour's fuel remaining.
Trying to be helpful, the controller told 68Q that he would provide
vectors to Garrett County Airport, since it was closer than Morgantown. The instructor agreed.

In another attempt to be helpful, the controller told the pilot that
the ceiling at Cumberland was 2,500 feet and asked if he would like
to try the NDB approach. Unfortunately, the controller's report was
third-hand information that an aircraft had just departed Cumber-

land and reported the ceiling as 2,500 feet AGL. The aircraft actually had reported the ceiling as 2,700 feet MSL, which meant that it was actually at 1,900 feet over the mountainous airport.

Compounding the situation was a misunderstanding between the controller and the pilot during the approach. When the instructor reported that he had the "beacon," he meant the Cumberland NDB. The controller, thinking the instructor meant the airport rotating beacon, stopped reading him the approach. As a result, the pilot didn't know the minimum descent altitude and actually descended below the MDA and circled in the vicinity of some very rough terrain while trying to spot the airport.

After the missed approach, the instructor finally took command of the situation by asking for guidance to Garrett County, but it was too late. The consequences of poor planning and decision-making had caught up with the flight.

2 | The Pilot's Age

"I'm Not Getting Older, I'm Getting Better!" What a marvelous philosophy of life, particularly as it applies to aviation; for most pilots, each aeronautical experience adds depth to the reservoir of skills and knowledge, and provides a good foundation from which to make the judgments required in this business. A seasoned pilot *should* be able to demonstrate more proficiency than a beginner, and a very large part of the veteran's touch on the controls and superior decision-making skills is simply the result of having "been there" more often over the years.

Unfortunately, there are some flaws inherent in "I'm getting better," because as the old bod ages, certain inexorable changes take place, changes which can play havoc with the way we operate aircraft.

Now before our more mature readers get upset, our objective in this section is not to point accusing fingers at older pilots, or to conclude that pilots should hang up their helmets and goggles just because they've reached some chronological milestone in life; rather, we will try to make you aware of some of the things to look for as the years roll by, and help you recognize some limitations you probably hadn't considered. Half the battle against the hazards of flight is won when pilots respect their own limitations, and adjust their aviation activities accordingly.

A court ruling several years ago said that professional pilots booted from the left seat of heavy hardware by the FAA age-60-and-out rule couldn't be denied the opportunity to downgrade to the flight engineer position, where the age limit is higher. Many feel this is a precursor to the eventual elimination of all rules specifying flying limits by age, and the beginning of performance-based testing to determine when it's time for a pilot to stop flying—whether commercially or recreationally.

A review of mishap rates suggests that there _is_ a relationship between age and the cause of mishaps, but the relationship isn't always what conventional wisdom might lead one to believe.

There's a fair bulk of research findings pointing to the dismal conclusion that several skills critical to flying do begin an inexorable downhill slide around middle age. The affected skills include processing incoming information and making quick judgments, resisting fatigue, performing in a high-stress environment and performing complex tasks rapidly. Many who accept the data but wish to deny the conclusion argue that increased experience counterbalances the decreased motor and mental skills.

The study, conducted by the U.S. Naval Safety Center, took a look at the flight records of all Navy pilots from 1977 to 1982. That amounted to around 16,000 pilots of fighters, attack planes and helicopters. The researchers found there were indeed certain types of problems associated with being certain ages. But the problems for older aviators had more to do with inability to cope procedurally rather than difficulties in the motor skill area.

The overall mishap rate didn't differ significantly between the over-38 age group and the 23-27 bunch. But the way they lost the planes was distinctive. For the 26-year-old fighter pilot group, which had the highest mishap rate at 9.43 per 100,000 hours, the leading causes were improper use of flight controls, failure to maintain flying speed, improper response, poor landing technique and loss of control.

Meanwhile, the over-38 fighter jocks were bending metal primarily because of violation of regulations or instructions, and poor judgment or inadequate evaluation of circumstances. So the young flyboys—those presumably having eagle eyes and sharp response rates—were having motor coordination problems while the old and presumably wise pilots were making dumb decisions.

Results were similar for the attack-pilot group, where the old, bold pilots got on the hit parade primarily for inadequate preflight preparation and a variety of factors that boiled down to inattention to detail. The youngest attack pilots, meanwhile, came in with failure to maintain flying speed, loss of control and poor physical condition of the pilot (stress, vertigo, etc.).

What it all means has yet to be fully sorted out. Some of the

differences could have to do with the differing mission types under-
taken by military pilots at different ages. On the other hand, these
data point at least tentatively to a conclusion that a lot of researchers
have been edging towards for awhile—what's needed is a good
functional aging index which will determine for any individual
aviator how well he is prepared to cope in the cockpit. Such a test
could serve as an early warning device for all pilots, identifying
physiological or cognitive weak spots which might cause a problem
if left hidden.

Use It or Lose It

Keeping sharp mentally and physically requires more than just
wishful thinking, particularly as the body ages. According to a report
at a recent meeting of the American Geriatric Society, there's
certainly something to the old saw of "Use it or lose it."

A psychologist tested 94 men, ages 25 to 69, all of whom were
practicing architects. She used a variety of tests to measure their
cognitive function, and the findings were encouraging. Mental abilities which have been shown in many studies to diminish with age can
be maintained until late adult years when used regularly. Unimpor-
tant skills decline while important skills, used frequently, are maintained. In another study, mental reaction time—a vital piloting
skill—was found to be equal in old and young joggers.

While it's clear that using both mental and physical resources
keeps them available and sharp, what's less clear is whether delaying
until later life and then jumping on the bandwagon can still save the
day. Numerous studies present conflicting evidence on whether a life
of mental and physical sedentism can in any way be reversed by a
sudden commitment to activity in later life.

The best bet appears to be flying often to make frequent use of
one's mental skills, and getting regular exercise to make certain the
supporting body functions are there when called upon.

Slowing with Age

Numerous studies have led to the same conclusion—as a person ages,
response to complex situations becomes slower, and where the pace
is forced to be maintained the older people have fewer correct
responses than their younger cohorts.

The long and short of it is that the older the person, the less
efficient he or she is at perceptual and motor tasks, and the degradation grows worse as task complexity increases.

There is no cure for growing older, but for pilots an awareness of what is happening to the varied skills needed to keep them flying can help. And for those who design airplanes and systems, knowledge of the workload attached to a specific task could be used to create a safer and more manageable "front office."

The problem, however, has been in determining with any meaningful precision how great a workload is imposed by a given task. As a first stab, a researcher studied the workload imposed by a tracking task performed by two groups of people—one group was 18 to 22 years old and the other was 48 to 67.

Each person was asked to "chase" a moving square on a computer screen with a light pen. There were three levels of complexity, determined by how fast the square darted around.

While that was going on, a secondary task in the form of a single digit was displayed on another computer screen. The job was to "cancel" the digit by pressing the corresponding key on the keyboard.

When all the buttons were pushed and the figures figured, the workload index showed that for a given task, the older subjects were facing about twice the load of their younger counterparts.

"The present results clearly demonstrate that the same task imposed a greater workload on the older subject. More effort was required on the part of the older individuals to perform the primary task," said the study's author. "Because the same task imposes a greater workload on the older operator, the operator could be at a distinct disadvantage in systems requiring manual control."

Age and Alcohol

Alcohol and pilots make a poor mixture at any age, but the older a pilot is the more likely his performance will deteriorate with any ingestion of booze. That was the major finding from a study conducted by the FAA Civil Aeromedical Institute. They recruited 25 men, 12 of whom were 30 to 39 years old, and 13 of whom were aged 60 to 69, and got them somewhat sloshed (blood alcohol levels just below the legal limit of drunkenness in most states) before administering a battery of tests that included mental arithmetic, pattern identification, tracking, and monitoring of warning lights and meters.

When the results were tallied from all the tests, the conclusion was crystal clear (which is more than can be said for the pilots): "The older subjects," the government researchers conclude, "performed significantly more poorly than did the 30- to 39-year-olds on all composite measures of performance, on all the individual tasks except pattern identification, and at the higher levels of workload. Alcohol produced significant performance impairment for both age groups, but the 60- to 69-year age group was more negatively affected."

Look Out, Old Eyes

Give two pilots of differing ages the job of spotting traffic in good VFR conditions after staring at the panel, and they'll do a pretty equal job of finding the bogey. But let the light get low, or conditions otherwise degrade, and the younger eyes will have a big edge in finding what they seek outside the window.

That's the conclusion of research conducted by investigators at Boeing. They gave 35 men, from 22 to 52 years old, the task of reading some material at close range and then trying to look up and accommodate their focus to a distant object (in this case a laser-generated pattern which appeared to be in random motion when properly focused on by the eyes). The amount of light available was varied from high illumination (550 lux, about average for an office) to 55 lux (comparable to a dimly lit restaurant or stairway).

"Age effects are most pronounced under the most degraded conditions," the researchers concluded. Under both good and bad conditions the length of time required for refocus was about equal for the younger group (22-32 years old), while the older group (42-52) slowed more than 300 percent when confronted with the task under low illumination conditions.

"We are impressed by the resilience of the young eye's accommodative system to generally poor viewing environments," said the researchers. "We could find no significant differences between the three youngest age groups for any variables influencing the time to accommodate."

On the other hand, they report, "The speed of accommodation in older subjects seems especially susceptible to degraded viewing environments."

Heat Shedding and Age

Cockpits are many things, including pressure cookers. That can literally be true when temperatures start to rise. With their wide expanses of glass and submarginal (at best) ventilation, conditions can pass rapidly from uncomfortable to worse when the thermometer really starts to soar. Many a student pilot, particularly in the warmer areas of the country, has heard the command to "Climb and maintain 70 degrees."

It turns out that command may be a critical one for older pilots. Medical people have known for a long time that as age increases, people have a harder and harder time shedding heat load. That's why senior citizens are generally less comfortable in hot weather than their younger counterparts.

For many years the assumption (largely untested) was that this differential somehow related to varying abilities to sweat, since sweating is the main means by which the body effects temperature adjustments. But like many time-honored but untested assumptions, it's just not so. Recent research finds that the sweating mechanism doesn't change with age. What varies is blood flow, which decreases with increasing years. Much like a car radiator with some of its small passages plugged, an older person simply can't move the same volume of heat-carrying blood to and from the body's surface, and thus isn't able to adjust temperature as readily.

To study what was going on, investigators put a group of older women (63-74) and a group of younger women (20-25) on exercise bikes in a lab where the temperature was 106 degrees. After resting in the bake box for 45 minutes, their core temperatures were very similar. But when each group performed a half hour of exercise, the older women's temperatures rose significantly higher. Both groups sweated at about the same rate, but blood flow to the skin of the young women was higher.

Older pilots need to be aware that they can't get rid of heat as easily, and are thus much more prone to the enervation and incapacitation that can come with an elevated core temperature. Being too warm is not just uncomfortable, it can lead to mental confusion and even complete incapacitation.

It's Up to You

Short of the rules which govern airline pilots, there's nothing in the FARs that prevent a senior-citizen pilot from doing his thing in the sky just because he has reached a certain age. Is the writing on the wall? Many states are moving toward closer regulation of older automobile drivers, and who's to say that it can't happen in aviation?

In the meantime, the older, *smarter* pilot—not necessarily the bolder one—will take pains to be cognizant of his condition, and limit his aerial activities accordingly.

3 | The Pilot's Vision

Lack of adequate vision has probably stymied more aviation careers than any other single physical frailty, while good vision keeps most of us out of trouble in the sky, and excellent vision has made aces of otherwise ordinary fighter pilots. Sight, and the maintenance of good vision, is definitely a large factor in the development and continuation of one's flying skills, and it behooves us to understand and protect the visual capabilities we have.

Over the years, *Aviation Safety* has published a number of articles dealing with vision—how it works, how it's examined, how it can be improved and protected with eye-glasses, ways to use it more effectively when you're flying, and so on—but before we get into that, a review of some general principles of the human visual system is in order. This is a very general review, with more detail on most of these subjects later on in this section.

Here's How It Works...
And Some Tips for Helping It Work Better

Inside your eye, at the back, is a photo-film called the retina, which does your seeing for you. The circular retina has two kinds of receptors. One is called the "cones," for that is the general shape of each one; they are densely packed around the focal center of the eye directly behind the pupil. As they spread out from the focal center, the cones become less numerous until they are entirely replaced around the outer part of the retina with "rods." These are (have you guessed?) rod-shaped and increase in number toward the periphery. There are no rods at the focal center and very few cones toward the edge of the retina. The cones are the main source of your day-time vision, enabling you to see fine detail and distinguish color. They are at their best in bright daylight or strong illumination up to the point of glare.

The rods do most of your seeing at night, detecting movement and picking up shapes in shades of gray and black. They begin working when illumination decreases to that of a full moonlit night and are the only part of the eye that can sight an object in starlight. Mainly thanks to the rods, the flare of a match has been seen at a distance of 25 miles.

Your visual system has a very interesting shortcoming when it comes to night vision—you have a blind area in the focal center your eye at night. This is where the cones are concentrated, an area which involves about 5 degrees of your visual field. All that you will be able to see at night will be picked up by the rods outside of this central area; therefore the best night vision will occur when your eye is directed approximately 10 degrees away from the object you'd like to see.

To use your rod (night) vision, you *must* look to one side of the object you are trying to see. This doesn't mean looking out of the corner of your eye; it means looking *past* the object. Then you can see its size and shape. In short, don't look directly at what you are trying to see at night, for then you are trying to see with your day vision. Off-center vision something you can learn easily with a little practice.

Maximum night vision also requires *dark adaptation.* You know that when you go from the sunlight into a dark room you are almost blind at first, but in a few minutes, you can see things clearly; you have gone through a period of dark adaptation. Within 30 minutes of walking from bright light into the dark, you can see a light about 10,000 times dimmer than you could when you first came in. The net gain will vary from one individual to the next; one person may be able to see with only one tenth of the light needed by another, regardless of how good either one's daylight vision may be.

In any event, your dark adaptation goes right down the drain when your eyes are again exposed to bright light. So when you get ready to fly at night, give your eyes an opportunity to adjust to darkness, operate with the dimmest possible panel lights, and be careful not use bright white lights any more than absolutely necessary. (It may surprise you to find out that blue and green lights are most easily seen at night; red and orange, least easily seen.)

The retina of the eye is more sensitive than any other part of the body to an insufficiency of oxygen in the blood. Technically speaking, this insufficiency begins as soon as you leave the ground, and will make a noticeable difference in your night vision by the time you reach 5,000 feet. When you breathe air (i.e., no supplemental oxygen) at 8,000 feet, your night vision is reduced 25 percent. The answer is to use an oxygen mask at 5,000 feet and above, but that's impractical for most general aviation pilots; in lieu of that, or when you're unable to keep a pressurized cabin below 5,000 feet, be aware of the impairment your night vision has suffered...and look all the more carefully!

Because the blood absorbs carbon monoxide more readily than it does oxygen, carbon monoxide really plays hob with night vision as well as the keenness of your eyesight in general. Smoking three cigarettes in a row will give your red blood cells a 4-percent saturation with carbon monoxide, with an effect about equal to your visual sensitivity at 8,000 feet, or a loss of 25 percent.

You may have heard talk of taking Vitamin A to improve your night vision. The facts are these: Vitamin A is essential to good night vision, and any nutritional deficiency in Vitamin A will impair it. But if you're already getting enough Vitamin A, you can't improve night vision by taking more.

It's easy for your eyes to play tricks on you at night when you stare at a single light source—perhaps the nav light of another airplane—for a period of time. What happens is technically known as *autokinetic movement,* and it can make for some uncomfortable and potentially dangerous illusions. The solution to this problem is obvious; don't stare at lights at night. Keep your eyes moving.

One last tip on seeing at night is to keep your windshield scrupulously clean. Dust, grease, water droplets, scratches all obstruct your view, night or day...and wouldn't it be frightening to watch as a "speck on the windshield" grows into an airliner approaching head-on?

Sunlight reflecting from water or snow, direct sunlight in the clear air at high altitudes, and plain ordinary sun when you fly into it are all sources of glare requiring the use of sunglasses. "Shades" are great, but remember that glasses which cut down the light reaching your eyes always represent a compromise with good vision, which depends on visible light. The same problem exists in instrument panel and cabin lighting. Dark adaptation, necessary for seeing outside of the airplane, is destroyed by light, which is needed in sufficient intensity to enable you to read maps, charts, and checklists.

It is a common misconception that the eye "takes a picture" of everything within its field of view. This is simply not true. Pick out any word in this sentence and then move your eye to the next and then the next. You will discover that you can no longer read the first word after having moved your eye about five degrees.

You see best in daylight with the cones in the center of your eye and the eye sees by moving in short jumps. It is not a sweeping but a jerking motion with which you see details around you. This is of the utmost importance when you are scanning the sky for other aircraft. Experiments have shown that the eye sees nothing in detail while it is moving. It sees only when it pauses and fixes an object on its retina. In scanning the sky, do not deceive yourself that you have covered an area with a wide, sweeping glance. The correct way to scan is to cover an area with short, regularly spaced movements of the eye.

Depth perception—judgment of distance—is done subconsciously in a combination of ways. Close up, we depend on binocular vision, each eye seeing an object from a different angle. At distance beyond binocular range, which is usually the case in flight, we judge it on a one-eye basis:

A. From the known size of an object and how much of our visual field it fills.

B. From our knowledge of perspective and the convergence of parallel lines at a great distance.

C. From overlapping—an object overlapped by another is known to be further away.

D. From light and shadow—an object casts a shadow away from the observer if the light is nearer.

E. From aerial perspective—large objects seen indistinctly apparently have haze, fog, or smoke between them and the observer and therefore are usually at a great distance.

F. From terrestrial association—objects ordinarily associated are judged to be at approximately the same distance.

G. From motion parallax—when the observer fixes his sight on one object while his head or body moves, other objects apparently moving in the same direction as he are judged to be more distant, while those apparently moving in the opposite direction are judged to be nearer.

So much for the quick review. What follows is a wealth of information covering a wide range of visual problems and situations, with procedures and suggestions to help you deal with these circumstances in your special situation as an aviator. Your sight should be Number One on the list of human factors you need to protect and maintain.

Visual Side Effects

It may be hard to look for side effects from prescription and non-prescription medications when those side effects are in the eye.

There's a tendency to think of drug side effects as things along the lines of dizziness, rashes, upset stomachs and the like. What many don't realize is that a fair number of drugs wreak at least temporary havoc on the visual system.

For example, some of the beta-blockers (drugs used in treating heart and high blood pressure conditions) cause reduced tear secretion. This can result in a painful and irritated "dry eye," especially when aggravated by continuous airflow from an airplane's overhead air duct.

Indocin (indomethacin, an anti-prostaglandin drug used to treat pain and swelling) has been reported to cause corneal deposits, as does the antimalarial drug chloroquine. Those receiving gold injections for rheumatoid arthritis may experience deposits of dust-like granules in the cornea.

The very widely used antibiotic tetracycline, as well as sulfonamides and antihistamines, have on rare occasions caused temporary nearsightedness. This is thought to be a function of the eye's lens temporarily absorbing more than a normal amount of water and thus thickening. No matter what the reason, a normal-sighted pilot who suddenly went myopic could be very unpleasantly surprised when it came time to land the airplane.

It is also possible for certain drugs to precipitate glaucoma in those who are susceptible but who haven't previously been symptomatic. Among the drugs known to have caused this problem are antihistamines, atropine, and several drugs used to control gastrointestinal spasms.

Since ocular incapacity could be devastating to a pilot's ability to function, extra caution is in order when beginning drug therapy. In the case of prescription drugs, if the doctor isn't an Aviation Medical Examiner, pilots might remind him or her of their desire to fly and ask for additional information on all known side effects, even those reported to occur rarely.

For non-prescription drugs, each first-time use by an individual must be looked on as something of an experiment. While an idiosyncratic adverse reaction is improbable, it is never impossible. Such experiments might best be conducted from the safety of the ground.

Without decent vision, you'll be piloting from the ground. Here again, the FAA specifies certain requirements, and there are drugs that represent a threat to your making the grade.

The book says that for a third-class certificate you must have 20/50 or better vision in each uncorrected eye. If it's worse than that, it must be correctable to 20/30. There can be no "serious pathology" of the eye, and you can't be so color blind that you can't distinguish white, aviation signal red and signal green.

For second-class privileges the numbers are 20/20 (uncorrected) or no worse than 20/100 correctable to 20/20. In addition, you must have a normal field of vision, sufficient accommodation (ability of the eye to adjust to a change in range) to read aeronautical maps, and no pathology. For a first-class medical the same requirements plus more precise criteria on near vision and permissible problems apply. You also have to have normal color vision—no compromises here.

Many drugs have an effect on the optic nerves and pose a risk. Probably the most commonly used is tobacco. Heavy smokers have been shown to suffer "tobacco amblyopia"—dimness of vision. And on a short-term basis, tobacco ties up the hemoglobin with which your blood gets oxygen from hither to yon. The eyes are particularly sensitive to fluctuations in oxygen level. High altitude and night flying compound the problem.

Cortisone and its derivatives (prednisone, prednisolone, dexamethasone and others) are extremely powerful drugs used to control severe inflammation (from athletic injuries, arthritis, or a bursitic shoulder), tissue rejection (in organ transplants) and histamine-type reactions that can cause unbearable itching. Unfortunately, when used in large doses over long periods, these drugs can also lead to changes in the eye's lens, and can even cause cataracts. While a bit of cortisone cream used to reduce the swelling from an insect bite won't make you go blind in a day, caution is in order if the prescription is for long-term, internal use of any of the cortiosteroids.

Bifocals and Trifocals for Pilots

For most pilots, there is a requirement to have competent vision in three main areas: (1) over the instrument panel for distant vision outside the aircraft, (2) the instrument panel itself, usually slightly beyond arm's length, and (3) near vision for reading maps and charts.

The problem may be solved with the use of trifocals, in which the top part of the lens is for distant vision, the middle part for the panel and the lower part for near vision. The center lens, sometimes referred to as the trifocal lens, is 8 millimeters from top to bottom.

This 8 mm center lens is not too common—most of them measure only 7 mm. The trick is to find an optometrist who is willing to try something new and convince him that a trifocal lens is available with a center lens of 8 mm. After that, have the prescription of the center lens made especially to accommodate the instrument panel distance in the airplane you fly most frequently.

Another important point is to accurately locate the vertical position of the center lens so that there is little or no up and down head movement required to properly scan the panel. One way to do this is to take a pair of glasses, preferably similar to the trifocals being ordered, and mark them with a felt pen while sitting in the aircraft being flown the most. While sitting in the properly adjusted pilot's seat, mark the glasses with a horizontal line indicating the top of the highest instrument on the panel. Bring the marked lens to the optometrist and have him locate the top of the center lens at this line.

Sometimes there is difficulty getting the lab making the lenses to accommodate. Persistence pays off and should result in a very useful pair of glasses. Of course, for those of you who need only bifocals, the same procedure works just as well; sit in your plane and mark the lens at the glareshield line with a felt pen. After several tries, you'll find the level where it is most comfortable looking at both the instruments and outside; this line is where you should have the optometrist split the lens.

Don't Let the Smoke Get in the Pilot's Eyes

Every pilot knows, or at least has been taught, that carbon monoxide (CO) is not an aviator's friend. A colorless, odorless by-product of combustion, CO can enter the cockpit oh so quietly, which is just the way the pilot exits shortly thereafter.

While the threat of cockpit incapacitation is the context in which most pilots think of carbon monoxide as a threat, those who smoke might take a moment to ponder the results of research showing that they face a second and perhaps more insidious CO menace—impaired night vision.

Inhaled carbon monoxide, no matter what its source, competes with oxygen for a ride on the hemoglobin molecules that circulate through the blood. Unfortunately, it's a competition carbon monoxide always wins, so in the presence of CO, tissue hypoxia is inevitable. And the human eye is one of the structures that is most sensitive to any shortfall in its oxygen quota. This is particularly true at night, when the eye has an even higher level of oxygen consumption.

To probe for impairment of night vision, researchers tested both smokers and nonsmokers by giving them air, via a mask, that contained 5,000 parts per million of carbon monoxide and then running a variety of standardized tests designed to measure dark adaptation and sensitivity to contrast.

Carbon monoxide combines with hemoglobin to form carboxyhemoglobin (HbCO); as the concentration of this entity rises, oxygen available to tissue decreases, and performance decrements might be expected. "A surprising finding," the investigators note, "was that the disadvantage of smokers was greater than would be expected from the HbCO levels alone. This was true for both mean dark adaptation time and threshold light sensitivity." In the adaptation measurement, smokers were worse off *before* artificial CO exposure than were the nonsmokers after they'd been given a 100 ppm dose.

"Noteworthy," the researchers say "is that even in young healthy men with a smoking history of three to five years and consumption of a third of a pack to one pack per day, an effect was observed on the visual performance that was significantly greater than a correspondingly high but short-acting CO poisoning of nonsmokers." In other words, for equivalent blood levels of CO, long-term smokers have worse night vision, suggesting that they have been subjected to some kinds of biochemical changes that result in greater impairment for any given level of carbon monoxide ingestion.

Pilots who wish to see their way clear to fly safely at night would be well advised to be nonsmokers.

Seeing Red over Color Vision Testing

Everyone who has had a proper FAA medical has jumped through the color vision test hoop. That usually consists of peering at cardboard plates with colored dots, some of which form numbers for those with normal color vision.

Like other aspects of the visual testing done by AMEs, there's often a gap between the ideal conditions under which the tests are supposed to be administered and real conditions in a doctor's office. Reality usually gets the worst of the deal, and so do the pilots who peer at the plates under less than the specified lighting levels, for less than the prescribed time, or at the wrong distance.

Pilots who'd like to turn the tables and ask their AMEs a few questions might casually toss out one like, "Say, Doc, how far away from my eyes is the Ishihara plate supposed to be, according to the specs?"

If he knows it's 30 inches, be surprised. Most physicians haven't a clue. Nor do they know it's supposed to be shown to the hapless pilot under either natural daylight or an artificial light which is balanced to daylight color values. Fluorescents are not the right color. A penny for every Ishihara plate viewed each year by examining-room fluorescent lighting would pay for an airplane, even at today's prices.

While the Ishihara plates are probably the most widely used, there are several other color vision testing systems and each has its own set of illumination, distance and duration specifications. In reviewing a number of studies recently, two investigators concluded that "A significant number of color-normal subjects will be misdiagnosed as color defective by some of the standard tests with even relatively minor variations from standardized viewing conditions. These results appear to have strong implications for the use of the tests in many applied settings in which precise control over viewing conditions is difficult."

Any pilot who has problems with the color vision test would do well to demand that the AME check on and adhere precisely to the conditions set forth for administering the test. The kind, color or duration of light can make all the difference between passing and failing the color vision test.

Contact! (Lenses)

Few are the pilots who will get much beyond their 40th birthday without some degradation of visual acuity. As the body ages, the ability of the lens to accommodate (bend light rays in order to focus them on the back of the eye, where they're detected) decreases. That means an almost inevitable need for glasses, or, in the case of probably a majority of pilots nowadays, contact lenses.

Contacts have many advantages, but the FDA recently warned that those who choose the new "extended wear" contacts should remove the lenses at least every seven days.

When contacts first came out, a long time ago in a galaxy far, far away, they were removed every night. Nobody would think of wearing the old style, thick contacts to bed. Even falling asleep with them in was a painful experience that few people were likely to repeat if they could avoid it.

Recent innovations have permitted creation of a lens that can be worn for long periods of time without being removed from the eye. The new extended wear lenses are approved for use up to 30 days without removal, but the FDA now says that's way too long and poses "too high" a risk of developing corneal damage that can lead to permanent blindness.

Research has shown that wearers of extended use lenses develop ulcerative keratitis at five times the rate of those wearing conventional one-day-at-a-time lenses. Ulcerative keratitis is a painful infection that results in the formation of lesions on the cornea—the transparent tissue that's the outer coating of the eyeball.

Extended wear users are also cautioned by the FDA to take particular care in the cleaning of their lenses. The extended period of wear can permit the buildup of proteins on the lenses. If not properly and completely removed by cleaning, these protein buildups can cause infection or mechanical abrasion of the eye.

Knowing the inevitable when they see it (as well as the potential for lawsuits), most industry sources and eye care professionals are bowing to the FDA's request that they re-label the lenses and instruct patients to remove and clean the lenses at more frequent intervals.

Eyeball Exercise

All of us over the age of 40 struggle with the reality of changes—usually for the worse—in our bodies. One of the most obvious of changes is that in our vision.

As we age, the eye muscles are less and less capable of making the myriad adjustments needed to get everything both near and far into sharp focus. At rest, the eye naturally focuses at a distance of about 20 feet. Seeing things up closer or farther away takes some work.

So, is there a magic set of exercises that will make old, tired muscles spring back to life and snap those eyeballs to attention when you want to get a sharp look at airplanes far away? Lots of such plans have been put forth over the years, always with the suggestion that just doing the exercises would magically restore youthful vision.

Don't count on it. Yes, people do occasionally report miraculous achievements; but the results are never substantiated by any large-scale tests. In medicine, such individual or anecdotal tales are very frequent—and very suspect. Eye exercises won't do any harm, except for the possible lightening of your pocketbook. But don't expect to see (so to speak) much change. You'll probably still wind up getting a pair of glasses.

Cockpit Design and Night Vision

Once color movies came along, it became fashionable for dramatic cockpit scenes to be played out under red light, the better to preserve the hero's night vision. Generations of pilots, too, have been schooled in the notion that they will see better at night if they're seeing red.

Nobody, however, has paid much attention to what the pilot needs to actually see. Looking out the window is a fine and highly recommended pastime, but a pilot unable to read either the panel or a map is not necessarily better off for his or her "better" night vision.

Two academic researchers, aided by two researchers from General Motors, decided to take a close look at what looked good at night to people presented with an automobile instrument panel and a simulated road task.

Forty people took part in the experiment. They were divided into young (19-30), middle (31-50) and old (51-73) age groups. Their task was to guide a simulator car along a projected nighttime scene. While "driving," they were occasionally presented with written words flashed on the panel, approximating the information which might have to be read at night on a real panel.

The experimenters decided to look at color, brightness, and size of the characters as important variables. Each volunteer "drove" under a variety of color, light, and type-size combinations.

In a preliminary experiment, younger and older subjects were asked to sit in the simulator and adjust the brightness level for each color until it made reading words with medium sized letters comfortable. This level of brightness was then used throughout the appropriate age group.

One of the first and most interesting findings to emerge from this preliminary experiment was that older people required a considerably higher level of brightness to comfortably see the written words when they were displayed in red and orange colors. What's often overlooked by the red partisans is that red tends to exacerbate nearsightedness, which gets worse with age as the eye's lens loses its flexibility and thus its ability to bend and focus light on the rear of the eye, where it's detected.

The preliminaries completed, the researchers launched into the main study. They diddled and twiddled and fiddled, with each subject making 16 ten-minute "trips" during which data on response time, deviation from the driving lane, and time spent glancing at the panel were all recorded.

Besides the hard data, each driver was also asked for his or her subjective judgment of how attractive and comfortable each set of conditions was. Blue was found least attractive. Red, blue-green, and green had neutral ratings. Orange, reddish orange, white, and amber were scored the most attractive. There were no significant differences in the comfort rankings.

The objective findings were that when all was said and done, character size appeared to be the most important of the variables studied here, and its limits were imposed by older drivers. Four letter sizes—1.5, 3.5, 3.7 and 5.5 millimeters—were used. The 3.5 mm size yielded very good performance for younger and middle-aged drivers. But for the older drivers, a substantial decrement in performance was observed with this size.

The researchers also noted that in the experiment the contrast between the letters and the background was very high—probably far higher than is normally achieved in most instrument panels. They conclude that the 5.5 mm size has the best chance of being seen, a fact that must be lost on those who write things on aviation instruments and panels.

While the drivers had the color preferences, as noted above, when it came to performance, color did not appear to have a significant effect on driving and reading performance for the two larger character sizes at the two brightness levels tested in this experiment. Red, the traditional favorite, neither helped nor hindered.

The Perfect Panel, like the perfect flight, has yet to fly. If it did, it would apparently have all dials and other lettering at least 5.5 millimeters high, the panel brightness would be moderately high, and the interior lighting would be amber, reddish-orange, or white.

Glaucoma: Vision Robber

One of the greatest visual threats to older pilots is glaucoma, a disease which strikes about three percent of those 65 or older. It's the leading cause of blindness in this country.

Glaucoma can actually be caused by several different problems, any of which result in a buildup of fluid in the eye which increases pressure on the optic nerve, which is eventually injured and progressively destroyed if the pressure isn't relieved.

What makes glaucoma particularly insidious is that it comes along unfelt, causing no pain but slowly robbing peripheral vision. Untreated, the pressure builds, the damage grows, and eyesight is eventually lost in the crucial central portion of the optic field.

While the standard aviation physical does not normally include measurement of eye pressure, which is the definitive means of detecting glaucoma, most AMEs do test for adequacy of peripheral vision and this is how many pilots first discover they're suffering the early stages of the disease.

Fortunately, if detected early glaucoma can usually be successfully treated with a variety of drugs. The most frequently used today is a beta blocker called timolol. The FAA considers all glaucoma cases on an individual basis for waiver.

The FAA recommends, but does not insist, that AMEs do an eye pressure examine on all applicants over the age of 40. Pilots should, for their own protection, have a regular eye exam including such a tonometric check, a simple procedure which can be done in the doctor's office.

As to your flying status, the FAA will grant a waiver if you have open-angle glaucoma (the most common type) and the pressure can be controlled with small to moderate doses of one of several drugs. You will require an exam by an ophthalmologist, and the information will have to be evaluated by the FAA before your certificate is granted. There may be some limitations pertaining to night flying, depending on the type of drug you are given to control the pressure.

Those with closed-angle glaucoma will generally be denied, because in this form of the disease there can be very sudden rises in pressure which could lead to blurred vision, incapacitating pain and a variety of other impairments which would be hazards to safe flight.

If glaucoma is confirmed, it is *extremely* important to get treatment immediately. Glaucoma represents a very real and significant danger to your vision.

Hot Cockpit May Mean Not-So-Hot Eyesight

Sweating away in the cockpit on a hot day, a pilot can almost feel that razor sharp edge draining away. It's a good thing he can feel it, because when the going gets hot, the eyesight gets going, and the pilot may not be seeing anywhere nearly as clearly as he would be under more moderate conditions.

This finding came from a fun gambit in which willing volunteers got three hours exposure in either a room-temperature room (29 degrees Centigrade, 40 percent humidity), a hot/dry room (50 degrees C, 10 percent humidity), or a warm/humid room (38.5 degrees C, 65 percent humidity). Vision was tested using the Landolt C patterns, in which a person must identify which side the opening of the C is situated.

Both high heat conditions caused a degradation of vision, with hot-and-dry being the worst offender. Most of the decline takes place in the first 30 minutes of exposure.

Vision may prove to be the weak link. In general, most research on human factors suggests the body is capable of maintaining fairly constant performance in non-physical tasks over a great range of temperatures, up to some threshold limit at which there's a precipitous decline.

In the case of visual sharpness, though, the decline appears to be a slow and steady one with heat exposure. When the heat is on, suggest the German researchers who did the experiment, "relatively small changes in visual acuity may seriously degrade performance."

On the Periphery

When approach control calls 747 traffic at 12 o'clock, five miles, most pilots expect to see something big out there. Chances are they will, since straight ahead is where the eye is set up to see the best, at least during the daytime, when light stimulates the foveal system. This eyeball focal point is primarily responsible for pattern recognition.

Peripheral vision, on the other hand, hangs out on the visual sidelines, but for pilots it's indispensable, because it's mostly peripheral vision that provides information on motion and locates objects in three-dimensional space. It is also information from the outer edge that informs the brain about attitude (the plane's, not the pilot's), as well as giving vital clues about altitude just prior to touchdown (or bouncedown, if the peripheral cues are incorrectly interpreted).

University of Washington researchers wanted to follow up on earlier research which showed that detection of apparent motion gets progressively worse the farther an object is from the visual centerline. Ten volunteers sat surrounded by a device that allowed various apertures to be opened and lit sequentially, creating an apparent motion in one of four directions (horizontal, vertical, left oblique and right oblique). The volunteers' task was to identify the direction of motion using their peripheral vision while focusing their eyes straight ahead.

The experimenters found that the more the motion varied from straight ahead, the more accuracy suffered. At 25 degrees off center, accuracy in detecting motion was 97 percent. This declined to 80 percent at 40 degrees and to 67 percent at 70 degrees. The researchers also found that the greater the apparent motion, the greater the accuracy with which an observer can see it taking place.

"Simulator engineers and training specialists," they concluded, "should expect pilots to perceive the direction of fast moving aircraft more accurately than slower aircraft when viewed at the same eccentricity from the line of sight."

Pilots, in turn, should be aware that the admonitions to keep one's head on a swivel while flying are best taken to heart, since the motion of what lurks out there on the edge of the visual field is not so keenly visible as that which lies in one's immediate path.

The View on Cataracts

The effects of some cataracts can be dealt with optically (i.e., with progressively stronger eyeglasses); but if the thickening and clouding of the eye's lens gets beyond that point, a lens implant may be indicated, and a pilot should have some concern about the FAA's position on granting a medical certificate after the surgery.

Although any surgical procedure must be looked on as having some risk, cataract surgery involving lens implantation has become about as routine as any surgery can be. Assuming a relatively uncomplicated situation, and assuming the patient is otherwise in good health, the operation is about as ordinary as a touch-and-go whirl around the field.

Because the operation is done under a local anesthetic, it doesn't entail the risks which go with having a general anesthetic. What will be done is to make a small incision, remove the old and clouded lens, and replace it with a synthetic lens ground to provide you with good vision. It's almost as easy as it sounds. You will be instructed to avoid all strenuous exercise for several weeks, and to avoid bright light for the same period, which obviously means no flying.

That brings us to the question of how the FAA will feel about your newly adjusted vision. The local examiner will defer or deny certification and pass the case along to headquarters, where you will have to make a case for what's known as a Statement of Demonstrated Ability (a waiver, to those not part of the government bureaucracy).

A complete opthalmological evaluation will be required to obtain a waiver. The purpose is show that you have indeed had a successful procedure which has restored vision to satisfactory levels and which is stable. Getting a waiver for a Third Class medical with a lens implant should not be a problem, other than dealing with the paperwork. Once the waiver has been granted, your local AME can issue subsequent medicals assuming there have been no major changes in your condition.

Speaking of Eye Surgery, What About Radial Keratotomy?

Whether what you see is what you get continues to be a significant question for those contemplating visual correction via radial keratotomy. The controversial procedure involves making a series of radial slits which permit the lens to change its shape and thus restore normal vision to the nearsighted. Recent results of an ongoing long-term study didn't do much to lessen the shouting match. If it works as advertised, radial keratotomy promises patients a chance to see without glasses or contact lenses.

In reporting on Year 3 of their continuing study, researchers said that the 410 patients had a 57 percent chance of getting close to correct vision; 27 percent still needed glasses for distant vision, though in some cases they were less myopic than before; and 16 percent had overshot the mark and required reading glasses.

What's disturbing those who question the procedure is that many patients report considerable fluctuations throughout the day, usually starting out the day close to normal and then becoming more nearsighted from morning to evening. There are also many reports of patients having considerable problems with glare and light flares, particularly at night. Because the cornea, in which the incisions are made, heals very slowly, it is not certain whether such problems are short-term, long-term or permanent.

More encouraging was the finding that most of the patients had achieved stability in their vision. Almost nine out of ten showed little or no change from Year 1 to Year 3 of the study. The study also reports a very low incidence of severe complications (two patients).

The consensus at this point seems to be that radial keratotomy is a promising but immature technology which needs considerable research and fine tuning before it will be a consistent and reliable answer to the vision problems of most people who wear glasses.

How to *Really* See What's Out There

Information on how simulators can better simulate may also be throwing some light on what makes an airplane more—or less—visible to a pilot looking for it in the real world.

In an effort to see what it would take to build a better mousetrap—in this case, a better simulator for training fighter pilots—a group of researchers found that Navy and Air Force simulators suffered from one common deficiency. Their pilots were often unable to discern the orientation of an aircraft at anything like the distance at which they could see it in the real world.

They saw that *something* was out there, but they just didn't know which end was up. Such a lack of knowledge can prove to be very rapidly fatal for a pilot trying to decide whether an enemy plane is headed away from or towards him. And it may not be much more healthy for the general aviation pilot who's trying to figure out whether that blip out there is a descending 747 or a retreating Ercoupe. While the GA jock gets a bit more time to ponder his decision (neither 747s nor Ercoupes generally carry missiles), he still needs in at least some cases to decide fairly promptly what he's seeing and where it's headed.

The tests used four people and one simulator. The latter was programmed to present some combination of four headings, two pitch angles and two roll angles, for a total of 16 possibilities. In a series of 100 trials, the targets appeared at various orientations and differing distances, starting at 4000 feet away (a simulated 4000 feet, of course). If a person managed to correctly discern the orientation of the target aircraft, the next image was "moved" five percent farther away. An incorrect answer moved the target five percent closer in.

The researchers offered up the targets under a variety of luminance, background luminance, and target resolution conditions. What they wanted to know was whether it made any difference how light the target was, how sharp its display was, or how much contrast there was between target and background.

All this simulated flying around produced a huge mound of data. Reduced, it revealed that with high resolution, a luminance contrast of 25:1 produced better performance than lower contrasts.

Improving contrast, though, had the greatest influence on performance. While the difference between best and worst resolution was 20 percent, the gap in successful rate of detection between the best contrast condition and the worst was 40 percent.

In measurable terms, the differences amounted to being able to see an aircraft at a simulated distance of four miles under the best condition, and only 1.5 miles in the worst. Those who remember their high school algebra can quickly calculate how long it takes a 747 approaching a 172 at 500 miles/hour to cover 1.5 miles, and how welcome those extra seconds might be if the plane could instead be spotted four miles out and the pilot could figure out it was headed his way. Contrast is the key.

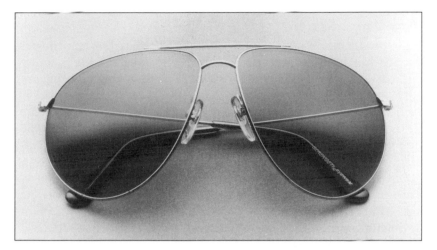

As sunglasses for pilots go, Serengeti drivers get high marks for blocking both UV and up to 86 percent of total light transmission.

The early morning sun reflected with a blinding glare off the sides of California's Mount Baldy. The pilot had decided to take a short sight-seeing flight after the fresh snowfall of the night before. The scenery was dazzling, but now he couldn't see it—the glare off the snow was even more dazzling.

Squinting, he tried to cut down some of the brightness and relieve his smarting eyes. He knew the mountain was close, but the brilliance of the sun was making it difficult to see. Finally, he reached over to the glove compartment for the sunglasses he knew were there.

Too late. With a crunch and a bang, the Cessna 140 hit the mountain 10 feet below the crest. The main landing gear caught the ground, then the nose, and the Cessna flipped, sailing backwards and upside down for another 20 feet before hitting again and sliding to a halt. The pilot emerged unhurt from the wreckage. NTSB listed the probable causes of the accident as the pilot's failure to maintain the proper altitude and his misjudgment of his clearance from the mountain.

But "failure to wear sunglasses" surely could have been a valid factor. In a very real sense, had the pilot worn sunglasses, the accident might not have occurred.

More Than Macho

For many people, pilots and non-pilots alike, sunglasses are considered more of a fashion accessory than a flight safety device. In many instances, they're chosen for the style, and what they add to one's looks, with the impact on vision and visibility secondary considerations. The macho image of James Dean in his sunglasses, or the flashy good looks of Eric Estrada in a set of mirrored "shades" may be the main criteria in the minds of many purchasers at the sunglass rack in the local drugstore.

But even for those who dispense with cosmetics and are primarily concerned with seeing better under bright conditions, how can the best set of sunglasses be found? What are some of the important parameters which pilots should be looking for in choosing "shades"? What can the wrong set of sunglasses do?

There is a substantial risk, from "rays" of several varieties. Our look into the subject of eye protection turned up concerns about:

• Ordinary visible light (including blue light)

• Ultraviolet light

• Infrared radiation.

• Polarized light

What's more, we found experts don't always agree on the potential danger of each kind of radiation, or the method of prevention.

Eye See

Exposure to bright light, especially sunlight, can have effects which go beyond what most people anticipate. These can range from simple contraction of the irises according to the brightness of the light, all the way to serious eye damage and long-term deterioration of vision.

As most people know, the irises act like the f-stop on a camera, closing in the presence of bright light to limit the amount reaching the retina. As a primary reaction to light, this works without any conscious input. But as the brightness of the light increases, the ability of the human eye to limit its input is reached. The next step is squinting. This has much the same effect as the contracting iris, cutting down the amount of light entering the eye. It, too, has its limits, and it tends to fatigue the eyes rapidly when you have to squint for a prolonged length of time.

This fatiguing effect affects not only the eyes, but the rest of the body as well. The eyes account for almost 25 percent of the body's energy use under normal conditions. The extra energy required to keep the pupil contracted and hold the eyelids in a squint raises this figure. Obviously, pilots do not need an additional source of energy drain during flight. Also, squinting limits the field of vision, which is obviously undesirable whether on the beach or in flight.

But the effects of exposure to bright sunlight go even deeper. Testing has shown that only a few hours of exposure to bright sunlight without proper eye protection can reduce night vision by as much as 90 percent, according to some sunglass makers. For pilots facing a night approach after hours of flying into a bright setting sun, such a decrease in night vision can be disastrous. Even more dramatic is the possibility that this loss of night vision can persist for days, weeks, even up to a month, depending on the length and severity of exposure. (For example, a week's vacation on a bright beach with no sunglasses can reduce night vision significantly for up to a month.)

Long-Range Effects

Especially over the longer term, exposure to sunlight can lead to permanent eye damage from the ultraviolet area of the spectrum. Exposure over the long-term to the level of UV associated with sunlight can lead to the formation of cataracts and other ocular disorders.

Studies by the federal Food and Drug Administration show a relationship between UV exposure and the incidence of cataracts. Some estimates are that not wearing sunglasses can double the chances of cataracts later in life; others say it's only ten percent. By whichever estimate, exposure to sunlight without protection is not healthy for the eyes over the long term.

The blue-light portion of the spectrum is also suspected of causing eye damage from long-term exposure. Researchers at the University of Kansas Medical Center have found that prolonged exposure to blue light will cause retinal damage after only 20 minutes of exposure to higher intensities of shorter-wavelength light, particularly the blue and near-UV portions of the spectrum. These levels of exposure are roughly equivalent to sitting on the beach for four to six hours and staring at the sand with no eye protection.

One of the researchers said, "To the general public, I would recommend sunglasses that filter out shorter-wavelength visible and

UV light. It hasn't been proven that sunglasses actually help, but to me it's intuitively reasonable to suspect they do."

Heated Debate

It's not easy to decide about the effects of infra-red, or heat radiation (IR). One of the premier sunglass makers, Bausch and Lomb, in a pamphlet titled "Sunglasses and Your Eyes, A Consumer Guide on Sunglass Selection and Uses," cautions sunglass wearers about the dangers of exposure to infra-red, but weaves it into the same sentence with a warning about UV rays. The pamphlet says both are "potentially dangerous to your eyes. If your unprotected eyes are exposed to these rays for long periods of time, they may suffer from burning or stinging sensations to intense pain. In extreme cases even total blindness, temporary or permanent, can occur."

As far as *Aviation Safety* could determine, however, these may be problems associated with UV and not with IR. We could find no concrete scientific evidence that common exposure to IR radiation is harmful to the eyes. As one sunglass industry observer noted, "Basically, the scare about the effects of infra-red radiation is nonsense. It can do harm if you get too much, and in effect cook your eyes, but otherwise, it makes no difference. I'd like to see some scientific proof that infra-red is harmful."

Straddling the fence on this issue was the FDA's Committee on Visual Health, which has been wrestling with suggested standards for eye protection. Their findings: "It is unclear whether any danger to the eye results from exposure to the levels of infra-red radiation which are used presently in industry. Since the average person is exposed to broad-band optical radiations, infra-red radiation may enhance the effects of exposure to other radiations by the elevation of temperature."

Eventually, we located a spokesman for Bausch and Lomb who conceded, "There is no indication that infra-red does anything to the eye. IR is just heat, and the level of heat from environmental IR is much less than the eye can handle. The eye will disperse this small amount of heat easily."

Polarization

Another issue for many is the effect of glare from polarized sunlight. When first introduced, sunglasses which were polarized were lauded as the true recreational sunglass. They were touted as eliminating or drastically reducing reflected glare off water, windshields, etc.

But polarized lenses have fallen out of favor in the eyes of the major sunglass makers. None of the major brands are polarized.

The primary reason cited for this is the supposed ineffectiveness of polarization when the reflected light is outside a certain angular range. As explained by Bausch and Lomb in its pamphlet, polarizing lenses "completely eliminate glare reflected from *flat* surfaces at a certain angle, depending on the type of surface. On water, for instance, the angle is 53 degrees, four seconds. Thus a fisherman, looking at undisturbed water at exactly this angle, will be able to look right down into it, unaffected by surface glare. Looking at water at any other angle, closer or farther away, diminishes this filtering action until at a 90 degree angle it is zero. The requirement for a specific angle is the reason why polarizing sunglasses have little or no effect on glare from curved or uneven surfaces."

Yet, many pilots and fishermen swear by polarized sunglasses. While it is true that the polarizing effect is limited to a rather narrow angular range of reflected light, a significant portion of the light reaching the eye under most circumstances seems to be in this range.

In sum, it appears that visible light, UV and perhaps polarization are primary concerns when shopping for sunglasses.

An Eye-Opening Experience

Armed with this knowledge, a pilot might head straight for the local drugstore in search of sunglasses. He finds himself confronted with racks of eyewear. Some of these glasses are plainly silly. But the rest all seem to melt into a melange of acrylic—how to pick the best pair? What to look for in things to look through?

Colored eyewear can be broken down into two primary categories—sunglasses, and what industry spokesmen call "funglasses." Sunglasses provide protection; funglasses provide style or fashion, but may not offer any protection.

A poor pair of funglasses may be worse than no eyewear at all. Insufficient lens tinting (lightly tinted lenses) will make the wearer squint almost as much as not having anything to protect the eye. Even worse are funglasses which are dark enough to prevent the wearer from squinting, but offer no protection from UV. Protected from the brilliance in the visible portion of the spectrum, the pupils dilate and allow more of the damaging UV rays in.

Poor quality control by the funglass manufacturer can allow distorted or imperfect lenses to reach the retailer. Eyestrain from trying to look through distorted or imperfect lenses can lead to dizziness, nausea, and permanent eye damage in severe cases.

Funglasses can generally be recognized by their light lens coloring. As these are sometimes intended to be worn indoors as well as out, the lenses tend to be rather lightly tinted compared to a real sunglass. Also, funglasses come in a variety of colors which are not recommended for sunglasses—pinks, blues, pastels and such.

While one might imagine that funglasses can be readily detected by their price too, this may not be the case. Some "designer label" funglasses cost more than a good set of sunglasses. Thus, price is no determinant of effectiveness.

Real Sunglasses

Standing at the rack, our pilot knows what he doesn't want. "But what should I be looking for?" he asks. "How about this $6 pair here? What makes them any different from this $60 pair?"

Real sunglasses should have several readily apparent features. Perhaps the two most important parameters are the lens color and density. Lens color can be of paramount importance in determining the effectiveness of a pair of sunglasses. For years, the school of thought has been that true sunglasses should have neutral gray or green lenses. While many in aviation, including the Air Force, still swear by these lens colors, testing by some manufacturers is showing that brown or yellow tinted lenses may be the best for pilots. One Army researcher has stated that the proper color for a sunglass lens would be yellow-amber or yellow-green.

Real sunglasses will have lenses which are one of these colors, with the gray or brown lenses being the preferred colors.

Lens density (which determines the amount of light which will be transmitted to the eye) is another determinant of true sunglasses. For maximum protection and easing of eyestrain, sunglasses should allow between five and 20 percent of the light to reach the eye—i.e., blocking 80 to 95 percent of the light. Current Air Force specifications call for sunglasses which will permit only 18 percent of the light to pass through.

Complementing this is a study by the U.S. Navy's Submarine Medical Research Lab. It tested a variety of neutral (gray) lenses on 60 volunteers to determine what density of lens the wearers found most comfortable. Surprisingly, most of the participants favored lenses which were much darker than what is normally available. The preferred densities, according to the researchers, allowed between 2.5 and 8.9 percent of visible light to pass through. Additionally, for most users tested, lenses of these densities would not adversely affect visual acuity.

Real sunglasses should also offer protection from UV. While this can't be determined by simply looking at the lenses, the major brand-name sunglasses do expressly offer UV protection. When dealing with unknowns, there is a dual hazard presented by some lenses.

Sunglasses which offer no UV protection but allow the wearer to look out at the world comfortably without squinting permit more UV to enter the eye, as discussed previously. But of even greater concern is a finding that the rear surface of some of these non-UV filtering lenses may actually concentrate the UV onto the lower eye.

More Miles

The lenses of the right color will filter out much of the blue light which reaches the eye. Not only will this prevent blue-light related eye damage, but, theoretically, it will also enhance visual acuity and can even increase the distance a pilot can see under hazy or marginal conditions.

This is due to the scattering effects produced by haze and dust. Small particles suspended in the air tend to reflect blue light better than other wavelengths (thus giving us the blue sky). This same scattering effect is what makes haze and dust so hard to see through. By filtering out all the scattered blue light, visibility will seem to increase.

Indeed, reports by pilots who have tested blue-filtering lenses seem to support this contention. One pilot told of being able to see the runway several miles before his copilot, who was not wearing blue-filtering lenses.

Tests by manufacturers have shown that sunglasses with blue-filtering capability offer improved visibility and visual acuity under marginal VFR conditions. One pilot even claimed that glasses with these type of lenses increased his ability to see through haze to the extent that five-mile visibility without the glasses suddenly increased to some 30 miles with them.

Shopping List

Pilots shopping for sunglasses should be looking for the following characteristics:

• Color: Lenses should be brown, yellow-amber, gray, or sage green.

• Density: Lenses should be fairly dark, cutting out between 80 and 95 percent of visible light.

• Protective Qualities: The lenses should block all or most UV transmission. Polarization may be a preferable enhancement. Claims about IR protection can be ignored.

What About Lens Material?

Plastic lenses may have an edge over the traditional glass lenses, which weigh more, and have less impact resistance than plastic ones; they also get more expensive as prescriptions become more complicated.

The accuracy of the lens is also said to be better with plastics. By grinding one perfect lens to make the mold, perfect lenses can be mass produced. Glass lenses, on the other hand, must be ground individually. To keep the price from getting astronomical, accuracy may be sacrificed. Advocates of glass lenses claim that with tempering, the impact resistance of glass becomes as good as plastics. Also, because of the manufacturing method of grinding each lens, quality control is better. Glass tends to be more scratch resistant than plastics, and it is impervious to most chemicals.

In the end, it would seem to be a toss-up, with good and bad points on both sides of the argument. The purchaser's personal preference is the final factor of the choice.

Information, Please

"Now I know what I'm looking for," our pilot says, "but I still don't see the difference between these $6 glasses and these $60 ones."

It is unfortunate, but true, that our pilot will probably remain in the dark about his sunglass choices. There are no labeling standards for sunglasses as yet, although some are being contemplated.

It is not a quest without hope, however. Most of the major manufacturers are willing to provide information about how much of which kinds of radiation their sunglasses will let through. At least one of the smaller manufacturers of sunglasses has now begun including transmittance information with its sunglasses on the rack, issuing tags with each pair of sunglasses which detail the items of importance for the consumer. These tags give information on the amount of visible, UV, and IR light transmitted by each pair.

Sunglasses at Night

While most people would not consider wearing sunglasses at night, there are occasions when it might be wise to break out the shades after sundown.

For protecting night vision, sunglasses can come in handy during those refueling stops. It is known that degradation of night vision can persist for hours after exposure to bright lights. This exposure can be minimized by slipping on the shades before taxiing to the lighted refueling area or walking into the FBO. Funglasses might be better for this purpose, as regular sunglasses may be too dark (it's no fun tripping over the counter).

Counter Testing

Selecting a few pairs of sunglasses from the rack, our pilot ponders which to buy. He tries them on, and decides on this nice set of aviator-style shades with acrylic lenses. He heads for the checkout, whistling the theme from *The High and the Mighty*. But wait—there are some simple checks he should be making before he checks these out.

Imperfections in the lenses are of paramount concern. Distorted lenses, or lenses with waves, wiggles, injection marks, or uneven density could be uncomfortable at least, disastrous at most. How can our pilot detect these in the store? Imperfections can be readily detected by turning the glasses over and getting some overhead lighting to reflect on the inside of each lens. By slowly rocking the lens back and forth, any imperfections will be apparent as the reflection will wave or wiggle as it passes over it. The reflection should be unchanged as it travels across the lens.

If our pilot has chosen a set of glasses without any transmission information provided, he can determine if they are dark enough by putting them on and looking in the little mirrors often found on the sunglass rack. He should not be able to see his own eyes clearly through the glasses. At best, he should see the outline of his eyes, but not be able to see the eyes themselves.

Unfortunately, there is no way for our pilot to determine if these lenses are UV-blocking. There is some comfort in knowing that the most common windscreen materials (Plexiglas, acrylic, etc.) will filter out much of the UV in the cockpit, so a pilot actually cuts down the danger the minute he gets into the airplane. UV blocking is vital, however, if these sunglasses are intended for all outdoor activities.

Who's Who?

Disgusted with the lack of information provided at the sunglass rack, our pilot puts back his selections. "Who makes *good* sunglasses? I want to know what I'm getting is good for flying, fishing, or golf," our pilot proclaims.

Name-brand manufacturers come to the rescue. The big eyewear makers offer not only quality sunglasses, but the information needed for intelligent buying decisions.

Bausch and Lomb, makers of Ray-Ban sunglasses, offer a wide variety of lenses and frames. Pilots should be looking for Ray-Bans featuring the G-15 or G-31 lenses. Available in gray, green, or brown, these lenses will filter out at least 99 percent of UV and 85 percent (for the G-15s) to 92 percent (for the G-31s) of visible light.

These lenses are made of optical quality ground glass, and polished to eliminate any distortions or imperfections. They are available at many FBOs, through several mail-order firms, and at many opticians.

Corning Optical markets "Serengeti Driver" sunglasses. Like Ray-Bans, these are made of optical quality glass, ground and polished. Serengeti Drivers are a photochromic lens, meaning that they darken upon exposure to light. Unlike earlier photochromic lenses, which reacted to UV (and would therefore remain almost clear unless the wearer kept his face in the sun), Serengeti Drivers react to visible light, allowing them to darken in the cockpit.

The Driver lenses are copper-colored, filtering out much blue-light and theoretically cutting through haze. In all conditions, they will cut out 99 percent of UV. At their darkest, Drivers will filter out 86 percent of visible light at the top of the lens.

Serengeti Drivers are also offered with *gradient lenses.* The top of the lens is darker than the bottom. These lenses, at their darkest, will filter out this much visible light: Top of lens—94 percent, middle—92 percent, bottom—86 percent.

Younger Optical of California offers sunglasses which are touted as "probably the best sunglass available." The main features of the Younger PLS 540 lenses are their ability to filter out 100 percent of UV radiation and more than 95 percent of blue light.

Despite the Younger company's claim that these are sunglasses, due to their rather high transmittance of visible light (they will pass about 45 percent of visible light), they cannot really be considered true sunglasses in their original density. They can, however, be tinted by an optician to bring them up to the 80 to 90 percent filtration of a true sunglass.

The PLS 540 lenses are brownish-colored, leaning a bit toward the red. This lens color will, it is claimed, allow better vision under hazy conditions. At least two wearers we spoke with claim to have found significant improvements in visibility. One pilot, for example, claims to have observed a 30-mile increase in apparent visibility with the Younger lenses. In our own very limited testing of these lenses, however, we found it difficult to detect any noticeable improvement in visibility under any conditions—hazy, foggy, or otherwise.

Additionally, some people who tried these lenses at our request reported mild to moderate color distortion, most notably in the greens (vegetation, for example, became a brilliant yellow-green, and mercury-vapor streetlights became stop-light green). Others reported that the lenses produced headaches and eyestrain.

The Younger PLS lenses do have some specific applications which are notable. They are, for example, recommended for eye patients with certain problems like developing cataracts, corneal dystrophy, diabetic retinopathy, or glaucoma, to name a few. Also, they are highly recommended for those whose occupations expose them to higher-than-normal levels of UV radiation, such as lab workers, video terminal users, and veterinarians.

These lenses are available through optical laboratories, opticians, and eye-care specialists. They can be matched to any prescription, or are available in flip-ups for use with untinted prescription lenses.

Cheap Sunglasses

Sunglasses need not be very expensive to give the pilot all the protection he needs. Hudson Universal, of Englewood, New Jersey, offers "cheap sunglasses" which claim to match the performance of most of the higher-priced models. Marketed under the name HiLex, the line offers a wide variety of eyewear at an equally wide range of prices.

Surprisingly, Hudson's product line includes two very good sunglasses at very reasonable prices. At the upper end of the price range is the S'Ombr/1 Gradient Density Lens sunglass. They cut out 80 percent of visible light, 10 percent of infra-red, and 99 percent of UV.

At the lower end of the price range, Hudson offers perhaps the best pair of "cheap" sunglasses. The Coquille Mirror Lenses filter out 90 percent of visible light, 80 percent of infra-red, and 90 percent of UV.

There is no free lunch, however, and Hudson's sunglasses are not without their problems. Chief among these is the quality of the frames. The pair of Coquille Mirror sunglasses we tested had metal frames which were not well finished, with some rough spots. Also, these frames seemed to be a little weak and were too easy to bend. They do not seem likely to stand up well under prolonged use.

The S'ombr/1 sunglasses we tried had plastic frames. We found them to be extremely comfortable. They were light on the face and almost unnoticeable after a few minutes of wear. But the all-plastic construction did not permit these glasses to be bent to conform to the wearer's face without special treatment (i.e., heating the frames in boiling water to soften them and permit bending). For an average-sized skull, these glasses should do fine.

The Eyes Have It

Our pilot steps out the door of the store and into the bright sunlight. He dons his new sunglasses and feels comfortable in the sun.

He also feels confident in his choice. Through careful selection, he has protected himself from harmful UV radiation, screened out the blues, improved his visual acuity, and he still looks good, too.

Swaggering like Jan Michael Vincent, he strolls off into the sunset—without squinting.

Eye Moves

Out the window, down to the instruments, out the window, down to the instruments. Up and down, in and around, thus go the eyes of a pilot. How well they do their assigned task is eventually measured in the safety records.

It was also measured in the lab of two scientists who decided to see what the eyes see when confronted with the need to both scan the outside world and monitor the gauges. In this case, both "the outside world" and "the gauges" were displays on a Macintosh computer. The upper half of the screen showed a large circle which had within it an X that had a tendency to walk around randomly on its own. The task consisted of watching the errant X and, when necessary, dragging it back to the center of the circle.

Meanwhile, in the lower half of the screen, three gauges were also on the move, conducting excursions in one direction or another from their ideal values. The gauges were marked at their top and bottom quarters with a black warning zone, into which the quivering markers were not to be allowed to wander.

There were two experimental conditions. In the first, the instrument pointers were always visible. In the second, the pointer became visible only when the instrument was selected using the computer's mouse. All eye movements of the half dozen people taking part in the experiment were recorded using a specialized camera so that the researchers could later sit down and figure out just where a person was looking every instant.

The tracking task—keeping the X at home in its circle—was performed quite successfully. On average the X was within 10 percent of the diameter of the circle from the center. Instrument monitoring was evaluated by the length of time the gauge dropped or rose into the forbidden black zone. "Results showed that performance was better in Condition 1 and that there are significant differences between subjects as well as between instruments for some individual subjects," the researchers write. They do note that the percentage of time the three pointers dropped into the black zone ranged from 0.03 for the best subject in Condition 1 to 0.3 for the worst subject in Condition 2, so overall performance here was quite good also.

The investigators found it noteworthy that "there were marked individual differences in frequency, mean duration, and patterns of visual sampling as well as manual sampling. These differences, especially in transitional patterns, reflect different strategies with which subjects achieved a required level of performance."

Second, and perhaps even more significant, the way people looked at the two different conditions varied. "Visual attention was more homogeneously distributed in Condition 1," the scientists report. "In contrast, eye movement patterns were far more constrained in Condition 2. The constraint obviously originates from fixations required for observing responses, which seem to have a stronger tendency to become patterned than visual sampling. This tendency could be a pitfall in a CRT-based console on which the operator may have to call up displays as required."

That will be familiar to any pilot who has ever diddled the dials of a multi-page Loran display, and the makers of such displays as well as the designers of equipment which will eventually give even GA pilots a "glass cockpit" might well heed the researchers' warning that "Special care should be paid to avoiding potential human errors caused by stereotypically patterned allocation of attention when designing a new CRT-based task."

The Pilot's Hearing

C ommunication is generally defined as the transfer of information from one person to another, through some sort of medium, or channel. If the signal is distorted, or blocked, or misperceived because of some interference between transmitter and receiver, "communication" doesn't happen. In aviation, a breakdown in communication can be uncomfortable at best, disastrous at worst...and annoying whenever it takes place.

Noise is generally defined as anything that gets in the way of communication, and, Lord knows, we have enough of that in general aviation airplanes; have you ever considered how much more pleasant flying would be if only it were *quiet?* Unfortunately, that's probably not going to happen; good headsets and noise-attenuating construction techniques help, but airplanes will continue to be a noisy way to travel—it's the nature of the beast.

We believe that understanding and prevention are a pilot's best weapons in the battle against noise. In this section of the *Command Decisions Series,* you'll find general information about hearing, hearing protection, and the results of research which might help make your hours aloft a bit easier on the ears.

A Tough Problem

The noise that we experience as pilots (and passengers, too) represents a lot of energy from a number of sources; noise from propellers, noise from engines, the noise of air rushing by, and of course the noise of leaky cabin doors and windows...the list goes on and on.

Bigger and faster airplanes don't solve the problems, either; easy communication in all types of airplanes presents bigger problems as we get more and more power and go to higher altitudes at greater speeds. You might argue that it's the jets which go the fastest and highest, and that they are quieter than prop-driven airplanes. In some respects jets *are* quieter, but what noise there is comes right in the frequency range you need most to hear speech clearly.

Any way you look at it, the voice you find so effective when "flying your desk" will simply not do the job when you take to the air. There are three general parts to the problem; how your hear, how you speak, and what you do about the interference or noise.

Here's the Way It Works

Sounds of varying pitch (wave-lengths or frequency) and loudness (volume and decibels) reach the ear as the result of pressure waves set up in the air by almost everything that moves—from a set of vocal cords to the compressor of a turbojet engine. The normal ear, under ideal conditions, drinks in every vibration with an efficiency 100 times greater than that of the best microphone.

The ear does it by picking up the pressure changes on the ear drum, that delicate membrane which separates the middle ear from the outer canal. The vibrations are carried across the middle ear by a series of three tiny bones and are then transmitted through another membrane into a spiral-shaped tube filled with fluid—the inner ear. This tube is divided length-wise by a membrane lined with tiny hair cells. These cells connect with the auditory nerve. The sensitive hair cells react to the pressure waves in the fluid and set up nerve impulses that let the brain know what all the shouting is about. That, in a thumbnail, is hearing.

There Are Limits, However

The ear simply doesn't pick up sounds outside of its frequency range, which is about 20 through 20,000 cycles per second for a young, normal-hearing person. Furthermore, sounds louder than it is accustomed to will tire the ear and make it less sensitive. Ordinarily, this loss of hearing is temporary. Its duration depends on how much noise the ear has to stand, what kind of noise it is, how long the noise goes on, and the durability of the ear itself. In many individuals, repeated exposure to fatiguing noises produces permanent impairment of hearing—hence the expressions "boilermaker's deafness" and "aviator's deafness."

These losses begin in the frequency range above that needed to hear speech, so you may have such a loss long before you are aware of it. A nuisance feature is that you might find it impossible to tell by listening if your wrist watch is running. You have to look at the second hand. A convenient feature is that you might find it impossible to hear the baby's cry in the middle of the night.

The most important feature of a hightone loss if you have one, though, is that it marks you as an individual who should be careful to protect his ears during future noise exposures, lest from not hearing the high-pitched cry of a baby you progress down to not hearing the boss's low-pitched bark!

Some Noises Are Worse Than Others

Because of tremendous variations from individual to individual, it is impossible to say how much noise an ear can take short of permanent hearing loss. Levels well below those which feel unpleasant can damage some ears. Levels high enough to hurt have no lasting effect on others. But for all, a noise containing an outstanding pure tone, such as the whine of a turbojet at idle rpm, is more annoying and has a greater damage potential than a noise of equal loudness which does not include a peak of this type.

Noise levels in the cockpit vary not only among airplane models, but with conditions of flight. The type of noise also varies. In general, prop-driven aircraft have noises which are most intense in the frequencies below those important for hearing speech. For any one type of aircraft, the noise is highest on takeoff and climb, and varies directly with power in level flight.

Now if you're one of those who fly jets and are convinced they make no noise, you may be surprised at what follows. True, there's seldom much low-frequency noise or vibration as with props. Aside from the "rumble" which is typical of some engines, you get noticeable low-frequency noise only when you extend the landing gear or wing flaps, or when something's drastically wrong with the airplane. But there's a great deal of wind or "whoosh" noise covering the entire frequency range. The level goes up with airspeed, but down with altitude. So as long as you do your really fast flying up high, slipstream noise won't hurt too badly.

Good Transmissions Are Important, Too

When you try to listen to two sounds of similar pitch but different loudness, you will discover you cannot hear the quieter one at all— the louder sound blocks out or masks the softer one. This is the big

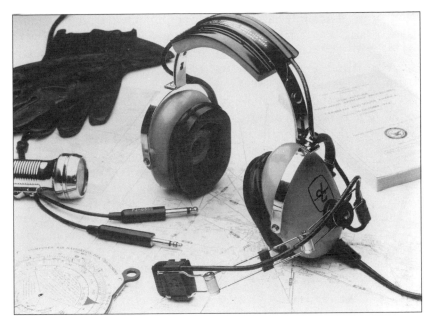

Given the noise level in most light aircraft, a good-quality, noise-attentuating headset is required safety equipment.

problem in airplane communications versus airplane noise—many sounds compete with one another.

And it's not only speech we're concerned with; consider the landing gear warning horn, the stall warning horn and so on. Although not very loud at any distance, these signals are pitched above the peak of the prop noise, and stand out clearly when they go off. (By the way, the noise spectrum of many jets mask these signals rather effectively, since the signals fall in the same frequency range as the peak of the jet noise. For that reason—among others—you'll find different kinds of warnings, such as flashing lights, spoken words or other attention-getters installed on contemporary jets.)

For good communications, the first thing you have to do is dust out your speaking tube, so to speak. Speech is generated by the bellows-like action of the lungs, forcing exhaled air over the vocal cords. These generate sounds which are modified by the resonance of the throat, nose and mouth cavities and shaped into words by the tongue, lips, and teeth.

Those of us who are not trained in public speaking (which means most of us!) speak imperfectly, to say the least. The carefree mumble-jumble we commonly call talk is thoroughly understandable to the listener under ordinary conditions, because he can take a series of hints and make sense of what he hears by mentally filling in what he did not actually get. In direct conversation, the job is made easier by facial expression and gestures.

This hint-and-guess game is not so easy when done via microphone and headset in competition with airplane noise. So it's a good idea to learn to make the best possible use of the communication system in your airplane.

Dynamic microphones and earphones have really hi-fi frequency responses when compared to the equipment of not too long ago. But you'd never guess it to listen to the way some folks use them.

Most microphones today incorporate a noise-canceling feature. That is, they are constructed so that much of the sound reaching them from any distance is canceled out, so it doesn't get carried to the headset or loudspeaker on the other end of the circuit. If, however, you don't keep the mike very close to your lips—almost touching them, in fact—much of your voice is also canceled. The person on the other end receives "tinny" unclear words liberally intermingled with noise. So if you're using a boom mike, pull it up close to talk.

How loud should you talk? Your normal conversational volume will do quite nicely, thank you. When you really raise your voice—perhaps even *shout*—into a mike, your words get badly distorted, and the message becomes even more difficult to understand.

There is one thing to remember when you're in a particularly noisy spot, however. The microphone has to have a minimum signal-to-noise ratio before it can separate out the speech properly. We've already said that the signal is distorted or lost when the mike is held too far from the mouth; but when the noise level is very high, the signal can also be lost even though the mike is positioned properly, unless the speech is quite loud. In speaking up, make sure you don't also distort; here's a time to talk slowly and articulate carefully; screaming will only make things worse.

Minimizing the Problem

So much for talking under noisy conditions. Let's consider what you can do to cut down the amount of noise reaching your ears. Any reduction will improve the ease with which you hear in flight, and lessen the possibility that you'll not hear so well later on the ground.

The first thing to do is adjust your headset so that it seals as well as possible around your ears. This is especially important with the new earphone cushions which surround rather than compress the ear. The large volume required to insure minimal touching of the outer ear, and thereby far less discomfort, prevents a really efficient coupling of receiver and ear canal. If, then, the muff does not seal closely around the ear, much of the signal is lost.

There is another aid to cutting down noise in flight and improving hearing—the insert ear plug. The plug is sealed in the ear canal and so reduces the level of the noise and of the signal reaching the ear drum. Surprisingly, even without changing the volume control you will hear speech more clearly. Also, if you wish, you can then turn up the volume and have a much better ratio of speech to noise than is possible without the plug. Now the speech signals tend to mask the noise rather than vice versa.

The one disadvantage of a well-sealed ear plug in flight is that it produces an airtight cavity between the plug and ear drum. During changes in altitude, this is subject to the same pressure imbalance as is the air space in the middle ear, but there is no natural equalization channel to correspond to the eustachian tube.

On ascent, the expanding air tends to push the plugs out a little and to escape around them. Then you simply reseal the plugs. On descent, the plugs tend to be sucked in. Since movement inward is not possible provided they fit properly, an uncomfortable suction beneath the plugs may be experienced. This is easily avoided by loosening or removal of the plugs prior to descent.

Help for Those Who Can't Help Themselves

The problem of how to protect a very young child's hearing from the damaging noises of flight has been raised a number of times before, but it takes on increased urgency with a recent (and very preliminary) finding that when newborn lab animals were exposed to high noise levels they suffered brain damage. While nobody is at all certain what the implications are (if any) for humans, it certainly raises a caution flag about exposing the very young to a harshly noisy environment without adequate protection.

What that protection should be remains a problem. You're right, the chances of getting David Clarks on an infant are not good. In fact, until kids are old enough to talk with you and see the headset as part of a fun game, it will be a struggle getting them to keep the headset on for any extended period.

That leaves ear plugs. If you are going to take a very young baby (less than a year) in the plane, you should consider a combination of ear plugs and some kind of an earmuff, to reduce as much as possible the impact of the loud noise. This will also increase the chances that the baby will share your pleasure at being airborne, rather than being terrified by all the noise.

Ear Block

A reader (who may be asking a question in many pilots' minds) wrote to us several years ago, "I am a student pilot hoping to be a commercial pilot or ATP. I love flying more than driving, but there's one condition that I don't enjoy: My ears hurt every time the plane starts to descend. If you know the cure for this problem, please help me. I don't want to give up my career because my ears are plugged up."

And the doctor answered: There's an excellent chance you can get rid of your problem. For one reason or another, your eustachian tube—the small passageway that connects the middle ear with the back of the throat—is not opening properly and allowing pressure to equalize between the ear and the outer world. As you ascend, ambient pressure drops. As you descend, pressure increases. Since you can't equalize, you're left with high pressure on the outside of your eardrum, pressing in—as you've painfully discovered—on the area of lower pressure.

You could have a chronic, low-grade ear infection that results in material blocking the eustachian tube, or you could have a tube that's dysfunctional for any of a number of other reasons, including that it just happens to be shaped a bit uniquely. In most cases, the problem can be alleviated. You should find a good otolaryngologist (ear, nose and throat specialist) or an aviation doctor with experience in handling such problems.

Hear This Warning

There may be more danger in the cockpit than in the sky. The results of an extensive study on cockpit noise suggest that more meets the ear than pilots would care to hear. "Even when the potential for injury to hearing may *appear* evident, too many fail to comprehend the seriousness where noises are routinely encountered," concludes a researcher who presented the results of more than a quarter-century of cockpit noise measurements.

The 528 fixed-wing aircraft he tested ranged from single-engine airplanes up through four-jet giants. The noise numbers on most were not good news. Once upon a time, severe hearing loss was taken as the mark of a pilot—an airborne version of the boxing pug's cauliflower ear. Unfortunately, according to these results, noise hasn't gone down as fast as airplanes have grown up.

The mean noise exposure level in single-engine aircraft was just under 98 decibels, and more than a third of the 92 planes in this category registered cockpit noise levels at or above 100 dB. Under OSHA standards, the 98-dB level is unsafe at an exposure level in excess of 79 minutes per 24-hour period. "Generally, aviators who encounter the magnitudes of (sound levels) evident throughout the foregoing summaries have reason to be concerned about the potential for auditory risk, especially when encounters are frequent and when personal hearing protection either is not used or is not adequate," writes the investigator. "Noises encountered in cockpits of most aircraft do represent a potential risk to unprotected hearing."

The answer, if pilots could hear, is ear protection. But that's easier said than done, as the study's author notes: "Education without motivation is of very limited value. Aviators must be convinced to avoid any and all unprotected encounters with excessive noises in and out of the cockpit."

As an example of the safety to be found behind a hearing protector, there may be ear plugs or headphones with a Noise Reduction Rating of 29 dB (the Noise Reduction Rating for hearing protection devices is normally printed on the package or given on an enclosure). Discounting the rating by 25 percent, to allow for the difference between lab tests and the real world, results in a reduction to 22 dB of protection. This would bring the 98-dB cockpit noise figure down to 76. At 76 dB, the permitted exposure while remaining within safe bounds is in excess of 24 hours.

Hearing loss is a slow, insidious and cumulative process. Each unprotected exposure does its little bit of damage, until the threshold is reached where hearing impairment becomes apparent. Those who wish to prevent it must start long before the time when people's lips seem to move without making a sound.

In Harm's Way Every Time We Fly

Most pilots undoubtedly would say an unblemished accident record equals perfect safety in the air. But there is one way in which every pilot can suffer serious injury, without ever crashing. Despite some advance in the use of protective devices, it is reasonable to estimate that tens of thousands of pilots at the present moment are regularly causing themselves harm, every time they fly.

The hazard is hearing loss, and practically every pilot who flies a piston-powered airplane is exposed to some risk. And, as we'll discuss, even some pilots who think they have protection, may not have total protection. Worse still, there is no practical way to tell if hearing damage is occurring, until it has already occurred.

One of the reasons for confidence in predicting at least some hearing loss in all bare-eared pilots is simple: there is virtually no production piston airplane in existence which does not deliver an ear-damaging dose of noise to the heads of its occupants. Over several years of spot-checking, *Aviation Consumer* magazine has never found a piston airplane with a cockpit noise level that can be considered safe from the standpoint of noise exposure.

Indeed, although individuals vary in their hearing loss, there are many piston airplanes with cockpit noise levels high enough to guarantee hearing damage to pilots who fly them regularly without ear protection. And, sad to say, the engineering difficulties presented by the interior noise problem are so tough that there is little likelihood of general aviation ever seeing a piston aircraft that is acceptably quiet—"sound-proofing" modification kits notwithstanding. Among the quietest cockpits we've measured, noise levels at cruise still are above 87 decibels. This is a lot quieter than some at 105 decibels, but still quite sufficient to create hearing damage in, say, flight instructors or paid pilots who spend time daily in the airplane.

Beyond the kind of hearing damage in which the person simply cannot hear certain sounds, there looms a much more disturbing specter: tinnitus, or ringing in the ears. This is commonly a high-pitched whine which commences one day in a person's life (often in middle age) and may never stop, day or night, ever. Since noise exposure damage is cumulative, both hearing loss and tinnitus may not show up until years after the start of the damaging exposure.

Although there is growing awareness among the general public of the ill effects of noise exposure, little is being done to deal with the problem in the general aviation cockpit, and pilots are largely left to individual answers on the extent of the danger or preventive measures they could take. The good news is that once pilots are convinced to take action, there are many effective ways of reducing the risk, and improving the safety of other aspects of their flying as a spinoff.

Deafening

It can be said that one is "wearing out" his ears throughout his lifetime. Exposure to excessive noise simply accelerates the wear.

Some in the medical field have posed that the human ear is

actually too sensitive for modern times. Eyes and noses may have atrophied since man needed them for hunting, but the ear performs at a level still comparable to that of a jungle animal. Human ears (with "perfect" hearing) can detect sound levels starting very near zero decibels, all the way up to the threshold of pain, an increase in sound energy of a trillionfold. Perfect ears may have a frequency response between about 200 cycles per second (Hertz or Hz) all the way to about 15,000 Hz.

These functions are accomplished by the ear in an elegantly simple way, although the hardware of the task may appear complex. Sounds arrive at the outer ear, enter the ear canal and cause the eardrum to vibrate. Connected to the inside of the eardrum is a chain of three bones that transmit the vibration to the cochlea, or inner ear.

Inside the spiral-shaped cochlea are thousands of tiny hairs. For a given frequency, a given set of these hairs will begin to vibrate in response to the incoming signal. The hairs now convert the vibration into essentially an electrical signal and transmit it through nerves to the brain.

Nature has provided very little in the way of a protection mechanism. There are two muscles within the ear which can respond to certain loud sounds by stiffening the eardrum and disconnecting the middle ear's chain of bones. However, these protective muscles have a response time that is slower than many modern explosive sounds (i.e., gunshots, or lightning crackle over a phone line). Thus, by the time the muscles can react, the sound has already gotten to the cochlea to do its damage.

Each human being has slightly different ears, and the shape and composition of the individual ear can affect the way certain frequencies of sound are transmitted. Particularly, harmonic resonances may change from person to person.

According to some experts, an ear commonly receives best at about 1200 Hz, does well at 500 to 800 Hz, and has a quarter-wave amplification at about 4,000 Hz. This 4,000 Hz frequency is remarkable, in that typical hearing loss also begins around 4,000 Hz.

There are many obvious ways to damage one's hearing. A blow to the head, an infection, something stuck into the ear, a single-event, extremely loud noise (i.e. standing next to a cannon), and even an excess dose of antibiotics can cause partial or full hearing loss. However, the vast majority of hearing loss and tinnitus cases are caused by longer-term exposures to noise.

Chiefly, this kind of damage affects the hairs of the cochlea. The damage is cumulative, and depends on the intensity and duration of the exposure. A moderately loud environment for many years will cause hearing loss; so will a very loud environment for a few years. The hairs of the cochlea will become "fatigued" and no longer resonate, or they may actually break off (short, high-intensity sounds like a gunshot can actually cause the hairs to break off instantly).

Temporary Losses

When the hairs are just fatigued, they can recover somewhat, so that a hearing loss can be only temporary (although long-term wear and tear on the hairs has also occurred.) Again, individuals vary widely, but researchers have found that as a rule of thumb, an eight-hour exposure to noise of 100 decibels or greater can cause a temporary hearing loss of as much as 40 decibels in the auditory threshold (i.e., what you could hear at 30 decibels you now can't detect until 70 decibels). If the exposure is to typical industrial noise, the largest area of hearing loss will be about 4,000 to 6,000 Hz. And, recovery from temporary hearing loss usually occurs within the first two hours after the noise exposure has ended.

Over the long haul, however, the hairs of the inner ear are suffering from every loud exposure. As one doctor put it, they are like blades of grass: "You can walk on them a little and they spring back, but if you trample them too hard or too often, they flatten and die."

Permanent Losses

Americans generally are exposed to a lot of noise, and a typical adult in this country may suffer at least a mild permanent hearing loss by the age of 40.

The trouble is, conditions and individuals vary, so there is no reliable way to correlate a level of exposure, a duration, and the amount of hearing loss. Numerous studies have eventually produced a table which the Occupational Health and Safety Administration uses as the basis for limiting noise exposure in the workplace. However, some individuals seem to keep their hearing despite exposure to more noise than the table shows, while some suffer damage at a lower noise level.

Still, if the exposure is well above 90 decibels (and it usually is in the lightplane cockpit), any individual can virtually guarantee he will lose some of his hearing.

The FAA, in Advisory Circular 91-35, speaks of Civil Aeromedical Institute (CAMI) findings as follows: "Pilots of helicopters and of aerial-application aircraft are particularly susceptible because of the relatively high levels of noise found in these cockpits—and, in the case of aerial application, because of the long durations of noise exposure.

But according to the CAMI tests, even the general aviation pilot (or crew member) who is in the air for more than three hours a week is likely to find himself slightly deaf after several years of flying. Two other rules of thumb are that the hearing loss will be greatest at the high end of the scale, and that by the time the person realizes he can't hear as well as he should, a lot of damage has occurred.

Very few people become concerned about the few violin high notes they are missing in a symphony, but when they begin to have trouble separating voices in a crowd, making out words to songs on the radio or hearing voices of women or children, then it becomes noticeable.

At this point, it is also too late. By this time, the lost hearing cannot be restored, and the remaining hearing will have to be preserved or it too will go.

All this makes it sad to consider the plight of certain young pilots— flight instructors are a prime example—who begin a life of flying without any warnings about their hearing, rack up thousands of ear-splitting hours in the cockpits of light trainers and do much of the preliminary damage that will years later result in hearing losses. When they graduate to the cockpit of an airline jet—which is much quieter—the rules unfortunately require them to have better hearing than if they were back in the lightplane.

Tinnitus

There is still worse news than that, however. Those who suffer permanent hearing damage may go on to suffer tinnitus, or ringing in the ears. Most people (94 percent, according to one study) may have noticed a low-level, high-pitched whine in one or both ears upon occasion. It is likely temporary.

But after hearing damage (in an estimated one in five cases) there may be permanent tinnitus. The whining noise may commence one day and simply never go away. It may start at a level that is only annoying at bedtime, but become loud enough to be heard all day. It's estimated that as many as 37 million Americans may suffer from chronic tinnitus. The tinnitus sufferer may look for all kinds of cures, but not much is available. Some people with severe cases may go to the extreme, asking their doctors to destroy their hearing surgically.

Unfortunately, this may not solve the problem. Although there is not universal agreement, it appears the ear-brain connection doesn't work that way. It has been postulated that the human brain scans the auditory system at regular intervals, looking for a "signal on the wire." Normal hairs in the cochlea produce a certain "static" signal. If the hairs for a particular frequency have been broken off, the brain apparently "invents" the noise those hairs would have transmitted, had they been vibrating.

Even if the auditory nerve is severed, it appears the brain replaces the missing signals with a perception of noise. The ear may no longer be functioning at all, but the "sound" is louder than ever.

In some cases, tinnitus sufferers get some relief by wearing "maskers," or devices which produces another noise as a distraction. But in many cases, the tinnitus is untreatable—and unbearable.

Other Hazards

So far, we have only seen the damage to the auditory system. Excess noise has also been linked to hypertension (high blood pressure), stresses that can lead to ulcers, physiological fatigue, and more.

Specifically for pilots, the FAA has noted that cockpit noise can do two things to make a flight less safe: it may cause pilot fatigue, and it may render radio transmissions unintelligible.

Words from the Head Shed

The FAA says, "Cockpit noise is particularly detrimental to speech intelligibility because the engine and exhaust noises are at a maximum in the same frequency range where speech has its maximum energy. Pilots often report that, although the volume or gain control on the receiver is turned all the way up, tower transmissions are garbled or covered up—masked—by the engine noise. Tests at CAMI showed that, under takeoff conditions, the intelligibility of the tower controller can fall from 100 percent to zero.

"The extent of fatigue—particularly how to quantify it—has so far eluded researchers, but recent research has been making inroads. Part of the problem is that a steady loud noise (although loud enough to be doing damage to the ears) can be tolerated by a person, provided there are not other stressful factors.

"Part of the problem is explained by another CAMI study that showed the fatiguing effects of noise to be increased in a listener, such as a pilot, who is mentally active rather than resting. Since a pilot in command cannot rest safely during a flight, the noise may affect him more than, for instance, a passenger who is relaxing," the FAA says.

In fascinating studies that are still under way, Dr. Harvey Wichman at the Aviation Psychology Laboratory, Claremont McKenna College, has been seeking to quantify the stress that pilots undergo. The Claremont, California, psychologist, who is also a CFII, has found evidence that three factors may combine together to create stress in a pilot. He believes the required vigilance of having to control the airplane, monitor the instruments, navigate and the like is one factor. A second is a "general ill-at-easeness in pilots once they get into the air—even long-time, experienced pilots." (Many pilots would assert that flying is relaxing. Upon close examination, they probably would agree that they mean they feel very relaxed after a flight.)

The third factor is noise. Laboratory studies using a tape-recording of a Cessna 172 at the actual loudness of the cockpit appear to show that, if one is not actually flying in the airplane, one can accommodate to the noise alone.

However, using a technique to measure breathing rate—an indicator of stress levels—Wichman found in an in-flight test program that the noise appears to pile a significant extra burden onto the stress of flying—and can be reduced easily with proper protection.

Noise-Stress Study

Ten low-time pilots were breathing at an average of 18 breaths per minute at rest before their test flights. On each of three 45-minute flights involving takeoffs, touch-and-goes, stalls and slow flight, their breathing rates were measured.

One flight was conducted without hearing protection. The test subjects averaged about 24 breaths per minute. For comparison, Wichman said in an interview that 25 breaths per minute is "on the verge of hyperventilation."

On another flight, the subjects were given ear plugs that effectively reduced noise exposure. They now averaged about 23.5 breaths per minute. Wichman believes even though the noise was gone, the subjects experienced some stress because the ear plugs were new to the wearers, and they complained about not being able to hear engine and airspeed sounds (more on this question later). However, on a second flight, with the subjects accustomed to the ear plugs, the average breathing rate went down to 22.5 breaths per minute.

As Wichman concluded, "This study not only established that ear plugs are effective in reducing pilot stress but it also quantified the degree of effectiveness. Notwithstanding the concerns for the long-term protection of an aviator's hearing, it seems that an easy-to-use, inexpensive device that will reduce a pilot's stress level by 9 percent is well worth use by general aviation pilots. This is particularly noteworthy because the 9 percent overall savings translates into a saving of approximately 25 percent of the stress that flying without ear plugs adds to the baseline stress level.

"This study also demonstrated that there is a brief time necessary for one to adjust to using the ear plugs, but even while using them the first time there is a savings of about 6 percent in stress level. Finally, the study reminds us once more that, at least for low-time pilots, flying is a very stressful experience, with aviators showing about a 30 percent breathing rate increase over baseline when they fly without ear plugs.

"Even highly experienced pilots may want to consider the lesson in all this. Perhaps a pilot is not concerned about noise and stress as he sets out on a fine VFR day for a one-hour hop. But let him fly for three hours into the night, shoot an IFR approach and fail to break out at minimums. Now, as he executes that missed approach (which, chances are, he is not used to performing) and the engines go to full power and the controller issues a series of rapid-fire instructions into his noise-deafened ears, the questions of noise and stress will take on poignant meaning.

Getting Protection

Assuming the pilot has been convinced to take steps to reduce the noise and stress, there is lots of good news. He can effectively reduce almost all the risk for less than $2. Depending on his preferences, he can also spend as much as $500.

Obviously, the equipment to do the job falls into two categories: ear plugs and headsets.

But, setting out to shop for such items is fraught with difficulty, for there is a vast array of both ear plugs and headsets on the market. The buyer soon becomes entangled in a mass of claims about comfort, performance, noise attenuation (reduction), and more. And there is the chance that a poor product or an ill-fitting one will leave the customer with a false sense of security, thinking he has hearing protection when he does not.

In recent years, the market has also seen products which combine the ear plug and headset features, appropriately called "ear sets." These also have good and bad points.

Some items to consider when looking at headsets, ear plugs, and ear sets: As a rule of thumb, some protection is better than none at all. The typical lightplane flier who submits to a 95 decibel environment and then turns up the cabin speaker so he can hear the radio above it, is simply asking for trouble.

While it is true that almost anything worn on the ears will offer some noise protection, there are a few cases where headsets ill-suited to aviation can actually amplify certain frequencies of noise in the cockpit. Also, certain ear plugs that do not conform well to the ears can be next to useless for noise attenuation.

Although it should seem obvious to the manufacturers of the devices, the one-side-only model of ear set or headset—still often seen for sale—is a waste of a pilot's money if used alone. It leads the wearer to turn up the volume in the set to compete with the cockpit noise coming in the other ear. Used with a good ear plug in the other ear, it makes sense, although pilots often try it and find they are more comfortable with two-ear headsets.

Comfort may seem like a minor consideration, but in fact it may make the only difference between a device being used or not. Headsets are often perceived as heavy, too tight on the sides of the head, and apt to cause sweating around the earmuffs. Ear plugs and ear sets can cause irritation and pain in the ear canals.

Even though a device might be a good product, if the customer finds out quickly that it doesn't afford him the comfort required to wear it for a three-hour flight, he is best advised to return it to the manufacturer and seek a refund. Otherwise, it will just gather dust back in the baggage compartment of the plane.

Headsets

There are dozens of headsets on the market, ranging in price from under $100 to nearly $1000. They are usually touted for their frequency response in the headphones, and their dynamic, noise-canceling microphones—features that are fine to have, but do not address the hearing protection question. Often, manufacturers have models which offer good or excellent protection, and other models with little protection. Reputable manufacturers also will point out that unless the headset is worn correctly, the noise protection may be next to nothing.

A good headset can take a 95 decibel cockpit racket and drop it to about 65 decibels in the wearer's ear. A further point about headsets is that they don't offer protection from sudden loud transmissions, radio static, the "pop" of aircraft strobes or lightning, or the roar of air from the cabin vent onto the headset microphone. Far from attenuating these noises, the headset actually pipes the din directly into the user's ears. Driven to its maximum, a good headset can deliver a dose of 120 decibel noise—the threshold of pain in many people.

Some experts believe this is far more of a hazard than had been thought. Particularly because explosive sounds do not register in the brain fast enough to reflect the true sound level (by the time you realize it was a very loud pop, it's over), some believe long-time headset wearers are doing damage to their ears because they wear headsets. A San Francisco company has developed a device which automatically limits such sounds to 80 decibels (by compression, not by "clipping"). However, this equipment, though small and relatively inexpensive (about $65), so far has required a separate source of voltage, and the company is still working on a model that can be a mere adjunct to the headset cord.

Finally, switching to a headset can do a lot of good for the pilot, but does nothing for his passengers. To some, it is an advantage that the pilot stays insulated from the cockpit conversation. However, when it is deemed useful to add a second pilot in the "loop," or the passengers, it is necessary to buy more headsets and an intercom. This can easily run the tab up to $500.

Ear Sets: You Get What You Pay For

The advent of featherlight, cheap ear sets has allowed many pilots into the "headset" game at a cost they can afford, and do away with headset weight and "squeeze." However, many ear sets are sold with only one-ear protection, and often with round, plastic eartips. These eartips must fit properly to get any real protection, and they often don't. And a lot of users find the round eartips give them a sharp pain in the ear canal after just a half-hour of use.

For these reasons, we strongly recommend not buying such ear sets. Superior ear sets will have two-ear protection, and the eartips will actually be individually molded plugs that conform to the user's own ear canals. These offer genuine noise attenuation performance of up to 40 decibels.

There are several ways to obtain such ear plugs. If a pilot already owns the type of set where the sound is delivered through a plastic tube, he can go to a local hearing aid store and be fitted for ear plugs that will mate with the ear set tubes. The process involves making molds of the client's ear canals, then having soft plastic ear plugs made to match the molds. This will cost around $50.

One company provides the customer with the materials to make his own molds. He sends these to the company and a couple of weeks later has his ear plugs back in the mail. Ear experts strongly advise against an individual's creating his own earmolds. We would recommend that you take the kit to an audiologist or hearing aid shop and have a trained professional make the molds.

Another company specifically instructs the customer to go to a nearby hearing aid center for the mold-making. This model of ear plug has several features which make it a truly superior product, to wit, a built-in sound filtering device which provides upwards of 30 decibel protection when worn simply as an ear plug. It easily adapts to receive the plastic tube of an ear set, and a kit to do this is provided. The company keeps the earmolds on file for three years, so that if a customer loses his ear plugs, a new set can be shipped within days.

Foam Ear Plugs

Finally, while all of the above devices have advantages, there is one product which simply cannot be beat for performance, comfort and especially, price.

The foam E.A.R. brand plug is decidedly one of the best deals in aviation today. The user merely rolls it into a tight cylinder and inserts it into the ear canal, where it slowly (takes about two minutes) expands to fit. It provides at least 29 decibel protection (more at some frequencies). And it costs less than $2 a pair, with quantities bought in bulk coming down to as little as 25 cents a pair.

Pilots in our office who have worn these plugs over many hours in a variety of airplanes have come back with the same report: they are comfortable, easy to use, and they work.

Best Insurance

In summary, we would recommend any protection over none at all. As a bare minimum, we urge use of E.A.R. plugs in all flying. The user will benefit immediately from a vast reduction in noise and fatigue.

Despite their weight, we would next choose conventional headsets over ear sets, since even used alone, they provide lots of hearing protection, and they lead to a quieter cockpit for everyone aboard, since the cabin speaker does not have to blare. We would use foam plugs (and we do) under the headset for extra protection. Were we to use an ear set, it would definitely not be a one-ear unit, nor one without ear-conforming plugs.

A final word: some pilots complain that use of ear protection cuts their ability to hear important sounds, such as the gear warning

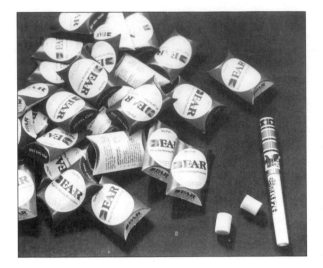

Expandable foam earplugs used alone or in conjunction with a headset, provide a significant amount of noise protection.

horn, stall warner, airspeed noises, etc. As the FAA points out, these sounds are not cut out—just softened. It will take an hour or two to get used to the quieter cockpit warnings, but the advantages easily outweigh the drawbacks.

The FAA has a suggestion for pilots to prove it to themselves. Advisory Circular 91-35 says, "Demonstrate the effectiveness of the (ear) plugs by wearing only one during a flight of an hour or more. After shutting down the engine, remove the plug. The difference in hearing in the two ears will almost make it seem as if the ear that was open during the flight is now quite deaf. It is not, of course. It is only less sensitive because of the noise exposure, and it will recover after a little time. But that loss of sensitivity is an indication of how the noise can produce permanent damage to one's hearing." In view of the consequences, it would appear that some form of hearing protection is one of the cheapest kinds of insurance in aviation.

Accidents?

Even though many safety experts agree that cockpit noise has a bearing on lots of accidents, a review of thousands of NTSB accident reports will reveal virtually none which mention the cockpit noise problem, let alone tag it as a factor in a crash. The NTSB has recently been concentrating more investigative power on the human factors areas, but even so, "pilot fatigue" is about the only NTSB computer bin where the noise problem might be included. But this factor is usually not used unless there is strong evidence of the pilot being overly tired—not just fatigued from "normal" cockpit noise.

This is ironic, since many hundreds of accident reports that we've seen have many "say again?" exchanges between controllers and pilots, even though neither side reports anything wrong with the radios. Due to the inability of the investigator to examine cockpit voice tapes (as in airline crashes where, even with much lower noise levels, there are often unintelligible remarks on the tape), the general aviation accident defies proof of cockpit noise as a factor.

However, when lightplanes at takeoff are known to make more noise than the cabin speakers can overpower, when pilot stress and fatigue due to noise becomes a measurable phenomenon, and when a decrease in hearing threshold of as much as 40 decibels is known to occur after a long flight, it perhaps becomes obvious that noise is making an unreckoned contribution to crashes.

Quieting the Unwanted Voices

Through prolonged exposure to noise, many pilots (particularly those whose flying time largely predates the extensive use of ear plugs and headsets) have developed tinnitus—ringing or other sounds in the ears. For some, the sound is continuous; for others it's intermittent. For all who have it, tinnitus is an unwanted and oft-times maddening companion.

Tinnitus has proved easier to get than to get rid of, but four researchers report success in reducing tinnitus by using a feedback technique that has the added psychological benefit of giving sufferers a feeling of control over their situation.

In the experiment, people suffering from tinnitus were placed in a soundproof chamber and presented a synthesized sound which was matched in frequency and loudness to duplicate as closely as possible the tinnitus noise. Once a match was achieved, the person was told that the synthesized sound would be reduced slightly in loudness and that they were to concentrate on matching that reduction by decreasing the tinnitus. When this was successfully done, the artificial sound was again reduced slightly. The process continued until the patient could not achieve a match on five successive trials.

Those tested achieved significant reductions in their tinnitus, a reduction they were eventually able to duplicate on their own outside the experimental setting.

"Of major importance in this study," write the researchers, "is the fact that it gave the subject the opportunity to gain control over his/

her own pathology, providing not only significant relief from the tinnitus but psychological benefit as well." One person, for example, "reported during the follow-up that as a result of being able to control his tinnitus, he was hopeful for its eventual elimination. He further indicated that there had been a marked improvement in his life, as he now was able to sleep, work regularly, and enjoy recreational activities that previously were not possible due to the persistence of the tinnitus."

For Some, A Serious Problem

Some people have such bad cases of tinnitus, day and night, that they choose to have operations which may destroy hearing in one ear. Is this a valid idea? If a pilot could only hear in one ear, would he pass his medical? This question was posed to an aviation medical examiner, who answered it this way: "Let me take the easy question first. Yes, a pilot who can only hear adequately in one ear can pass a Third Class medical.

"Now for the tougher part of your question. Tinnitus, or ringing in the ears, can range from just a slight and occasional noise to a constant echo and hissing which threatens to literally drive the sufferer crazy. It's little wonder that those afflicted with tinnitus say they'd do anything for relief—and sometimes they do go to great extremes seeking the sounds of silence."

Surgery that leaves one deaf is a pretty extreme cure, and we would certainly hope that a lot of alternatives were explored before using that option. Many people find they get sufficient relief by having a machine that creates background "white noise" to help mask the sound in the ears. Others find refuge in an old reliable treatment, nicotinic acid, or with the use of biofeedback.

The best bet of all, of course, is prevention. For pilots that means making use of adequate ear protection whenever flying. Don't wait until your hearing deteriorates noticeably. The time to use hearing protection is *all* the time.

Muffled Muffs

Heeding the ads for lightweight earphones, pilots would be led to believe that the single largest factor in earphone comfort is weight. Yet according to a recent study, the weight of muff-style hearing protectors plays little role in determining whether or not people will perceive them as comfortable.

Fifty volunteers went to earmuff heaven in a lab where they

donned four different types of muffs and an additional three types of "earcaps"—essentially devices that pushed something into the ear without surrounding or covering the part of the ear which normally flaps in the breeze.

While wearing the devices, these lucky volunteers answered a battery of 23 questions designed to elicit their feelings about what they were feeling. They were asked to differentiate pairs of terms (such as hard/soft, loose/tight) on a seven-step scale. They were also asked to rank each device for general comfort, ease of donning, personal preference and estimated eight-hour day preference.

When the results were tallied, all the muff-type hearing protectors rated ahead of any of the earcap types. The most highly ranked muff had a liquid and foam cushion filler, a padded headband, a fairly large cushion area and a relatively low clamping force. It was also the lightest, though the difference was slight. The problem was that this best-of-show earmuff also offered the lowest noise reduction.

"Contrary to popular belief," the researchers write, "the weight of the earmuffs had little influence on rated comfort whereas the compressive 'tightness' of the headband spring and the conformity of the cushion to facial contour were important influences on comfort."

Attention, Frequent Fliers

Noise is on every pilot's mind, which is exactly the problem. While things have improved a bit from the days of the P-51 and other super-loud flying machines, which could deafen one almost on sight, even the most modern general aviation cabin doesn't earn high marks from a hearing point of view.

Now comes a bit of hope. Researchers have discovered hearing is much less likely to be hurt by loud noise if the insult is only periodic. Biomedical researchers at Los Alamos National Laboratory and the Central Institute for the Deaf (CID) in St. Louis report that hearing is likely to recover from the effects of loud, continual noises if the sound is cushioned by periods of quiet.

The research strongly suggests that pilots (even those not using hearing protection) may suffer only temporary hearing loss provided they give themselves a break from the cockpit once in awhile.

"Our work," says Don Sinex, a neurophysiologist in the Life Sciences Division at Los Alamos, "shows that the inner ear has tremendous recovery powers. Hearing recovers even while the noise continues."

Previous research had shown that hearing recovered after the noise completely stopped, providing the noise wasn't too severe. The current study showed that the healing process begins quickly and continues even when the noise resumes.

Using the chinchilla as a model, because of the similarity of its ear to that of a human, the researchers exposed the animals to noise at 500 Hertz at 95 decibels, which is about the level found in many general aviation cockpits. The animals were exposed to this noise for periods ranging from four to 40 days, in a constant cycle of 15 minutes on, 45 minutes off.

"Their hearing," Sinex says, "returned to within 15 decibels of normal. That's not debilitating by any means."

While optimistic about the ear's recuperative powers, the researchers note that risks are believed to increase with months or years of exposure.

Even If You Can't Hear, Perhaps You Can Hear Again

A lot of pilots don't hear well. Some pilots, particularly those whose flying dates back to "the good old days" (loud engines, no hearing protection) scarcely hear at all. Until now, hearing loss was irrevocable, but a new technique is providing people with artificial ears.

"There has been a real revolution in the last few years, and the impact has yet to be felt," says A. James Hudspeth, professor of physiology and otolaryngology at the University of California, San Francisco medical center. "In five or 10 years cochlear implants may be as routine for the profoundly deaf as pacemakers are for heart patients, and they will even be extended to help those who still have a little hearing left."

Hudspeth is conducting research he hopes will actually help prevent hearing loss or cure it without the need for an implant. His studies center on the hair cells in the inner ear. It's these minute organs which translate vibrations into electrical signals that the brain processes and understands as sound. Noise damages these hair cells, and results in hearing loss.

At the moment, the artificial implants consist of a few channels, with each channel carrying one frequency. Investigators are still experimenting to find out how many frequencies are needed to provide a reasonable semblance of normal hearing, at least for purposes of understanding speech.

"Losing your hearing is worse than losing any other sense, including eyesight," Hudspeth says. "Now, for the first time, there is the hope of being able to restore hearing. The psychological benefits will be great."

Getting Closer to the Real World of Flying

The problem with laboratory studies is that they're conducted in laboratories. Labs offer neatly controlled conditions, which is just the problem when it comes to studying hearing.

In the case of hearing studies, most determinations have been made by feeding the pilots pure tones, at various frequencies, in a completely quiet lab. It's an exercise that yields data of questionable applicability to the real world of the cockpit.

How true that is was reaffirmed by a study in which investigators sought to find out how well aviators who have some hearing impairment hear under conditions more closely approximating those of a real cockpit.

To do that, they studied 100 people, all of whom had some degree of hearing impairment. One-third of the group was given a standard word recognition test in which they were asked to hear the human voice against a quiet background. Another third were asked to perform the same task but with background noise of 70 dB, about what would be found in some of the quieter general aviation cockpits, while the final group got background noise at 80 dB.

The results showed that, not surprisingly, scores decreased with increasing noise no matter how severe a person's hearing impairment. What was surprising was the finding that the decrease in scores with an increase in hearing impairment was less in noisy than in quiet conditions. The researchers speculate that in something more akin to a real-world environment, people are able to do better than predicted because they are listening with both ears, and thus capturing information that isn't reflected in traditional hearing tests, which focus on threshold levels in each ear separately.

Valsalva: A Hidden Maneuver

The Valsalva maneuver is supposed to clear a pilot's ears, and properly performed it will usually do just that. But some pilots who are trying to blow their ears open could wind up with a blowout of an entirely different kind.

What few pilots realize is that the Valsalva maneuver causes significant physiological changes. By raising pressure considerably in the chest cavity, it causes a series of changes in blood pressure and cardiac function. In fact, the Valsalva maneuver is used by physicians as a diagnostic technique to discover certain kinds of heart problems.

For example, those with congestive heart failure will not show the normal decrease in blood pressure during the straining phase of the maneuver, but will instead show either no change or a slight increase. And the Valsalva maneuver is widely used to establish the diagnosis of heart murmur.

What pilots need to be aware of is that the Valsalva maneuver has a small but perceptible risk attached to it. It can, first of all, cause fainting, particularly in older pilots whose reflex mechanisms aren't quite as responsive to sudden changes in blood pressure.

Second, the maneuver can precipitate heart rhythm irregularities as a reflex response to the decrease in blood pressure. In those with underlying heart disease, this could set off a cascade of problems.

While these rare side effects are hardly reasons to abandon a simple technique that provides quick relief to thousands, pilots would do well to be moderate in their application of the Valsalva maneuver. If it's going to work, it will usually work when done quite gently. A couple of light puffs against the closed airway will generally open any eustachian tube that's going to open. Any great amount of straining and grunting add to the risk without adding to the likelihood of getting relief.

Expectancy and Hearing

Eh? What? Say again? Was that for us? The cockpit of a general aviation airplane redefines the term "hostile environment," particularly for the aviator's ears. These sensitive sound-gathering instruments were not designed for long exposure to high levels of noise, and the result of years in the cockpit is often a pilot who doesn't hear well.

However, according to recent research, when it comes to understanding what's said on the air, even pilots with substantial hearing loss are all ears for aviation communications.

This discovery was made by two researchers at the National Aerospace Medical Centre in The Netherlands. They were struck by the fact that even though many of the airline pilots they regularly examined showed evidence of hearing loss, as measured by tone audiometry and a standardized speech discrimination test, the pilots rarely, if ever, complained of problems understanding what was said to them over the radio.

In order to see what the pilots were hearing, the researchers gave a group of pilots both a standard radiotelephony (RT) speech discrimination test and a variation of the test that they devised for the research. The pilots averaged more than 14,000 hours of flying experience.

In the standard test, the pilots were presented with a spoken list (normally about 20 words long) of phonetically balanced, monosyllabic words. In the flying version of the standard test, the researchers challenged the pilots with one of 20 sentences, each of which had several words or numbers that could be varied. The sentences were of the sort familiar to every pilot, such as, "Maintain 6,000 feet; it will be an ILS approach for Runway 27."

Each pilot was tested by having the sentences delivered through a set of David Clark headphones to one ear while the other ear remained uncovered. A total of 32 pilots lent the investigators their ears. Half had unimpaired hearing. The other half suffered from substantial hearing loss as measured audiometrically.

When the last sentence had been spoken, the results showed that the hearing-impaired pilots did as well or better than the other group in understanding aviation talk. This was true even though these same pilots had scored as low as 65-70 percent in understanding the non-aviation words of the standardized test. When spoken to in their own language—plane talk—all the pilots heard either 99 or 100 percent of what was directed at them.

These favorable results may, in fact, be measurements of the experience of the pilots. This appears to be confirmed by the researchers' findings that in a group of young pilots-in-training, the intelligibility score on the aviation word test dropped to an average of 72 percent, even though all of them had excellent hearing, according to electronic measurement.

Experience is a good teacher, and after thousands of hours in the cockpit, pilots have an excellent idea of what to expect in a given radio communication. It may take only a word or two for the pilot to understand the entire sentence...or think he's understood it. The problem with such context-driven word discrimination ability is that it opens the door to expectancy error—the strong tendency to hear what a person expects to hear, rather than what is actually said. It's the type of error that occurs when a pilot makes a familiar approach and fails to hear that, on this day, the controller said something different.

5 | The Stress Factor

"Lazybones, sleepin' in the sun; how you gonna get your day's work done?" This line from an old song asked a question which "Lazybones" probably would have answered, "If I don't get the work done today, I'll think about it tomorrow."

A rather stress-free situation, in which this character was under no pressure to do anything other than sleep in the sun, and couldn't care less whether the work got done or not. Few pilots ever operate in such a care-free environment; we are just about always under some sort of stress.

An aerospace dictionary defines stress as (1) the force per unit area of a body that tends to produce a deformation, and (2) the effect of a physiological, psychological, or mental load on a biological organism which causes fatigue and tends to degrade proficiency. The first case is a strictly mechanical definition, but if you substitute "pilot" for "biological organism," the second case becomes very descriptive of the sort of stress aviators experience regularly.

How well we recognize and deal with the stresses of flying makes the difference between inconvenience and discomfort, and disaster. Recognition is perhaps one of the most important parts of the problem, because we experience stress as the result of a wide spectrum of emotions and circumstances that are defined by the complexity of the individual involved, and the impact of his environment.

The stories which follow are intended to share the experiences of fellow aviators, with the hope that you will learn to recognize similar stressful situations when they appear, and with the benefit of knowledge, be able to deal with them successfully.

How Stress Can Kill

Central Airlines Flight 27 was a Learjet 25, transporting cancelled checks from Chicago's Midway Airport to Newark, New Jersey. Flight 27 left Midway at 2:51 a.m. CST, on an IFR flight plan to Newark. Aboard were two pilots, both rated as captains in the Learjet.

The flight was cleared to start its descent into the Newark area at 4:56 a.m. EST, though it took prodding from ATC two minutes later before the crew actually began what was to become a high-rate, unstabilized approach. The weather was clear, visibility 15, the wind 340 at 9 knots.

The copilot, handling the radios, reported to Approach Control having Runway 11 in sight and asked for a visual. After being advised that the runway was "noise-sensitive" (i.e., pick another runway to keep the airport's neighbors happy), he agreed to a Runway 4R visual approach. Flight 27 was told to maintain 2,000 feet until on final and to contact the tower, which cleared the Learjet to land. That's the last anyone heard from Flight 27.

The accident was witnessed by several people, including the check airman who had given the pilot of Flight 27 his last proficiency ride. He was, by coincidence, on final directly behind Flight 27, flying checks for a competing company. What happened, he reported, looked "a little like an 'Indy' car hitting a wall."

Other witnesses, on the ground, reported that the plane dropped in from about 10 feet above the runway, bounced "pretty high," touched down again, rolled to the right, maintained runway heading for a while, then swerved off the runway where it burst into flames.

The airplane's final resting place was 750 feet to the right of Runway 4R. The fire was extinguished by the crash-fire-rescue crew within three minutes, but not before both pilots expired. Subsequent investigation showed nothing out of line mechanically. The approach, however, was far from normal. Radar information showed Flight 27 was considerably above the legal limit of 250 knots under 10,000 feet. In fact, the plane didn't slow to 250 knots until it reached 2,500 feet, less than three minutes before hitting the runway.

The plane turned final at 180 knots, and proceeded to follow a 5-degree glidepath at a 1,000-foot-per-minute de-

A Learjet is one of the fastest general aviation aircraft available. Either by intent or accident, the pilots weren't able to manage its impressive speed and crashed near the runway at Newark.

scent rate, averaging 140 knots on final approach (proper bug speed was 125 knots). That left the pilots 33 seconds from the time they aligned with the runway to touchdown.

At first glance, a simple case of a botched approach. Pilot error, with grave consequences.

But it wasn't quite that simple. The toxicology tests had something interesting to say. Both pilots tested positive, via nose swabs, for recent use or inhalation of marijuana, and the captain's urine tested positive for marijuana use within at least the 24 hours prior to the incident.

The captain, according to NTSB interviews with his friends, was a heavy marijuana smoker until about two years prior to the accident, at which time he (1) got married, (2) quit smoking cigarettes and (3) quit smoking marijuana.

However, several people reported the captain had resumed cigarette smoking shortly before the accident, attributing it to the stress of family matters and changing jobs. He had, in the weeks just before the accident, purchased a new house, gotten a new job, and found out he was about to become a father. Each is a major source of stress.

Hard to Figure Out

The crash of Flight 27 illustrates the frustration and difficulty of determining the role of stress in aviation accidents. There is considerable evidence the pilot suffered an extraordinarily high stress risk, and that his personal response was to try and reduce the risk by smoking marijuana. The accident is evidence that his stress-coping mechanisms may have failed, leaving him desperately error-prone— even in the absence of marijuana's judgment-clouding effects. Yet it's impossible to "prove" that stress was in fact the culprit here. And in most general aviation accident investigations, toxicological and personal history inquiries are either absent or limited, meaning the stress factors will rarely appear as the accident cause.

There's little doubt that stress is causing a substantial portion of pilot-error accidents. According the official NTSB findings, N351B, a Beech Queen Air, crashed as a result of multiple pilot errors, including fuel mismanagement, fuel starvation, improper emergency procedures, and diverted attention from operation of the aircraft.

Stress isn't mentioned. But perhaps it should have been. The ATP-rated pilot, with 5,300 hours, 100 in type, was flying to the 2:30 p.m. funeral of two friends killed a week earlier in an aircraft crash. He was to be a pallbearer, as was the private pilot passenger in the right seat. Also aboard was the girlfriend of one of the men killed in the earlier crash.

When the Queen Air departed Laredo International, the pilot called Center to pick up his IFR clearance, filed earlier with San Antonio Flight Service. Center informed him the flight plan had been cancelled since he'd been late departing and thus forfeited his 15-minute "block time" at destination Dallas-Love Field. Center, operating at that time under the General Aviation Reservation (GAR) system limitations, told the pilot he couldn't air file again with them and would have to go through Flight Service.

Flight Service said Center wasn't accepting any IFR arrivals for Love Field. The pilot offered to take anything in the area, and was told the next opening was between 4 and 6 p.m. At this time he was airborne and VFR; he elected to fly

on toward the destination and try to negotiate something
when he got closer.

Forth Worth Radio had nothing to offer after talking with
Center, which was accepting no additional IFR penetrations
of the Dallas TCA. The pilot tried a direct plea to Center, but
was told that under GAR there was no longer any such thing
as an "IFR pop-up." He was now faced with being absolutely
unable to land and get to the funeral on time, since weather
in the Dallas area was overcast, ceiling around 700 feet in
rain and fog.

"A short time passed," the pilot wrote in his report of the
accident, "and I changed the frequency to talk to approach
and suddenly noticed the two main tanks that were half-full
were now empty, although the other two tanks were still full.
Expecting the engines to stop from fuel starvation because
the selectors were on the empty tanks, I turned the booster
pumps to auxiliary and turned the fuel selectors to the
opposite tanks. The engines continued to run for 2 to 3 minutes; thereafter, the engines began to sputter and surge."

The pilot tried everything he could think of to restart the
engines, with no luck. After a descent through turbulence
and clouds, with the ground only intermittently visible up to
the last seconds, the pilot put the plane down in a wet field,
substantially damaging the left main gear, striking a fence
and adding substantial damage to the left prop, wing root
and stabilizer.

The NTSB investigator reached the crash site in a few
hours. He found the main tanks dry, no flight manual on
board, and noted that when interviewed, the pilot "did not
appear knowledgeable of the manufacturer's recommended
procedures for bleeding the air in the system if a fuel tank is
run dry." The Beech 65 manual notes that if a tank is run dry,
air will be drawn into the system and must be bled in order
to get a restart.

Mismanagement of fuel? That will go down as the "official" probable
cause. But why would an experienced ATP who flew DC-3s for a living
miscalculate fuel burn, not notice main tanks heading for empty, fail
to familiarize himself with aircraft systems and procedures, and
depart without the legally required flight manual on board?

Perhaps he wouldn't, except on a day when stress exceeded his ability to cope, thereby making him dangerously error-prone.

Taking the Measure of Stress

Stress kills pilots, not in a violent, visible way, but rather like a toxic gas—quietly, quickly, often leaving behind little or no trace of its presence and contribution to the tragedy.

Though it's much like catching ghosts, researchers are learning to measure the effect of stress, and are coming up with methods by which pilots can identify when they are at greater-than-normal risk.

In the late 1960s, a Navy researcher became intrigued with the idea that major changes in a person's life, and the associated stress, could be measured and that this measure could be used to predict the probability of illness and other problems.

The result was a list of 43 life events and their associated risks, expressed as "Life Change Units." The researcher's Social Readjustment Rating Scale has, in the intervening years, been extensively tested. Initially, investigators sought a direct link between Life Change Units and illness. Later, many realized that what was really going on was stress, filtered through an individual's own coping, defense and expression mechanisms. The result might often be as obvious as illness, but it could also be as subtle as attenuated performance in the cockpit.

That was the conclusion of one study made on naval aviators. Questionnaires were sent to flight surgeons sitting on official boards inquiring into the Navy's air crashes. Of the 501 questionnaires returned, 248 reported on aviators found to have committed an error which was a factor in their accidents; 230 questionnaires were for aviators not considered at fault, with the remainder covering incidents where no fault determination was possible.

When the groups were compared, significant differences emerged in their profiles and pointed a finger at stress. For example, the at-fault fliers were significantly more likely to have marital problems, to have recently made a major career change, to be currently having trouble with interpersonal relations (superiors or peers), or to have recently become engaged. Once again, it's clear that both good and bad events in a person's life can cause stress. The results, however, are the same in imposing a penalty on the body.

In an attempt to develop a rating device based more on common, day-to-day events, other researchers developed the Daily Hassles Scale. "Hassles" say the scale's developers, "are the irritating, frustrating, distressing demands that to some degree characterize everyday transactions with the environment." In other words, hassles are stressors, and by measuring how many of them a person has suffered, and how severe they were, it should be possible to get some handle on when a pilot is at risk. None of these scales is an absolute indicator. There is no stress litmus test, no positive indicator that stress has reached the danger level. Stress doesn't show up in the blood, or urine, just in the accident reports. But don't look for the word "stress" under "probable cause." Oh, it might be there, but hiding quietly behind the words "pilot error."

Speaking Out

Anyone who has ever monitored the frequency on a day when the weather is bad has heard the change of tone in the voices of both pilots and controllers. And virtually everyone has heard (and many have been) a pilot who was getting way behind the power curve suddenly go up an octave or four as conditions went from bad to ugly.

All this is of more than academic concern for a variety of reasons. First, of course, there's the question of being able to understand the communications of those under stress, which is what each of these situations has in common.

A more subtle concern is that of designers who are now at work on the speech recognition systems that will one day enable pilots (first of military craft, then commercial jets, and almost inevitably the operators of general aviation aircraft) to say what they want (within limits, of course) and have it happen. Instead of dialing dials and pushing buttons, a pilot will one day run the autopilot by simply telling it to "Turn left, heading 320, descend and maintain 8000."

In order to program George, he/she/it must have some notion of what "Turn left, heading 320" sounds like, a task that is far from trivial when it must be performed with 100 percent accuracy over the wide range of accents, inflections, and other speech variations normally found in the population. The stress factor definitely can not be ignored. "If speech recognition is to be reliable for the control of aircraft systems," writes one researcher who's taken a look at the matter, "it must be robust with respect to variability in the human speech signal; that is, recognition accuracy should not be sensitive to acoustic changes in the user's speech but should perform equally well when the user is busy and under stress as when the user is relaxed and operating under low task load." Yes, and pilots should all maintain altitude plus or minus 10 feet.

In an experiment designed to get at some of the effects of stress on speech recognition, the researcher found that under high task loads (and thus high stress) the speech recognition error rate zoomed, with 82 percent of the errors accounted for by the lack of pauses between words. "Certainly the error rates obtained here for an isolated word system would be unacceptable in a cockpit environment," the investigator concludes, "where pilots will be even more time stressed than they were in this experiment."

Judgment Under Stress

To err is human, to error is pilot. The vast majority of accidents get labeled "pilot error." Eliminate that category and the general aviation safety rate would make walking look dangerous by comparison.

There has been increasing recognition over the last few years that a somewhat squishy entity called "judgment" plays a substantial role in many of the accidents diagnosed as caused by pilot error. To see what effect stress has on pilot judgment, researchers used a microcomputer and some willing pilots to fly a simulated flight from Saranac, New York, to Logan Airport (Boston). Each "flight" consisted of some printed text at the top of a screen and a series of constantly-updating instruments at the bottom. As each scenario was presented, the pilot had to choose which of four diagnoses or actions seemed best. That led, in turn, to another scenario.

The pilots (all instrument rated) were divided into two groups. One served as controls, the other was subjected to certain stress conditions which included time stress, financial risk, an additional task to deal with at the same time, and noise. All four stressors were laid on during the same session.

For example, subjects in the control group were paid $5 per hour; those in the stress group were paid $8, but this could be decreased for failure to meet certain performance criteria—thus the financial risk. Just to appeal to the competitive nature of pilots, there was also a bonus for the best three flights in each group.

When the results were tallied, it was found that stress had an effect on the accuracy of performance. But the effect was not uniform. It was found that problems demanding use of spatial memory are particularly sensitive to the disruptive effects of stress.

Interestingly enough, problems that involved the retrieval of knowledge from memory were not sensitive to stress.

At this stage the groundwork is just being laid for an understanding of how pilots think and make decisions, and the effects of stress on those processes.

All Circuits Are Busy

Pilot workload is like pornography: Nobody seems capable of giving it an exact definition, but everyone thinks they'll know it when they see it. Meanwhile, thousands of hours have been spent and dozens of experiments have been conducted attempting to come up with a useful, repeatable means of answering the rather simple question, "Just how busy is the pilot right now?"

In an effort to measure the measures of workload, researchers rounded up 48 volunteer pilots (60 to 2,500 hours total time), a motion-base flight simulator, and lots of literature on assessing pilot workload, from which they chose 14 methods that authors claimed reflected the amount of effort being expended by a pilot.

The simulator had the usual instrumentation, including two fuel gauges, ammeter, oil pressure, oil temp and CHT, all of which could be redlined (or, in the case of fuel, placed on empty) remotely. There was also a carb ice warning light which could be illuminated remotely. Pilots were required to respond to any adverse situation by pressing an adjacent button to return the condition to normal.

Each "flight" was under instrument conditions, and one, some or all of the instruments would display danger conditions at some point in the run. Multiple failures were possible.

Of the 14 measures, seven turned out to be reliable indicators of pilot workload. Three of these were rating scales, in which the pilot rated workload immediately after the flight. It's a seemingly simple and novel idea to simply ask the pilot how hard he's working, but it succeeded.

Less successful were other kinds of measures involving physiological measurements and the ability to do another task while flying. Some of these yielded useful estimates of pilot workload, others didn't. Heart rate, pupil diameter and eye blinks, for example, didn't accurately reflect pilot workload. Neither did the number of control movements (aileron, elevator and rudder) a pilot made, a so-called primary measure. When all is said and done, it seems the best way to get information about how the pilot is doing is still to ask the pilot.

Interpersonal Relationships and Stress

Perhaps it goes without saying that concepts of "crew coordination" and "distributed workload" in the cockpit cannot work if the crewmembers are not even on speaking terms. Such a situation probably existed in a much-publicized crash of a Piper Cheyenne at

Baltimore, Maryland, but neither official reports nor nationally published accounts have called any attention to it.

> The case was bizarre in that the Cheyenne, making an approach to Martin Airport, struck powerlines and snagged two pieces of cable. (The impact also broke off one engine airscoop and one of the plane's two pitot tubes.) One 150-foot piece of cable then wrapped around a church steeple and pulled away from the airplane, while another 1,000-foot piece (estimated to weigh more than 300 pounds) hung onto the left main gear while the Cheyenne executed a missed approach, tried and missed an approach at nearby Baltimore-Washington International Airport (BWI), and finally crashed a quarter-mile short on the next attempt when the wire apparently dragged the plane into the ground. Only one of four people aboard survived.
>
> Accounts of the crash of Cheyenne N6123A have focused on events that occurred after the call, "Twenty-three Alpha's hit. Twenty-three Alpha's going down." High drama ensued, and the air traffic control tapes caught every detail.

In our opinion, the real story—how the Cheyenne got to the point where it struck wires nearly 400 feet below the MDA—has not been told. Even NTSB's official probable cause report lists only "improper IFR operation," which is an understatement in the extreme.

Contained in the Safety Board files, however, is a statement provided by the surviving passenger. Whether it may have been discounted because he was not a pilot, or because investigators did not feel there was strong enough evidence, we cannot guess. But it describes a cockpit atmosphere so frosty that we believe it cannot be ignored as a factor in the accident. In addition, there were all the familiar overtones of a decision to fly into obviously worsening weather, just to get back to home base.

> The Cheyenne was a corporate airplane, and the pilot in charge of flying it was a 46-year-old CFI with an instrument rating and 6,500 hours, including about 300 hours actual IFR and 136 hours in the Cheyenne. He would sometimes fly corporate trips as the sole pilot, and other times would have an acquaintance along as copilot.
>
> The acquaintance was a commercial pilot with instru-

The pilot, who reportedly had a reputation for ignoring minimums, flew the Cheyenne into powerlines. One line snagged the landing gear, eventually causing the airplane to crash short of the runway.

ment rating and had at least 830 hours (details were not available because her logbook was not found). She reportedly had attended Cheyenne training courses and was working on a CFI rating.

One passenger on the February 23 flight was the sales manager of the company that owned the plane. The second passenger was not only a fellow salesman taking advantage of an empty seat, but was also the copilot's husband. According to the survivor, the pilots and the other passenger were very good friends. Indeed, they had gotten "snowed in" and had spent the last five days prior to the flight together, and the three shared a ride to Martin Airport the morning of the trip. According to the survivor, the three would normally be "happy and joking" with each other.

But February 23 was not a normal day. As the surviving passenger related, "The weather that morning was not very good; it was foggy and rainy and the captain informed us that the windshield wiper on the aircraft was not working properly, and that he wanted it fixed before he took off. During our wait, it was apparent to me that the pilots and the other passenger were rather cool to each other. Normally, these people are happy and joking, but on this particular morning there seemed to be something wrong. No one was talking to each other very much."

After the delay, the four boarded the Cheyenne and left Martin for Roanoke, Virginia. However, they were told en route that Roanoke was closed by weather, so they diverted to Lynchburg, Virginia, and landed without incident. The survivor recalls the flight was mostly conducted on autopilot, and that "the pilots seemed to have very little to say to each other." The passengers rented a car and left to conduct their sales calls; they both had successful days and arrived back at Lynchburg Airport around 4 p.m. in good spirits. They found the two pilots sitting in the lounge, and again, the survivor noticed that they were barely talking.

THE STRESS BUILDS

The captain had been checking with the FSS regularly and were advised of lowering ceilings at Baltimore. He called again at 4:02 p.m. and got another forecast of poor weather, but current Baltimore observations were not available. At 4:56 p.m., the copilot called to file the IFR flight plan.

Unfortunately, they couldn't leave Lynchburg. An emergency was developing: a young VFR pilot in a Skyhawk was lost and disoriented. After several passes, the pilot would finally be led into Lynchburg for a safe landing.

When the Cheyenne was ready to go at 5:16 p.m., the pilots were told of the emergency and advised of a 15-minute gate hold. Two minutes later, the captain called and asked the nature of the emergency; the controller told him about the Skyhawk. At 5:25 p.m., the captain asked the status of the emergency, was told it was continuing, and advised he was shutting down for 10 minutes. He called again at 5:45 p.m., again at 5:54 p.m., and yet again at 6:00 p.m., only to be told of continuing delays. To add to the problems, weather was getting worse. Martin Airport was now indefinite 1,400 feet obscured, one-quarter mile in rain and fog.

The pilots had deplaned their passengers, and did not hear the controller phone at 6:11 p.m. to say they could start engines. The surviving passenger recalled this period in his

NTSB statement: "Thinking back on the whole thing, it sort of seemed like the pilots wanted to get home. They seemed to have a lot of tension between them, and while they were waiting around before we took off, they did a lot of quiet talking together which I didn't hear, but it certainly wasn't a pleasant conversation, or at least it didn't appear so from the expressions on their faces."

Finally, at 6:24 p.m., they reboarded and got permission to taxi—more than an hour after they had originally wanted to leave, on a flight that would take less than an hour block to block. The copilot handled the radios for the initial call-up, but the captain broke in to ask about a taxiway turnoff. They arrived at the runway at 6:29 p.m., only to experience further delays due to traffic and then, getting their IFR clearance.

It was not until 6:39 p.m. that the clearance came through—direct to a VOR, direct to another, out a radial to intercept an airway, down that to an intersection and direct to Martin. In the first readback, the copilot missed the first VOR and gave a confused version of the rest of the clearance. The controller read it all back again, after which the copilot asked, "After Victor 44, where do I go until direct Martin?"

The controller was not pleased: "You don't have any of it, Miss. You read back the wrong clearance from the start." He read it all again, the copilot got it right this time and the Cheyenne was finally cleared for takeoff, with instructions to report when established on course. However, five minutes later the controller called and found the flight was on course, but hadn't reported as instructed.

Once en route, the captain began to handle communications with controllers, until the flight contacted Baltimore Approach for the descent and approach. Cheyenne 23A was given vectors to CARNY intersection, the initial fix for a VOR approach to runway 14 at Martin.

During the descent, controllers informed the flight that Martin weather was now indefinite 700 feet obscured, three-quarters of a mile in light drizzle and fog. Minimums for the intended approach were 560 feet (536 AGL) and one mile; thus technically the field was already below minimums.

While being vectored for the approach, the Cheyenne was given a heading of 110 degrees, no doubt to smooth the intercept with the approach radial (134 degrees to the VOR, located on the field). However, after a couple of minutes, there was the following exchange, with the copilot talking from 23A:

ATC: Two-three Alpha...what is your heading now?

23A: Heading 134.

ATC: 6123 Alpha, turn left to zero nine zero.

23A: Zero nine zero?

ATC: Yes, ma'am, zero nine zero.

23A: Roger, we're showing an intercept on the final approach course.

ATC: 23 Alpha, you show on the, ah, VOR approach now?

23A: That's affirmative, we're showing an intercept right on the, ah, approach.

ATC: 23 Alpha, roger. Turn back to the right and, ah, one three zero. Cleared for the VOR approach runway 14 at Martin. I showed you a mile, ah, to the west of the VOR final.

23A: Okay. Thank you."

The flight was handed off to Martin Tower, which does not have the equipment to determine aircraft altitude. Consequently, no one outside the cockpit would know if the pilot busted minimums now.

A LITTLE BIT LOW

Martin Tower gave the wind and weather, and asked whether the pilots were aware of the runway conditions. The controller then informed them that portions of the runway and the threshold lights were obscured by snow. Two minutes later, the plane struck the wires.

The surviving passenger remembers the approach, like most of the flight, as a period of near-silence. "There was a lot of heavy air in the cockpit between the two pilots," he told *Aviation Safety*. Indeed, no one said anything until just before impact, when the passenger looked out his window and exclaimed, "We're going to hit the wires!" The plane did so before he finished speaking.

The final sequence of events was a heart-breaker. The Cheyenne staggered up to 3,000 feet, but soon lost altitude down to 1,500. It was given vectors to what the crew was told would be an ILS approach to runway 28 at BWI. In fact, however, the glideslope was not operating on that runway, and the approach was a surveillance approach. That failed when the crew apparently was unable to hold a heading at 600 feet (possibly because the wire was dragging along the ground). Executing a missed approach, the Cheyenne got slowly back to 1,500 feet and was vectored around for the ILS to runway 10. It was two miles away at 600 feet and appeared to have a chance of making it, when the altitude decayed and the airplane struck trees one-quarter mile from the threshold. Marks on the snow showed the wire had been dragging behind the plane.

In the aftermath of the crash, investigators interviewed people who had known the pilot. According to the FAA investigator who conducted these interviews, two pilots told him they "always wondered when he would 'get it.' It was his practice to go below minimums." Unfortunately, the investigator said, the two would not make statements on the record, so no hint of this appeared in the accident report.

In our view, the day started with an inauspicious feud raging between the pilot and copilot. Whatever the source of the disagreement, it could only have been compounded by the tension and distractions of their knowledge of worsening weather at Baltimore and their inability to get out of Lynchburg. We can imagine that the quiet, unpleasant discussion before takeoff concerned—at least in part—the wisdom of making the return flight.

Further, the copilot's flubbing of the clearance readback, her failure to report on climbout, and the mistake in lining up with the approach course may well have had a psychological effect on her, making her unwilling to raise doubts as the male pilot attempted the approach below minimums—not even to save her own life.

Pushed Beyond the Threshold

A subject of vital interest to all pilots is cockpit workload. Every pilot can handle a certain number of distractions and still be able to control the airplane and navigate successfully. But when the situation in the cockpit gets too complex, the pilot will start making mistakes, either in operating the airplane or getting it to go where he or she wants it to go. In an already tough situation—solid IMC at night in a complicated airplane, for instance—it won't take much to push the pilot over that threshold.

One young, 456-hour commercial pilot got into just such a tough spot one spring night a few years ago. He was flying a Beech Travel Air and had three passengers on board. The chartered twin was returning to Visalia from Salinas, both in California. Weather at Salinas was low IMC, with a solid overcast at 700 feet and five miles' visibility in fog.

The passengers were a family of three—including an 18-month-old baby—who had arranged to return to Salinas at about midnight. Before they boarded the Travel Air, the pilot obtained a weather briefing and filed a flight plan requesting IFR to VFR on top.

The four people boarded the airplane, with the father in the right rear seat, the baby in a child seat next to him and the mother in the right front seat. She recalled that after she slammed the door shut, the pilot didn't check to make sure it was latched. She and her husband also claimed that the pilot never gave them a safety briefing.

Shortly after takeoff, as the Travel Air was climbing through 1,000 feet, the cabin door popped open. According to the pilot, the passengers panicked and the baby started screaming. The woman immediately grabbed the door handle, but it broke off in her hand. Not knowing that air loads would keep the door where it was, she and her husband grabbed the edge of the door, trying to hold it partly shut.

The pilot told them he would slow the airplane at altitude and try to secure the door. At 6,500 feet, he reached over and tried to close it, but to no avail. He asked the woman to hold the controls while he tried again. "I was pretty scared and didn't know the first thing about flying a plane," she said, "I pulled back a little because he had to reach over me, and the plane went up. So we scratched that idea."

MISSED APPROACH

The pilot contacted ATC and advised that he had an open door. He asked for vectors to return to Salinas and conduct the ILS approach into the airport.

He never saw the airport, however, and executed the missed approach. Once back on top of the clouds, he asked ATC for an expedited approach back to Salinas, but the controller said that Monterey would probably be closer.

The pilot had his hands quite full. He recalled that the baby kept screaming and the passengers interfered with his control of the airplane. Furthermore, a torrent of air was pouring in through the open door, and the pilot was having a hard time with his approach charts.

The controller remembered that he instructed the pilot to climb to the minimum IFR altitude of 5,000 feet so that the Travel Air could be picked up on radar. However, the pilot refused, saying he wanted to stay at the lower altitude because of the open door. The controller told the pilot that he couldn't issue vectors to Monterey without having the airplane in radar contact. The pilot's recollections were different. He told FAA that he did climb to the requested altitude but ATC still could not identify the airplane on radar.

WHICH WAY

Eventually, the pilot reported that he was intercepting the localizer course to Monterey. But based on earlier position reports from the pilot, the controller believed he was actually picking up the back course. He told the pilot that since he was not in radar contact and did not have the approach plate, he should fly up to the San Francisco Bay area where it was VMC.

The passengers said the pilot seemed lost and confused after the missed approach at Salinas. After flying past Monterey, he turned to the east and descended to 3,000 feet.

At this point, the woman saw something out the windshield and asked the pilot what it was. The pilot said it was clouds, but they soon found out it was a mountain ridge. Just before impact, the pilot cursed, slammed the throttles full forward and pulled back on the yoke, stalling the Travel Air just before it hit the trees.

The woman panicked when she realized they were going to crash. She unbuckled her seat belt and was trying to climb into the back seat when the airplane hit the mountain. She landed on the floor behind the front seats. She survived with serious injuries, but her husband and the pilot suffered only minor injuries and the baby was unhurt.

Every pilot has a threshold at which his or her workload becomes excessive. In this case, poor weather conditions, the tumult caused by the open door, an inability to work with ATC and panicky passengers proved to be more than the young charter pilot could handle. However, in the end, he did have the presence of mind to cushion the impact, and his reflexes may have saved his and his passengers' lives.

Recapping the Problem

Pilots are no different from most other folks, in that our physical and mental condition influences and is influenced by every circumstance of our existence. However, in the case of the aviator, the results of stress—no matter how it's generated—can be catastrophic as likely as not.

There are some common-sense preventions and cures for stress; for example, making sure that you are as physically fit as is reasonable for you, that you don't fly when you're fatigued or when taking medication, and staying out of the pilot's seat when there's turmoil in your personal or business life.

And for those times when you're airborne and stress jumps up out of nowhere, you've obviously got to do something—you can't continue "sleepin' in the sun." This is definitely *not* the time to accept an approach to minimums, or try to land in a 30-knot crosswind, or stretch the on-board fuel supply to its limits. As never before, the first rule must be to fly the airplane; and do it in the most basic, fundamental, least demanding manner you can.

Managing stress is a lot like managing risk. It can be handled if you recognize the problem and take sensible steps to keep it from getting the best of you.

6

The Fatigue Factor

T he all-time classic report on the effects of fatigue is surely that of Charles A. Lindbergh, in *The Spirit of St. Louis,* the story of his epic New York-to-Paris flight in 1929. After 18 hours in the air, and nearly 36 hours without sleep, Lindbergh had this to say about his difficulties in controlling the airplane:

"...I'm thankful we didn't make the *Spirit of St. Louis* a stable plane. The very instability which makes it difficult to fly blind or hold an accurate course at night now guards me against excessive errors. It's again a case of the plane and me compensating for each other. When I was fresh and it was overloaded, my quickness of reaction held its nose from veering off. Now that I'm dreaming and ridden by sleep, its veering prods my lagging senses. The slightest relaxation of pressure on either stick or rudder starts a climbing or a diving turn, hauling me back from the borderland of sleep. Then, I fix my eyes on the compass and determine again to hold it where it belongs.

There's no use; within a few minutes the needle swings over to one side. No mental determination within my control has more than fleeting value. That third quality [mind and body were one and two, respectively. -ed.] has taken over. It knows and holds a limit I can't consciously define, letting my mind and body stay relaxed as long as the Spirit of St. Louis flies reasonably straight and level, giving the alarm to both when needles move too fast or far. So far, no farther, the nose can veer off course; so far, no farther, the plane can dive or climb. Then I react from my stupor, level out, kick the rudder back onto the compass heading, shake myself to half awakeness—and let the needle creep again. I'm asleep and awake at the same moment, living through a reality that is a dream." (From *The Spirit of St. Louis* by Charles A. Lindbergh, Charles Scribner's Sons, 1953.)

Lindy made it through the night, and through the storms, and through the icing, and managed to get the *Spirit* down in one piece on the unlighted Le Bourget Airdrome, to his everlasting credit. All of us have flown in a tired state, and perhaps some of us have even walked close to the edge of the kind of fatigue Lindbergh suffered...but *none* of us are made of the stuff he was, to say nothing of the sleep-deprivation training he went through before the crossing.

Which is to say that pilots need to know the effects of fatigue on their performance in the air. The operational flexibility of today's aircraft, coupled with the realization that we can get a lot more done with those machines if we "push" ourselves a little bit, sets the stage for a fatigue-oriented accident...and the pilot may not realize what is happening. Fatigue can be a lot like hypoxia—very insidious—and just as hazardous.

The machine will drone on and on, without knowledge or concern for how long it's been running. But the man? That's a different story. And in this section of *Human Factors,* we intend to make you aware of some sources and effects of fatigue. If you can stay awake as you read this, you'll be better off the next time you think about flying when you're tired.

Long Day's Journey into Night

Researchers continue probing mind and body in a quest to discover what makes both tick. Or miss a tick.

With aircraft, particularly the transport-category machines, growing ever longer-legged, interest has increasingly focused on the question of how well the pilots hold up when asked to fly for 12 or more hours, doing minor, inane and/or repetitive tasks.

Of equal concern has been the impact on performance of the type of long day often faced by the harried regional carrier pilot, whose work day can stretch from dawn to dusk (and beyond) with a mind-numbing number of operations under a wide variety of conditions, the whole scenario repeated day after day.

Nor are such concerns of no concern to the private pilot, for it's not unusual for the plane-owning business person to arrive at the airport at 6 a.m., fly for several hours, disembark, do a day's business, then fly home 12 or more hours after the work day got its start.

In an effort to look at the effects of such prolonged days, we can turn to research by a pair of National Institute for Occupational Safety and Health investigators. They were curious about how people perform on long days of repetitive tasks. The curiosity came from the recognition that there's a push in many quarters for so-called "compressed work" in which workers put in more hours per day for fewer days. But will that pattern work? Depends a lot on how much accuracy you demand.

Testing was conducted on 11 volunteers (all men). Their "job" was to sit at a computer keyboard and enter five-digit number strings as they flashed on the screen at a rate of one every three seconds.

The investigators established a 12-hour per day, five-day "work week," followed by two days off. During the "work" days the workers tapped away for just over 10 hours per day, with the rest of their 12-hour shift devoted to testing, a half-hour lunch, and occasional breaks. They were periodically tested on a wide variety of measures, from reaction time to digit addition to cognitive abilities.

On the "rest" days the workers reported to the lab where they read or watched TV and took the same test battery at the same time as they had on the work days. This regimen went on for two weeks.

When the results were tallied, most measures showed steadily declining performance through the five-day work week of 12-hour days. On Day 1, for example, the workers averaged 412 data errors. By day five the number rose to 454. The percentage of errors in the digit addition test went from 4.91 percent to 7.47 percent, while hand steadiness decreased, reaction time increased, and self-reported degree of sleepiness rose from 1.98 to 3.26 on a 1-7 scale.

In looking at the results of one grammatical reasoning test, the researchers found the results "suggest that long workdays reduced motivation to perform carefully. In generalizing to the work situation, we speculate that a worker in a fatigued state could be more likely to take careless shortcuts to completion of a job. This potential sacrifice of safe work practices might be likely in tasks that are tedious because of high cognitive or information-processing demands, or those with extensive repetition."

The results, they say, taken together, "imply that fatigue effects are more critical then circadian influences, at least within the day-shift hours observed in the present study."

Bottom line? That's easy—pilots who put in a long day are doing it at the price of safe operation.

FATIGUE — TIRED OF IT ALL?

The air-taxi pilot's task did not appear to be difficult. The night was dark, with an overcast layer at 4,600 feet, but visibilities reported as 30 miles. The 10,000-hour pilot at the controls of the Beech Baron had completed two legs of the six he was scheduled to fly that night, transporting checks around the state of Arizona. Having departed Phoenix for this leg at 12:45 a.m., he droned through the sky at 5,500 feet, heading for Tuscon.

The pilot had been through a full day, starting at 8:15 that morning. During the course of the day, he had worked and flown, giving another pilot a checkout in a Baron for about an hour during the afternoon. After going all day, he had returned home for dinner, but his respite was brief; he returned to the airport at 8:30 to begin his nightly bank-check runs.

After departing Phoenix for the third leg, he was cleared to Toltec intersection by Phoenix Approach. After this, Phoenix Air Traffic Control shut down for the night, and nothing further was heard from the pilot.

It was a little too routine. The Baron flew right by Tucson Airport and continued on course at about 5,500 feet. Losing only a little altitude, it slammed into the side of Mount Fagan in the Santa Rita mountains at the 5,200-foot level.

Fatigue—it's not always as obvious as this. It may not manifest itself as physical exhaustion. It may be dangerous in small doses. People may suffer from fatigue even though they have gotten plenty of rest. Pilots can find fatigue creeping up on them despite their sleeping habits or lifestyles.

Fatigue is insidious and pervasive. Its effects can range from simple tiredness to neurosis. But for aviators, it is an enemy which must be faced. It can be more dangerous than a level 6 thunderstorm.

How can pilots recognize, prevent, and treat fatigue before it becomes life-threatening?

Symptomatic

Perhaps the most important part of the battle against fatigue is recognizing its onset before it becomes overwhelming. In its earliest stages, fatigue is very subtle. According to various studies, it tends to begin with mental lethargy.

Aviation psychologist Dr. Chaytor Mason, of the Institute of Safety and Systems Management of the University of Southern California, told us that one of the first things to go is the "scan." The brain, becoming dulled by the constancy of inputs during steady-state flight, begins to shut things off—much in the same manner as wearing a wristwatch becomes unnoticeable a few moments after it has been put on. As a result of this shutting down of stimuli inputs, the eyes start to narrow their scan and eventually begin to fixate on centrally located items.

This is the start of a vicious cycle. Another pyschologist specializing in aviation, Dr. Harvey Wichman of California's Claremont-McKenna College, explained that as the brain begins to filter out the constant stimuli—things like engine noise and vibration, or the unmoving engine gauges—fewer external inputs reach the brain cortex. The narrowing of the visual scan tends to compound this by taking in fewer things, also providing less and less external inputs.

At this point, according to the psychologists, a general state of sloth sets in. With the reduced stimuli to the brain, the mind begins to avoid stimulating actions. Pilots will tend to sit more motionless than normal, making fewer head movements. They will tend to forego optional actions, such as confirming their position, giving or getting PIREPs and weather information, and so on. The pilot may become irritable, finding fault with the actions of controllers or his copilot. At night or in tough IFR conditions, such symptoms already are enough to cause fatal mistakes.

But now fatigue begins to take on more physical symptoms. As the body starts slowing down further, the eyes begin to get filmy and may start to feel like they're on fire (Lindbergh said that his eyes felt "like salted stones"). Physical motions start to slow as heart rate falls. The pilot may find himself staring blankly or fixing his gaze on a single instrument or object outside the aircraft. Mental activity becomes slower, and eventually drowsiness sets in.

Now the cycle picks up speed. Tired, the pilot does not want to move much or do much. The less he does, the less inputs the brain has to work with and the general slowdown of mental and physiological activity increases, making the pilot feel more drowsy and less like doing anything. Left to its own, this cycle will continue until, like the pilot cited above, the fatigued aviator slips into sleep.

The RAF Studies

In a study of pilots and fatigue, a group of British Royal Air Force aviators were given flights in a simulator. These lasted from two to six hours, and the pilots' performances were measured. This study found that, as the pilots grew fatigued, they were less likely to make errors due to misuse of controls—an interesting finding. But they discarded this advantage through loss of accuracy in timing and skill.

Critically, and perhaps the most deadly implication the study discovered, was that as fatigue increased, the pilots began lowering their performance standards. Things that would have been unacceptable at the start of the flight now became acceptable.

The study also found that the pilots became unable to integrate what their instruments were telling them. They tended to fixate on a single instrument and did not compare it to others or to the airplane as a whole. In some cases, the pilots would stop looking at those instruments which were not directly in front of them—a deadly development in IFR flying.

But perhaps the most striking finding of the study was that pilots would tend to relax considerably when the airport was in sight. At this point, they would already be operating at a lower standard of performance, and with the airport so close, they tended to lower these standards even further. The tendency was for the pilots to make ever-increasing numbers of mistakes, and accept ever-sloppier flying, as they perceived the end of the flight drawing nearer.

The Long Run

These are the effects of fatigue in the short term. Easy to feel and obvious in their impact, symptoms of this form of fatigue can be recognized and dealt with—usually by getting a good night's sleep.

But fatigue also acts over the long term. Extended periods of working hard, being under considerable stress, or working against the body's rhythms (or all of these together) leads to a far more insidious kind of fatigue.

It is well known that the stress reaction in humans corresponds to a state of arousal. Stress is known to produce a response akin to the "fight or flight" response. In short doses, this response works as intended, preparing the body for physical exertions. But when the response is maintained over extended periods, particularly when there is no outlet for the energies it creates, it is like connecting a battery to a ground—the body's energy is drained.

But because of the state of arousal the stress produces, often the fatiguing effects will not be noticed until the source of the stress is removed. For pilots, difficulties at home or on the job can produce such stress. Stepping into the cockpit often provides an escape from the source, allowing the body to transition from the stress-arousal of the initial source to the high arousal state of flying. This is when the fatigue slips in.

Silent and insidious, the mental muffling which fatigue brings poses a hazard which may well go unrecognized. The pilot may find himself taking longer to perform what should be simple mental calculations. Concentration suffers, and often attention wanders, drawn towards thoughts about the stress source or into daydreams as a means of escape from the stress.

This kind of fatigue shows itself in other ways, too. A study of Australian airline pilots found that the pilots were in a constant state of arousal during flight—they were under stress. This manifested itself, for the most part, in gastric troubles. In the study, about 50 percent of the pilots involved suffered some form of gastric distress (chronic indigestion, ulcers, etc.). The net result was the pilots did not feel 100 percent fit most of the time, and they found themselves having to make greater efforts to cope with day-to-day existence. The implications are obvious in a profession which demands so much perfection as flying.

This is one of the most difficult types of fatigue to combat. Coping with stress is largely an individual matter. Recognizing stress and its results is a good step towards mitigating the untoward effects.

Sleep—Too Much, Too Little

Perhaps the most obvious effects and causes of fatigue lie in sleep. Tired at the end of the day, most people go to sleep. Those who don't, or can't, simply find themselves getting more fatigued. At a certain point, it will be impossible to stay awake without chemical aid.

As a cure for physical fatigue, sleep satisfies just about everyone. For those who look a little tired, the age-old advice has been to get a good eight hours sleep.

But this advice may not be entirely accurate. Studies have shown that different people need different amounts of sleep. It has been found that people's nightly requirements for sleep can vary tremen-dously, from a low of around four hours per night to a high of up to fourteen (Rip van Winkle, perhaps?). The average, however, is generally considered to be eight hours.

Numerous studies have documented the effects of lack of sleep. One Army study found that sleep loss can make the subject slower physically and mentally. Worse, it tends to make his reactions erratic, even unpredictable. It can produce variations in reactions to situations which change from minute to minute. For example, where one minute the subject may be capable of catching or fending off an object thrown without warning, in the next he may allow it to hit him squarely in the head.

But getting *too much* sleep can also produce fatigue. Sleeping in excess of one's normal requirements tends to produce sluggishness which can last all day. Those who sleep too much can actually feel more tired than when they went to bed. This has been linked to a dropping of the body's basal metabolism from the prolonged sleep. In other words, the entire body—chemically, mentally, and physically—is moving more slowly. For pilots, this can mean slower mental and physical reactions, which can have fatal consequences in the flying environment. The extra seconds needed to compute a holding pattern entry, for example, can produce a collision with terrain.

Because each person requires different amounts of sleep, it behooves pilots to determine what their requirements are. Experts say this is most easily done by simply going to bed when tired and waking up when refreshed. It sounds obvious, but it's not necessarily easy to do in today's environment. The premise is to avoid an imposed schedule for sleeping and let the body signal its requirements instead. Once the correct amount of sleep time has been found, it should then be reinforced to produce a good strong habit pattern for sleeping. After a time, the person will probably find he no longer needs an alarm clock as his body will awaken him at the best time, usually right on schedule.

Rock Around the Clock

The notion of allowing the body to determine its own best sleep pattern presupposes that one's lifestyle will allow such a pattern to form. But some pilots find themselves working hours which vary considerably from week to week. Some are even working on rotating shifts, which has them flying during daytime one week, darkness the next. And of course, flights which traverse several time zones impose a similar condition.

The net effect of both of these circumstances is to throw off the body's internal clock. Commonly known as circadian rhythms, these internal clocks tell us when to sleep, when to eat, when to perform various bodily functions.

There is evidence to suggest that the circadian clock is set by the time cues supplied by the environment. The regular cycle of daylight and darkness determines when our bodies feel sleepy and when they feel awake. This is done, in part, by regulating the levels of various chemicals in the bloodstream. Certain hormonal levels change when the sun goes down. (It has been found that the level of melatonin in the bloodstream, for example, rises with the onset of darkness and increases until the individual is asleep. It remains fairly constant until morning, when the level begins dropping prior to waking up.) Body temperature also falls during the hours of darkness as the body prepares for sleep. It has been found that heart rate decreases during the early morning hours (usually around 3 or 4 a.m.).

A significant effect of consistently working against the circadian rhythm is its impact on the subject's health and social functioning. Psychologist Dr. Chaytor Mason told us that pilots working for some of the overnight package and cargo services have been experiencing higher rates of loss of medical certificates than their daylight-flying counterparts, and seem to be having more difficulties at home, too. Dr. Mason said he was not sure whether a factor in the home, such as a spouse's dissatisfaction with a pilot's night flying job, causes more stress in the pilot's life, leading to more health and personal problems, or whether the stress of working against the circradian clock causes the problem.

When someone is forced to work against his circadian rhythm, what can he do to minimize the adverse effects? This question, unfortunately, has no single answer.

Circumstances

It all depends on the circumstances which the individual is trying to adjust to. Flights across time zones will require different strategies than flights which are being made at "off-hours."

Flights which cross time zones present unique conditions. The body finds its external time cues shifted, with some resulting circadian confusion. It has been found that the human body will generally compensate for one time zone per day. Pilots who have just completed a flight to Europe may have to wait up to eight days for their bodies to adjust to the new time zone (if they have crossed eight time zones).

The effects of time zone changes are not as pronounced on flights from east to west. It has been found that people arriving in the U.S. from Europe have an easier time re-adjusting to the new schedule. While no reason for this has been confirmed, it is suspected that most people find it easier to adjust to the longer day which the east to west time-zone change produces than they do to the shorter nights which travel in the opposite direction brings on.

For pilots who find themselves working constantly changing schedules, however, the situation can be quite different. The body is still receiving the same external cues in terms of light and dark. But now it must be able to function at peak efficiency at any time. This kind of scheduling can lead to the body chasing the circadian clock but with no real hope of catching up. Those who work rotating shifts find themselves just settling into one clock setting, when they are called upon to reset the clock and transition to another shift.

The implications here are the same as those for crossing time zones—how can the pilot remain as sharp as he would during a normal day? The vast majority of those who work under these conditions find their own individual way to cope. There has been some input from the scientific community on this, however.

Dr. Charles Ehret of the Argonne National Laboratory in Chicago has espoused a dietary approach to overcoming this "shift-lag." This diet is intended to be implemented during the individual's off-duty days (i.e. weekend) and should enable him to transition from one shift to the next more easily. The diet consists of regulating the intake of proteins and carbohydrates while simultaneously shifting the sleeping pattern. Extended over the course of the weekend, it permits the body to be better adjusted at the start of the new work week.

The Crew That Plays Together...

Take a two-pilot crew who have done a full day of short-haul, commuter airline-type flying, run them through a simulator flight, including a mechanical problem, then compare their performance to that of a crew that has had three full days of rest. Which is going to perform better on matters related to flight safety, as rated by an expert observer?

No contest, eh? The well-rested pilots should clearly fly better than their stressed-out, tired-out colleagues.

They should. But they don't. That was the startling conclusion of a study conducted at NASA's Ames Research Center.

The post-duty pilot pairs were tested within a couple hours of ending their normal flying day, which consisted of anywhere from

eight to 13 hours on duty and from five to eight landings. All were
captains or first officers with a major U.S. air carrier operation. They
were tested in the company's simulator, flying a "normal" flight
segment, using their own charts, headphones and other familiar
cockpit equipment. The pre-duty pilots were tested after a minimum
of three days off (a real luxury for a commuter pilot).

The simulator flight was no piece of cake for the crews, what with
bad weather (including icing and turbulence), equipment failures,
and the discovery at the end of the flight that the "destination" was
below minimums and they were in many cases flirting with minimal
fuel. It was not fun, but all in all, probably not something most of the
crews hadn't seen many times in the real world.

The emphasis in the data gathering and analysis was on crew
performance. This resulted from the finding that most air carrier
incidents are a result not of lack of knowledge on the part of crew
members, but rather on failures to coordinate and execute.

There were two sets of ratings, both prepared by the expert
observer. One set rated each crew member on a scale of 1 (below
average) to 5 (above average) on a variety of tasks within each phase
of the flight.

The second set of ratings was more general, consisting of the
expert's evaluation of nine categories including crew coordination
and internal communication, external communication, motivation,
command ability, vigilance and overall performance.

To nobody's surprise, the crews with three days off averaged
considerably more sleep on the average the night before than their
working colleagues (8.5 vs. 5.7 hours), and the pilots coming off a duty
day were significantly more tired by self-report than their pre-duty
friends. All of which would make it quite understandable if the post-
duty pilots were to perform worse. All of which makes it less
understandable that they didn't.

"Duty cycle exposure had no apparent effect on any of the parameters associated with flight safety," the researchers report. "It is also
interesting to note that the positive effects on crew coordination of
some unknown amount of recent operating experience can be an
effective countermeasure to the levels of fatigue associated with the
duty cycles examined in this study. Whereas fatigue tends to be more
prevalent during the later stages of a given duty cycle, crew coordination may be better as well because of the increased familiarity of
crewmembers."

When it comes to improving performance, working together
appears to be even more powerful than rest. This finding substanti-

ates and validates the considerable emphasis now given by most airlines to the concept of crew coordination.

While a day in the cockpit may not replace a day off on any commuter pilot's wish list, the study's results point out the importance of the subtle effects of people working as a crew to get the job done. It might also argue strongly for longer-duration assignments of crew partners, as opposed to constantly changing assignments.

The Cat-Nap Versus the "All-Nighter"

Things have a way of happening just before a flight. Deadlines and demands that didn't exist will rear their ugly heads and force the pilot's nose to the grindstone in order to earn the precious air time.

Sometimes the tasks at hand grab a large chunk of time the night (or day) before a flight, and most pilots have faced the dilemma of a short sleep before a long flight. The question then becomes whether 'tis better to sleep, perchance to dream, or to pull one of the fabled "all-nighters" much beloved by college students, and plan on catching one's rest when once again on the ground.

Many people say they feel worse after sleeping a little than they do just going on without benefit of slumber, but there's now experimental data to suggest a pilot is better off taking the sleep when it's available, even if only a very few hours of such unpowered flight from consciousness can be snatched.

Investigators at the Royal Air Force Institute of Aviation Medicine in England and those at Henry Ford Hospital in Detroit cooperated in a study that looked at the effects of: (1) early evening sleep on overnight and subsequent daytime performance, and (2) morning sleep on daytime performance after overnight sleep deprivation.

Each of half a dozen volunteers completed nine different work/rest schedules of 48 hours duration, with a week between each experiment. During the "work" phase, the volunteers performed a number of standardized tests designed to measure their mental alertness and performance.

In the case of an overnight period of wakefulness preceded by an evening sleep of just four hours, performance on virtually all measures was improved compared to that for those who didn't sleep before. And when an all-nighter was both preceded and followed by a sleep period, performance during the next day did not differ from that seen when there was a full night of slumber.

"It would appear that relatively short periods of sleep have a beneficial effect on subsequent performance even in the absence of preceding sleep debt," the researchers said.

Controllers Have Problems, Too

It's 2 a.m. and all is quiet as the pilot drones along, content that he's got the additional protection of being in touch with a controller who will be ever-vigilant against the traffic a sleepy brain might not perceive. Perhaps. But the odds will be better if the controller is a coffee drinker.

British researchers explored the dark side of night when they went looking for performance differences between controllers on day (8 a.m. to 5 p.m.) and night (5 p.m. through 8 a.m.) shifts. As they note, such people have to share the more and less desirable shifts, which means they "have to cope with unusual patterns of work and rest," and yet do so in a way that assures high levels of vigilance while also letting these people live something resembling a normal social life.

To see how well the controllers coped, four were subjected to two weeks of testing. This consisted of two day-shift days (nine hours on, starting at 8 a.m.); two days of night-shift (15 hours, starting at 5 p.m.); and three days off. During the night shifts, some of the people were given caffeine in pill form; others got a dummy pill.

During their "shifts," the controllers were tested on a wide variety of tasks designed to measure their mental sharpness and vigilance level. Performance on virtually all the tasks declined on the night shift, with the onset of impairment obvious between 11 p.m. and 2 a.m. "The fall in performance during the night was pronounced," the researchers wrote. "Impairment of visual vigilance occurred within 9 hours after the beginning of the overnight work period, but such an effect was not seen at the end of the daytime work period which was of the same duration." Something was clearly going on—or not going on—at night.

Caffeine didn't make sharpies out of these sleeping beauties, but it did help to stem the tide of deterioration on most of the tests. "It had a beneficial effect on most aspects of performance overnight," the scientists said, "when impairment was marked due to both prolonged hours of work and falling levels of alertness."

Their conclusion about controller performance was a bit sobering for those who might be counting on help from that extra set of eyes at 2 o'clock in the morning. "It is clear that individuals working long periods from the late afternoon are highly unlikely to maintain reasonable levels of vigilance."

How Much is Less Important than How Good

Fatigue can also find its source in the quality of sleep. Restless nights with the sleep pattern interrupted often find the sleeper awakening quite tired from the night's exertions. Pilots with a baby at home have no doubt been subjected to this. Those without children have probably been awakened during the night by other causes. The effect is the same, however.

If the interruption is not consistent, in other words happening only once during the night, the effects will not be pronounced. But if the person finds himself awakened several times during the night, the effects can be dramatic. This will be true even if the person gets a total of eight hours of sleep.

The key is the amount of time which the person spends in (rapid eye movement) sleep. According to psychologists, this stage of sleep begins about 90 minutes after the person first falls asleep. It is considered one of the most critical stages of sleep, and it's during this period that the person dreams.

Several studies have shown that people deprived of REM sleep will awaken feeling worse than when they went to bed, particularly if the deprivation has continued over two or three nights. Thus, if the person's sleep is consistently disturbed before he enters REM sleep (the baby cries, an unmuffled truck passes by), the effect will be almost like getting no sleep at all.

REM sleep deprivation can be caused by things other than disturbed sleep. Sleeping too deeply, when under the influence of alcohol or drugs, for example, will prevent the body from reaching REM sleep. Psychologist Dr. Harvey Wichman tells us that the body will not enter REM sleep until all alcohol has been metabolized. Until the blood alcohol level drops, the body will lie in very deep sleep. For someone who has really tied one on, this could take all night, leaving the victim feeling not only hung-over from the alcohol but also sleep-deprived—even though he may have been unconscious for eight hours or more.

In the Still of the Night

For some pilots, such as those involved in air ambulance work, the call to fly can come at very odd hours, often in the middle of the night. For these pilots, there is no prospect of rolling over and going back to sleep. They must fly *now*.

Dr. Wichman suggests that pilots who find themselves in this situation be extra careful in their flying. As an aid to waking up, he suggests that doing light exercises before and during flight could help the pilot in maintaining his alertness. Fighting against both sleep loss and the circadian clock, these pilots must take steps to prevent themselves from falling into a torporous state through inactivity during the flight. The doctor suggests that talking to people (controllers or copilots) will help provide the needed stimuli to help keep the brain active.

Several psychologists we spoke with suggested that some forewarning of the impending flight could be used by the pilot to his advantage, provided this warning came far enough in advance to permit some small amount of sleep before takeoff.

Dr. Wichman told us that the mind has the ability to react to the anticipated sleep loss by accelerating the onset of REM sleep and maintaining REM for longer periods. To illustrate this, he used an example: Two people are driving long distance. They make a deal such that the first person will drive until he is too tired, while the other sleeps. Then the first driver sleeps while the second takes over. If the first person stays at the wheel until 2 a.m., when he awakens the second driver, the second driver is going to feel very tired. Chances are, he'll feel just as tired as the person who was driving all along. This is because he did not know when he would be awakened, and so his body could not "make up" the lost REM sleep.

But suppose instead, they decided the first person would drive until 2 a.m., then awaken the second driver. The second driver would probably feel much better, according to Dr. Wichman. This is because he knew he would be getting up in a short while and his body compensated for this by getting more REM sleep.

Studies conducted at Stanford University tend to confirm this hypothesis. These sleep studies involved awakening people just at the onset of REM sleep—never allowing them to achieve it. After several nights of this, the subjects were becoming increasingly irritable during the day and were hard to awaken during the night.

Interestingly, when the subjects were allowed to sleep undisturbed, it was found that they had more periods of REM sleep, as though their bodies were trying to catch up on what they had lost during the previous nights.

As applied to an air ambulance pilot, it has been suggested by several aviation psychologists that dispatchers who find they have to awaken pilots in the middle of the night could help the pilot considerably by calling as far in advance of flight time as possible. If the pilot could be warned a few hours in advance, he could go back to sleep for a short time. Knowing he would have to get up shortly, his body would attempt to compensate for the anticipated loss of REM sleep.

Is It All in Your Mind?

Fatigue can also come during flight from various aspects of the flying environment. While not very demanding physically (pilots certainly do not exert themselves physically as much as longshoremen do), the cockpit requires large amounts of mental activity. It also imposes its own special stresses on the body.

That long IFR flight, featuring several clearance amendments, routing changes, and tricky navigation problems, can tax one's mental abilities. Prolonged flight under these conditions can certainly promote reduced mental acuity, and has been shown to lead pilots into making mistakes.

More insidious, but just as fatiguing, is a flight where nothing happens. Long periods of scanning the instruments with little conversation or break in the scanning routine is, to say the least, boring...and boredom is fatiguing.

Fatigue can also be brought on by some of the cockpit and cabin amenities. Pressurized aircraft tend to have very dry air in the cabin at altitude. This leads to mild dehydration—a fatiguing state. Pilots often compound this by drinking coffee, cola and sweetened drinks. Coffee and cola both contain caffeine and both act as diuretics. They prod the kidneys on to greater efforts, drying the body out faster. The drier the pilot gets, the more fatigued he gets. The most obvious way around this trap is to avoid caffeinated and sweetened beverages. Since water is what is being lost, then water (or fruit juice) is what should be taken in to replace it, the experts say.

Another source of cockpit fatigue is noise. It is well known that noise is physically tiring. This is particularly true of continuous, droning type noise, such as aircraft engines. During World War II, a pilot ferrying a P-38 fighter across the Atlantic found the drone of the engines putting him to sleep. When the fatigue became too much for him to handle, he found relief by doing barrel rolls in the heavily loaded aircraft. The adrenaline boost he got from scaring himself was enough to let him finish the flight to Greenland.

While pilots do not generally fly aircraft which are capable of performing rolls safely, there are other ways of fighting cockpit fatigue. Breaking up routine is probably one of the best remedies for fatigue on the flight deck.

According to the aviation psychologists we spoke with, the trick is to have a variety of stimuli for the brain to work on. Dr. Wichman suggests that talking with people on the ground, like Flight Watch or some other airborne service, is probably one of the best ways to accomplish this. Not only does it provide a break from the routine of the flight deck, but also provides the opportunity to gather potentially invaluable information.

Another trick he recommends is to do small mental chores, like checking the aircraft's position using as many navigational aids as possible. This will help alleviate the boredom and fatigue and also enhance the safety of the flight. Likewise, checking groundspeeds, computing fuel burn, or any number of items which might otherwise get deferred until later in the flight can help reduce fatigue.

One way to both reduce fatigue and to prevent its further onslaught, according to Dr. Wichman, is to move around. Pilots tend to sit quite motionless at the controls. This tends to dull the senses and reduce blood circulation. Moving about, even if it is only flexing the arms and legs while seated, will tend to provide stimuli to the brain and aid tremendously in restoring circulation. It will also cause the release of small amounts of adrenaline, which will act as a short-term pick-me-up.

Dr. Wichman also told us that when strong symptoms of drowsiness set in, the key is to produce some sort of change in the environment. Long-distance drivers have used the trick of opening the window and letting cold air blow on their faces. Even Lindbergh used this trick—and it works. Eating a strong mint or candy will be effective in providing stimulus, as will pinching oneself or biting a lip. Dr. Wichman told us of one pilot he knows who places a rubber band loosely around one wrist. When the pilot starts feeling tired, he just stretches the rubber band out and lets it snap smartly against the wrist. The short, stinging pain this produces gets the adrenal glands going, providing a nice boost.

Wiley Post, who flew around the world solo in 1933, tied a wrench to his wrist with a short string. He held the wrench in one hand, and whenever he nodded off during one of his multi-hour legs, the falling wrench would snap him back to wakefulness.

An Ounce of Prevention...

Whether flying the Atlantic, or just flying the pattern, fatigue can be as deadly as an airframe failure. The only real cure is prevention—rest, relaxation, and proper planning. But for the aviator who is forced to fly when fatigued, being aware of his body's needs, of the effects of fatigue, and of some of the methods for combating it will make those tiring flights easier and safer.

Is Anyone Awake Up There?

It caused a fair amount of stir recently when a study revealed that substantial numbers of transport-category pilots have at some time or another gone to sleep while on the flight deck. The idea of a jumbo jet cruising the skies with part of its crew asleep is not comforting to those who pay to be transported safely and comfortably.

Sleeping is just one measure of fatigue, a pervasive and threatening problem for all types of pilots. Taken to the point where sleep imposes itself, fatigue is obvious and in a sense self-limiting. What is much more insidious is fatigue which does not announce itself quite so obviously yet which quietly erodes a pilot's skills to a point where he becomes a hazard.

Researchers selected from the NASA Aviation Safety Reporting System file 426 reports in which fatigue, workload, complacency, scheduling or time of day were mentioned as factors in the incident being reported. From this they isolated 77 reports where fatigue was explicitly stated or implied by the reporter. These reports were tested against 100 others drawn at random from the files.

One of the skills most affected by fatigue, the study revealed, is perception, particularly the ability to monitor what's going on. One airline crew was on its tenth landing of the day and got vectored to base leg behind another aircraft. They became quite busy maintaining adequate separation, preparing for landing, etc. After clearing the runway, the first officer pointed out to the pilot that they'd never talked to the tower! "I don't remember approach control turning us over at the outer marker, as is the normal procedure," the pilot reported. "Another case of too much to cover in too little time." And, he might well have added, after perhaps a bit too much flying.

What makes an aircrew suffer fatigue? It's more than just not sleeping; in fact, adequacy of rest or disturbed sleep were cited only 23 out of 137 times by reporting crewmembers. More than one-third cited excessive duty periods, including too many flight hours or being at the end of the duty period. Almost half had been on duty 12 or more hours. And a substantial number pointed to workload problems (either excessively high or excessively low, leading to boredom), night operations, weather or physical discomfort as factors.

Overall, the study found that fatigued pilots make the same kinds of mistakes as always, but more frequently. There's nothing unusual about the errors committed by tired pilots, but simply a greater risk they will experience a mental lapse with its potential for problems.

High Altitude, Low Sleep Don't Mix

Sometimes one plus one is greater than two. That appears to be the case when pilots mix high altitude flying and a short night's sleep. Researchers at the FAA's Civil Aeromedical Institute decided to see what could be seen about pilots who fly under the influence of inadequate rest. The results were not comforting, and suggest that pilots need to be a lot more concerned than most people about getting an adequate night's sleep.

A group of 30 men, 16 of whom were 30-39 years old and the rest of whom were 60-69, were recruited. They passed the equivalent of a Third Class physical, had normal pulmonary function, and had average or above IQs. The volunteers were first trained on a series of standard tasks used to create varied workloads and to force time-sharing, the capacity to do more than one task at the same time. The tasks included monitoring warning lights and meters, performing mental arithmetic, identifying targets, tracking a blip on a screen and problem solving. For each run of the experiment, a person was subjected to five 10-minute intervals of work involving various combinations of these tasks, weighted to produce either a low, moderate or high workload condition. For the experiment, each person either had a normal night's sleep or was kept awake for the whole night before the experiment. Those undergoing sleep deprivation were monitored to make certain there was no snoozing, and they were not permitted excessive caffeine or any vigorous exercise.

There were two possible altitude conditions—high altitude (about 11,000 feet) or ground level (about 1,000 feet)—both of which were created by varying the mixture of gases being fed the volunteers through a face mask. Altitude variation had little or no effect on the performance of people who were rested, no matter what their age. The sleep-deprived people, however, were an entirely different story. In short, they didn't do well, and they did even less well at altitude. And the older group was particularly affected by a combination of increasing altitude and increasing workload.

Decreased performance due to sleep deprivation and altitude combined was a statistically significant factor in overall scores as well as scores related specifically to monitoring tasks. "Detrimental effects of altitude appeared when subjects were sleep deprived," concluded the investigators.

"This finding supports warnings in the aeromedical literature that the effects of sleep deprivation may be more important for pilots than for other occupational groups because of the altitude factor. The data of this study corroborate the validity of those warnings for altitudes in the general aviation range," the researchers said.

Bad Sleep, Off Balance

While launching after a poor night's sleep (or no sleep at all) is generally thought to be a bad idea because the pilot isn't mentally sharp, often overlooked is the fact that sleep deprivation can have a wide range of physiological effects, some of which are as dangerous as the mental miscues.

FAA scientists decided to see what happened to the vestibular response—the inner ear signals that "tell" the brain whether your body is headed up, down, or around—when pilots were deprived of sleep for prolonged periods of time.

Twenty people volunteered for the experiment. Half were on a normal sleep-wake cycle. The other half were deprived of sleep for approximately a 55 hour period. Twice a day each person was loaded into a rotating device in a completely darkened room and spun (clockwise, for those who like such details). By depressing a switch, people indicated when they thought they hit each 90 degrees of turn, and when the turning motion ceased. After three minutes of going around in a circle, each person was told to tilt his head to the right and, later, to return his head to an erect position. The switch was used to signal the start and end of each "climbing" (head tilt) or "diving" (head return) sensation, and then each subject gave a verbal estimate of the number of degrees of climb or dive he experienced.

When the data were analyzed, the experimenters found that loss of sleep results in "a general decline in all measures of nystagmus produced by angular acceleration." Nystagmus is rapid, involuntary eye movements that reflect disturbance of the vestibular system. While a decrease in such movements might at first seem to be an advantage, the problem is that the response is different than what the pilot is used to.

Fatigue-induced suppression, the researchers conclude "may have effects, subtle or otherwise, on responses to a variety of motion environments. Survival in some flight situations may be dependent upon appropriate vestibular suppression and enhancement."

7 | Hypoxia and Hyperventilation

A breath is not just something you can take or leave. You take it—through the nose, throat, and windpipe into the lungs. Inhaling requires a small amount of muscular effort to pull the chest wall and diaphragm away from your lungs, reducing the pressure inside and permitting atmospheric pressure to push in and fill up your lungs—and you "leave" it, as soon as you relax the effort of expanding your chest; you exhale, a "no-effort" operation.

Ordinarily, you breathe 12 to 16 times a minute, although the rate will be slower when you are resting and faster when you are exercising. The average man inhales about a pint of air at a time, or from six to eight quarts per minute. When you really get excited, you may breathe as much as 50 to 60 quarts per minute.

The purpose of breathing is to get oxygen into your blood stream and carbon dioxide out. This exchange is made through the walls of millions of tiny sacs and blood vessels in the lungs. The importance of this function may be judged from the total surface of these sacs, estimated to be between 700 and 800 square feet, or 40 to 50 times the skin surface of your body. The walls of the sacs are only 1/50,000 of an inch thick, moist and porous, enabling air to be pushed through this barrier. It is also pushed through the walls of the tiny blood vessels surrounding each sac. These tiny tubes—capillaries—connect with a large artery carrying blood from heart to lungs and with veins carrying it back to the heart. The heart, of course, pumps blood throughout the body.

The blood does an excellent job of carrying oxygen, thanks to the red blood cells, or solid substance of the blood. These cells saturate themselves with oxygen. Normally, the red blood cells carry oxygen at about 95 percent of their total capacity, which amounts to about a pint of oxygen in every five pints of blood. The red cells pick up oxygen easily at ground-level atmospheric pressure, such as is found in the lung sacs, and release it quickly at lower pressures, such as are found in the body's tissues. As oxygen is released, the waste carbon dioxide is dumped into the air you exhale.

We live under an air pressure of 14.7 pounds per square inch at sea level. Oxygen makes up 21 percent of the air, and is therefore responsible for 21 percent of the pressure (about 3 psi at sea level). That much is needed in your lungs to keep your blood cells 95 percent saturated with oxygen, a normal level.

But climb to 10,000 feet and you will find that the oxygen pressure in the atmosphere has dropped to almost 2 psi, not enough to deliver a normal supply of oxygen into your lungs, but enough to keep your blood about 90 percent saturated. This deficiency is ordinarily of no great consequence. Get on up to 18,000 feet and the oxygen pressure in the air drops to 1.5 psi, or half that at sea level. This is not enough to keep your mental wheels turning properly, for the oxygen saturation of your red blood cells drops to 70 percent at this altitude.

Take an atmospheric pressure reading at 34,000 feet altitude and you will find it is 3.6 psi, which is almost down to the sea-level pressure of oxygen itself. For practical purposes, you do have a total air pressure about equal to that of the 3-psi oxygen pressure at sea level—if you subtract the pressure of water vapor and carbon dioxide in the air you breathe.

The thing to do is use a supplemental oxygen system to increase the percentage of oxygen to above 21 percent. By the time you get to 34,000 feet, you need to breath 100-percent oxygen to get 3 psi of oxygen pressure. Breathing 100-percent oxygen is sufficient to protect the human system up to an altitude 40,000 feet, where the atmospheric pressure is 2.7 psi. By breathing 100-percent oxygen at this altitude, the situation is comparable to that when you breathe free air at 10,000 feet—a mild deficiency in blood oxygen saturation ordinarily not imposing any danger.

Above 40,000 feet, the atmospheric pressure is so low that even 100-percent oxygen will not meet your body's needs. To fly above 40,000 feet, you must be able to increase the pressure of the oxygen reaching your lungs; this requires a pressurized cabin, a pressure mask, or a pressure suit. The latter two are pretty much the sole province of military aviators.

Blood Is Tricky Stuff

Other things besides low atmospheric pressure can cause a shortage of oxygen in your body. One is lack of enough red blood cells to carry the oxygen, which may occur if you are a blood donor and have visited the Red Cross just before flying, or if you have recently lost a lot blood for any reason. Certain chemicals, such as carbon monoxide in exhaust gas, can grab off the space normally occupied by oxygen in the red blood cells.

Carbon monoxide is especially dangerous, because the red blood cells hold it 200 times more tenaciously than they do oxygen. If the circulation of the blood slows down because of injury and shock, oxygen is not delivered to its destination in the tissues rapidly enough. Lastly, chemicals such as alcohol can create a tissue poisoning, or blocking, which tends to prevent the blood from unloading its oxygen when it arrives at the destination.

In general, you should remember that without protection (supplemental oxygen systems or pressurized cabins), the higher the altitude, the less the pressure on you. The less the pressure, the less oxygen in your blood. The less oxygen in your blood, the worse the effect on you. The longer all this goes on, the more the effects of oxygen deficiency—hypoxia—increase. You lose the good judgment you need to survive if you are flying at higher-than-normal altitudes, or when you are under the influence of any of the situations we mentioned which *effectively* raise the altitude at which you're functioning.

Though the effects of hypoxia vary with individuals, the results of oxygen deficiency may be generalized as follows:

• 8,000 to 10,000 feet for over four hours—fatigue, and sluggishness.

• 10,000 to 15,000 feet, two hours or less—fatigue, drowsiness, headache, poor judgment.

• 15,000 to 18,000 feet, one-half hour or less—false sense of well-being (euphoria), overconfidence, faulty reasoning, narrowing of field of attention, unsteady muscle control, blurring of vision, poor memory. *You may pass out!*

• Over 18,000 feet—above symptoms appear earlier, loss of muscle control, loss of judgment, loss of memory, loss of ability to think things out, no sense of time, repeated purposeless movements, fits of laughing, crying or other emotional outbursts.

Loss of consciousness generally occurs at 26,000 feet in 4 to 6 minutes, at 30,000 feet in 1 to 2 minutes, at 38,000 feet in 30 seconds or less, and above 50,000 feet in 10 to 12 seconds. These figures vary with the individual and the work being done at the time.

The eyes are really an extension of the brain and are therefore the first organs affected by hypoxia. This is demonstrated by a reduction of night vision at altitudes of 5,000 or higher.

Stop Panting! It's a Waste of Time

By this time, you may have gotten the bright idea that one way to get more oxygen in a hurry when atmospheric pressure sells you short is to breather faster. If you breathe in a pint of air 16 times a minute, you figure that you could take in 32 pints by stepping up your breathing to 32 times a minute. True, but it will also knock you out if you keep it up!

The catch is this: By forcing yourself to breathe more rapidly you eliminate carbon dioxide more rapidly. So what? It's a waste product. True enough, but it so happens that the amount of carbon dioxide in your blood is what controls the rate at which you breathe. For example, when you exercise, you breathe harder because muscular work increases the amount of carbon dioxide in your blood; as you breathe harder, you get rid of more carbon dioxide and take in more oxygen. Everything works automatically on the ground and it will continue to do so between 10,000 and 40,000 feet *if* you use a source of supplemental oxygen and it is working properly.

However, if you overbreathe as a means of getting oxygen to make up for low oxygen *pressure*—and not simply because your muscular effort requires it—you eliminate too much carbon dioxide and that brings on strange sensations. You get dizzy and see spots before your eyes; your fingers and toes will get numb.

You may breathe too fast (hyperventilation) especially when you are excited or scared. You need to watch your breathing at such times and slow down. Other than that, just forget it. Let the amount of carbon dioxide in your blood do your thinking for you. *Never force your breathing!*

Real-World Experiences

The symptoms of hypoxia and hyperventilation are, to some extent, remarkably similar—dizziness, eye-spots, strange sensations here and there—but the conditions that lead to these two respiration-related maladies are remarkably different. A waggish flight surgeon was once heard to tell a class of military pilots that "since you know that hypoxia is a lack of oxygen, and hyperventilation results from too much air, when you're not certain which you've got, just take a big whiff of oxygen; if you're hypoxic, you'll feel better immediately, but if you're hyperventilating, you'll pass out."

That's a lot of tongue-in-cheek, and in the latter case, the cure may be more hazardous than the problem. Pilots need to understand what's going on, even when flying at relatively low altitudes; remember it's the *effective* altitude you must consider. You don't have to be a high-flier to subject yourself to respiration difficulties, as one pilot discovered:

> I recently experienced an incident in which I had what felt like hypoxia even though I had a good oxygen supply. At the suggestion of someone else, I considered the possibility that the problem was hyperventilation, and after testing it I think that's exactly what it was. If I take several deep breaths, I get a slight sense of dizziness. The thing I should have done at that point was to make my breathing shallower. Instead, I did the opposite, by deepening my breathing when I thought I was becoming hypoxic.
>
> That, of course, made the situation worse. I got scared and descended quickly to a lower altitude, at which point I felt good again.

Hyperventilation sounds like a reasonable diagnosis in this case, and it's one pilots should keep in mind. The body uses the level of carbon dioxide in the blood as a kind of gauge about oxygen status, and as a signal to the respiratory center to breathe.

Under extreme conditions of stress, fright, or pain, people tend to "overbreathe." This has the effect of washing carbon dioxide out of the blood. The initial symptoms are dizziness, hot and cold sensations, and tingling of the extremities. If the hyperventilation continues, you may experience nausea, sleepiness and—in an extreme case—a loss of consciousness.

People vary in their sensitivity to hyperventilation. It's not a bad idea to try a test in the safety of your home to see how sensitive you are and just how your body reacts. Taking a few deep breaths rapidly through the mouth should give some indication of how hyperventilation will affect you. WARNING—don't try this in a standing position, just in case your threshold is really low and you depart consciousness for a while.

Another pilot experienced a strange physical problem, and suspected a lack of oxygen as the cause of his brief difficulty. In his words:

> I had been airborne at 9,000 feet for two hours, heading home at dusk after a business meeting. The first sign of a problem was spots in front of my eyes. I removed my glasses, thinking I might give my eyes a rest.
>
> A few moments later, ATC instructed me to change frequencies. Although I knew what I should be doing, I could not communicate intelligently for a period of what I estimate to be less than a minute. I couldn't state my N number or the assigned frequency. The numbers simply came out garbled.
>
> This condition cleared up as quickly as it occurred. At no time did I feel faint or queasy. Believing this was due to a lack of oxygen, I immediately requested an altitude change to 5,000 feet and continued the rest of the flight (another two hours) without incident.
>
> I am 58 years old and in very good health. I have never had this happen before or since, and am still wondering what caused my problem.

Chances are, lack of oxygen was the villain, but there's a possibility that another malady was to blame—a transient ischemic attack, or "TIA." These are brief episodes (often precursors to strokes) in which oxygen flow to some part of the brain is impaired. In this pilot's case, the power of speech may have been affected, thus his temporary inability to communicate with ATC.

TIAs usually strike middle-aged people. They're thought to be a result of bits of cholesterol plaque (the stuff that clogs arteries and causes heart attacks) that have broken loose and momentarily become lodged in an artery leading to the brain. Another possibility is that the brain arteries are subject to a momentary spasm.

If you suffer an experience such as the one just described, it is critically important that you see your physician immediately and get a complete neurological examination. While a TIA is at the top of the suspect list for symptoms such as these, there are other possibilities. A person who has experienced a TIA is at greater-than-normal risk of having a stroke, and this situation needs to be evaluated.

Suffice it to say that it would be considered *extremely* hazardous for a suspected TIA sufferer to fly until the cause of the problem has been fully explored.

There's Reason in Them Thar Rules

We often wonder why the FAA rule-writers chose certain altitudes when they assembled the Federal Aviation Regulations. For example, why are the rules for oxygen use so specific about the difference between 12,500 feet (where oxygen is required for anything more than a half-hour stay) and 14,000 feet (above which continuous use is required)? It doesn't seem like 1,500 feet would make that much difference. But as far as your body is concerned, it *is* farther from 12,500 to 14,000 than it is, for example, from 9,500 to 11,000 feet!

To understand why that's so, you need to know a bit about how oxygen gets around in the system. It travels as sort of a hitchhiker with the substance hemoglobin, for which it has a great affinity. At sea level every 100 milliliters (ml) of blood in the arteries contains about 20 ml of oxygen, which is around 97 percent of its theoretical maximum saturation.

As the pressure of oxygen drops with increasing altitude, the saturation decreases, but it doesn't do so in a nice, even fashion. At 5,000 feet it's still possible to squeeze around 95 percent of the theoretical maximum into the blood, and even at 10,000 feet the figure is still above 90 percent.

However, at that point things take a rapid nose-dive. What had been a gentle downward slope suddenly becomes a very steep plunge, with the oxygen-carrying capacity very quickly falling off to levels below what's needed to keep a pilot sharp and capable. The area from 12,500 to 14,000 feet is at the start of that steep plunge, which is why the rules get so specific, and why pilots are constantly cautioned that anything (such as cigarette smoking, fatigue, stress, etc.) that reduces their blood's ability to transport oxygen calls for supplemental oxygen at lower elevations.

High-Flying Might Make You Sick

We humans have lived for so long on the floor of our ocean of air that any displacement upward (or downward, for that matter—surely you've heard of the "bends?") can cause discomfort, or worse. "Altitude sickness" is a general term applied to the unpleasantness that may result from exposure to reduced atmospheric pressure and/or a deficiency of oxygen. Given the similarity of symptoms, how does a pilot know whether he's hypoxic, suffering from hyperventilation, or a victim of altitude sickness?

A reader's question in this regard several years ago elicited this response from an aviation doctor: "A headache is frequently the first symptom of acute altitude sickness. Facial swelling is present in 75 percent of the persons with acute altitude sickness; to my knowledge this does not happen with hypoxia.

"A pilot who has hyperventilated usually experiences an almost immediate clearing of symptoms on descent; this is not usually the case in altitude sickness, where cerebral edema (swelling) accounts for most of the symptoms and typically takes hours to days to clear.

"It's difficult to say what percentage of the headaches and other minor miseries experienced by pilots are the initial symptoms of altitude sickness. I know of no good systematic studies. Since pilots are normally exposed for relatively short periods of time, and under minimal levels of exertion, and since oxygen is required above 12,500 feet after half an hour, I don't think altitude sickness is a substantial problem for most pilots.

"However, I hasten to remind readers that we all vary considerably in our susceptibility to physiological incapacitation, and I certainly think it's likely that at least some pilots do have a minor amount of altitude sickness when they spend long periods above 10,000-12,000 feet without oxygen."

Pilot, Know Thy Equipment

Most of us don't have occasion to fly very often in that user-unfriendly environment above 10,000 feet—not without the benefits of a pressurized cabin or at the least, oxygen equipment of some kind. When you do approach that rare situation in which you intend to fly high and are not familiar with the equipment available, there are some things you should know.

At the outset, be certain that the system is capable of supplying the amount of oxygen you'll need. "Flow rate" is the operative phrase, and the universal language is liters per minute. There are wide variations in equipment, and the best bet is always to read the directions pertaining to the specific piece of oxygen equipment you're using.

To get the proper amount of oxygenation (that is, enough to keep your blood at least minimally saturated), be sure your oxygen system is capable of supplying at least 1 liter/minute at 10,000 feet; 1.5 liters/minute at 15,000; 2.0 liters/minute at 20,000; and 2.5 liters/minute at 25,000.

Above 25,000 feet, there's a big and terribly important change in the type of oxygen equipment required. Rebreather-type equipment (the type installed on virtually all light aircraft) isn't recommended; you'll need a much more sophisticated mask, and a regulator which senses changes in air pressure and adjusts oxygen flow accordingly. If you're going up to those altitudes you'd better make certain you know and understand the limitations of your gear, and the specific procedures for using the oxygen equipment. And things get worse the higher you go. If you should struggle up to 30,000 feet (not out of the question for some of our readers who challenge "the wave" in high-performance sailplanes), problems with the oxygen supply system could leave you with only one or two minutes of time during which you'll still be able to competently perform flight duties.

It's Decision Time...Now!

For the most part, aviation educators make it a point to teach their charges that when something goes wrong in the air, "fly the airplane, take your time to diagnose the problem and take the proper action."

But there's one situation that demands quick, if not instant action; we're speaking of an oxygen emergency, in a situation where the pilot is dependent on a continued adequate supply of the "good gas" for his very life. When the oxygen supply fails at altitude—for whatever reason—a pilot can no longer "take his time" to figure out what has gone wrong. The "time of useful consciousness"—TUC—is the time available for rational thinking, and it includes trouble-shooting the oxygen system itself.

A study of the time of useful consciousness at 25,000 feet led to both expected and unexpected results, some of which carry a caution-ary tale for pilots. Why 25,000 feet? Not many GA pilots find themselves wandering around that high, but that level was chosen because it's one at which previous research indicated that a pilot's ability to remain functional deteriorated fairly promptly.

The material used in the government's high altitude training course for GA pilots says that TUC at 25,000 feet is three to five minutes, and in the altitude chamber run given as part of the course nobody is allowed to remain off oxygen at 25,000 for more than five minutes no matter what color they have or haven't turned.

When researchers tested 17 subjects in the altitude chamber to determine TUC at 25,000 feet, they ran into an interesting question: Just what *is* useful consciousness? Seems there's been something of a failure to settle on an appropriate definition, so they decided to weigh the effects of hypoxia by deciding a person wasn't functioning if he could no longer correctly add two-digit numbers together. This assumed, of course, that a group of student pilots, 18-20 years of age, could add such numbers together *before* they became hypoxic.

The results were, on the one hand, not surprising. On average, the pilots lasted a little more than four minutes before 22 and 22 no longer added up to 44 for them. That's right in line with the generally accepted three-to-five minute value.

On the other hand, the experiment yielded one very surprising finding. There were two test runs made, a week apart. On the first, four people showed absolutely no sign of being unable to add the numbers up until the instant at which they stopped doing everything. On the second run, three people did a swan song with no advance evidence. "Their inability to continue the test," the researchers report, "was accompanied by trembling and almost total lack of response to the observers' instructions."

Other attempts to measure TUC, using other measures (such as handwriting), have also encountered this phenomenon. Some people, under some conditions, will give little or no notice that their cognitive functions are deteriorating until the instant at which they become essentially nonfunctional.

These results re-emphasize the importance of an altitude chamber "ride" for any pilot who is a regular visitor to the flight levels. What considerable research has made evident is that the response to extreme hypoxia is extremely idiosyncratic. Until a pilot has discovered his or her own pattern, the possibility exists that useful consciousness could exit without much prior warning.

Puff, Puff, Puff That Cigarette

A reader posed this question about smoking: "I know that smoking results in reduced oxygen-carrying ability of the blood, but a friend and I disagree as to just how reduced. He says there isn't all that much difference."

And a doctor came up with the answer: "It's not hard to guess who the smoker is. Tell your friend he's giving up a lot of vital oxygen to his cigarette habit. There is a finite amount of oxygen bound to hemoglobin (which transports oxygen to body tissues). Carbon monoxide competes with oxygen for those slots on the hemoglobin molecule, and it's much more efficient at gaining a place than oxygen is. A smoker usually walks around with a carbon monoxide level of about 5 percent. That smoker at sea level is experiencing the same oxygen deprivation effect as a non-smoker at 7,000 feet!

"Take your smoking friend up to 5,000 or 6,000 feet and he's physiologically at the level where he should be using oxygen in order to maintain full capability.

"As I'm certain you know, the situation is even more pronounced at night due to the extreme sensitivity of night vision to hypoxia. I wouldn't advise leaving the ground at night with a smoker who wasn't using oxygen."

More About Carbon Monoxide

Carbon monoxide is nobody's friend in the cockpit. And while most people might tolerate a very low level of this noxious by-product of combustion without dire consequences, research findings show that if a pilot has pre-existing (and probably undetected) cardiovascular disease, any exposure to carbon monoxide can trigger a dangerous and potentially fatal shortage of oxygen in heart tissue.

Carbon monoxide is insidious. Colorless and odorless, it can creep into the cockpit with no notice. The most frequent source is a leak in the exhaust system. When CO gets into the bloodstream, it ties up the oxygen-carrying hemoglobin.

Researchers at several medical centers throughout the country cooperated in a study of the effects of low-level CO exposure on people who had cardiovascular disease. All the subjects were men. They were placed on a treadmill in a chamber into which varying amounts of carbon monoxide were fed.

When people with cardiovascular disease exercise on a treadmill, they normally experience chest pain after a time, as the heart's demand for oxygen increases. The researchers were surprised, however, at the degree to which even minute amounts of carbon monoxide accelerated the onset of chest pain. The amount of CO required to cause problems was so low that it was well within the limits set for environmental exposure by the EPA.

The researchers point out that cigarette smokers, who are continually dosing themselves with a high level of carbon monoxide, are particularly at risk of cardiovascular problems when exposed to even more CO in the cockpit.

Do Mountain Dwellers Grow Bigger Lungs?

It would seem that all the recommendations for the use of oxygen assume pilots live at sea level. Has anyone ever given consideration to the folks who live at altitudes well above sea level? Since they are acclimated to high elevations (and thus less oxygen) they should be able to fly a lot higher before needing supplementary oxygen.

Sounds logical, and there is a bit of truth in that reasoning. Studies have been done on this subject, and sad but true, they suggest that living almost anywhere in the U.S. isn't going to help you out enough to make much difference.

The acclimatization effect at 6,000 to 8,000 feet is minimal, and there aren't a lot of places to live permanently, let alone fly out of, much above those altitudes. You will do slightly better at 10,000 feet than someone who's suddenly hauled up from sea level, but the difference isn't much and it will nearly disappear by 12,500 feet, which is where the FAA oxygen requirement comes into play.

Keep in mind that the reason for the FAA requirement is to assure competent functioning of one's *mental* machinery. The brain is a lot more sensitive than anything else to oxygen deprivation. While being acclimatized might give you a slight edge over a flatlander in terms of being able to perform physically on the ground at a given altitude, the same can't necessarily be said for brain function.

There's just no benefit in taking any risk when it comes to the question of oxygenation. Since acclimatization is a highly variable thing, it would be dangerous to assume yourself safe to fly above the prescribed levels without oxygen. You might make it. Then again, you might not.

Learn All About It...The Safe Way

Hypoxia and hyperventilation—a pair of problems that lurk in the background of every flight operation, and made even more hazardous by their insidious nature; you can be suffering from the initial stages of either, and not be aware. What's more, especially with hypoxia, you can easily get to the point where you don't care, and a pilot trying to operate in a state of euphoria is a pilot looking for trouble.

Here's one area of pilot operations that demands knowledge and training, and near-constant vigilance for the signs of impending problems. If you have no idea what your personal symptoms of hypoxia or hyperventilation are (and nearly everyone has unique reactions to these conditions), get yourself to the nearest facility that offers formal training. Any FAA office can supply a list of these facilities (most of them are military installations), and for a few bucks, you can learn a lot about your personal oxygen-supply system and its limitations.

This type of training is strongly recommended for all pilots, if for no other reason than the general aviation knowledge to be gained; it approaches the level of necessity for pilots who operate aircraft capable of regular and frequent flight above 10,000 feet.

8

Illusions and Spatial Disorientaion

T here are few—if any—aviators who have not been exposed to the "can't tell which way you're turning" illusion. Part of every pilot's early training, it involves holding one's eyes closed while the flight instructor smoothly sets the airplane into a gentle turn, and when the fluid in the channels of the inner ear settle down, the confusion begins. The pilot is convinced that the turn has stopped because the sensory inputs tell him so, when in fact the airplane and its occupants continue to turn; it's a simple matter of a sensuous perception conveying a false impression of what has been perceived—in short, an illusion.

The pilot beginning instrument training soon figures out that he *must* learn to rely on the indications of his instruments rather than what he feels; it's a conflict of the senses that can result in a monster illusion—and one that can proceed to total spatial disorientation. Even the highest-time pilots experience illusions and occasional disorientation, but it's the ability to recognize and overcome the false impressions that makes the difference between an unpleasant episode and an accident.

Some illusions are related to speed. As you climb to altitude, there is an illusion of going slower and slower although your forward speed is usually increasing. Flying through or very close to clouds creates a sensation of speed, as does flight through rough air; the increased speed illusion at very low altitude has caused many a pilot to slow down and stall out when he thought he was in fat city, airspeed-wise.

Increased engine noise is normally associated with increased speed or a climbing attitude. Taking off on a rough runway makes you feel that you're going faster, when in reality the speed is completely normal. Optical illusions are often produced by sloping cloud banks, curved glare shields, various types of airport lighting, and the lights of other airplanes.

Instrument flying and its complete dependence on artificial clues provides perhaps the most fertile ground for illusions. For example, a normal turn may produce an illusion of climbing, and you may feel you have entered a dive during the return to level flight; after slow, imperceptible changes in aircraft attitude, rapid corrections to level flight may result in an illusion of a positive movement in the direction of the correction.

Fatigue and lack of sufficient oxygen can cause their own brands of illusions, and the list goes on and on, limited only by the senses and circumstances involved, and the personal characteristics of each pilot; each of us must learn to recognize and compensate in his own way. So, given the wide range of causes and effects that might be attributed to illusions—no matter what the source—we will look at the problem in a rather general way, touching as many sensuous bases as we can along the way.

Keeping Things in Balance

Sight, hearing, smell, taste, and touch are the five senses you usually hear about. Balance, however, might be the aviator's *sixth* sense. Without a sense of balance you could not stand up, much less fly an airplane. You maintain balance in three ways:

1. Your eyes tell you where you are in relation to whatever is around you, and are probably of the greatest importance in keeping your balance. Eyes make corrections on the two other factors in balance.

2. Your "body sense" comes from changes in the pressure and tension on your tendons, ligaments, muscles, and joints. In other words, you *feel* what position you are in. This is the significance of the old expression, "Flying by the seat of your pants." Body sense, however, informs you only of the vertical and angular movements of your body. It doesn't tell you anything of circular movements.

3. Your inner ear contains something which in itself has nothing to do with hearing. Connected with that snail-like tube of your ear which sends auditory nerve impulses to the brain, this particular organ looks like a pretzel. It consists of three semi-circular canals, each in a different plane and containing a fluid. The slightest movement of your head causes this fluid to press in the opposite direction and stimulate the tiny hairs of the cells lining the inside of the canal. The stimulation causes nerve impulses to be sent to your brain telling you which end is up—that is, your position in life. Taken alone, however, this message may fool you.

Take a Tip From the Birds, Birdmen

The homing pigeon, born to fly on course without instruments, refuses to take a chance if he runs into a cloud and cannot see. He simply sets his wings for a glide to the ground. If a homing pigeon can't fly without visibility, certainly man can't.

Maintaining orientation and equilibrium requires interpretation of sensations from the eyes, the vestibular apparatus in the inner ear, and pressure or tension sensations from skin, muscles, and joints. In flight, the combined picture received from these sensory organs may be completely unreliable—like getting a TV picture from one channel and sound from another. Flying blind without instruments is similar to walking blindfolded. The tendency is to go around in a circle when the eyes have no fixed points of reference, and, in flight, the circle tightens and quickly becomes a spin or diving spiral. Sensations in flight are also misleading to the brain because the vestibular apparatus cannot distinguish between gravity and centrifugal force.

Before a pilot can develop real confidence in his flight instruments, or what he sees outside the windshield, the brain must be taught to suppress these sensory illusions. The first step in successful instrument flight (and to some extent, VFR flight as well) is to learn to ignore the sensations which, on the ground, you depend upon instinctively to keep from falling on your face. Disregard the sensations of going up or down, slipping, sliding, or turning, and let your flight instruments and *real* outside visual clues feed accurate, ungarbled information to your brain. That's the only way to get picture and sound tuned to the same channel.

Surviving Vertigo

"I've had vertigo once in the cockpit," recalled one high-time, commercial pilot. "I was with a student in a large twin at night, and it was blowing and raining really hard, with pretty strong turbulence and a hefty crosswind. We were shooting an ILS, and the moment we broke out at minimums it hit me. I saw the runway lights where I didn't expect them to be—out my side window—and the runway appeared to me to be inverted."

Needless to say, he survived the experience of becoming disoriented only 200 feet above the ground in bad weather. Another pilot was flying the aircraft, and he had the presence of mind to keep his hands off of the controls when he felt the disorientation set in.

High Fatality Rate

But not all pilots who have had the misfortune to experience vertigo—more properly called spatial disorientation—in the cockpit have lived to tell the tale.

An FAA report drawing on five years' worth of accident data shows that accidents involving spatial disorientation are more often fatal than not. Although spatial disorientation was found to play a role in only about 2.5 percent of accidents studied, it was a cause or factor in 16 percent of accidents *involving fatalities*. The evidence indicates that if a pilot does suffer spatial disorientation in the cockpit, the chances of survival are bleak: 90 percent of those accidents were fatal.

Loss of Orientation

"Vertigo," in the sense usually used by pilots, is a misnomer. True vertigo is a narrowly defined phenomenon that's actually part of the larger subject of spatial orientation.

Humans actually rely on several sources for information about which way is up. Of prime importance is vision, but touch ("seat of the pants") and sound also play a part. There also are the semicircular canals and otolith organs, which together provide a sense of balance. The semicircular canals detect changes in angular acceleration; the otolith organs respond to straight-line accelerations and gravity. The brain combines all of the cues to provide spatial orientation.

In an airplane, the environment conspires to disorient the pilot. Though open-cockpit pilots once derived useful information from the singing of their flying wires, auditory cues gained in today's aircraft are basically useless, and seat-of-the pants cues are inaccurate—the perceived direction of gravity isn't necessarily vertical. Pilots wind up relying on vision and their sense of balance.

When the two senses don't agree, disorientation sets in. There's a strong tendency to follow the sense of balance rather than vision—which is usually the wrong thing to do, since the sense of balance is often telling one that motion (like a roll or turn) is taking place, when it's not.

"All throughout life your body's been good to you," explained Charles Valdez of FAA's Civil Aeromedical Institute. "You tend to believe what you feel, rather than what you see." When the eyes trick a pilot—like the one who saw the runway upside-down—he or she gets disoriented and will often take the controls and try to bring the airplane "upright." In the case cited, the pilot fought the urge to grab the controls and looked at the instruments, instead. Seeing that the twin was still on the glide slope and tracking the localizer, he was able to re-orient himself with little problem.

False Cues

Disorientation commonly starts with what's being seen—or not seen. Either there's a total lack of visual cues, in which case the signals the inner ear is sending will likely be misinterpreted, or there's a confusing visual cue, one that disagrees with what the inner ear says.

An example of the first kind is a pilot who unwittingly allows a wing to drop slowly; he thinks he's level when he's really in a bank. He corrects suddenly, and his inner ear tells him that he's now in a bank in the opposite direction. False cues from the inner ear also can occur during acceleration, which can be perceived as a pitch up, or deceleration, sensed as a pitch down—a particularly insidious hazard in airplanes that alter pitch with flap extension.

Disorientation from confusing visual cues can occur during a night flight with no visible horizon, when the pilot mistakes a chance line-up of ground lights as the horizon. Sloping runways can also cause problems, particularly in low-light conditions. Landing uphill, the pilot might think he's too high and descend below the glide path.

Relative Motion

Simple vertigo often is spurred by the operation of the balance organs. When the body is accelerated, the fluid-filled inner ear moves, while the fluid it contains tends to remain still (like the ice in a glass of ice water—rotate the glass and the ice stands still at first). Hair-like cells in the inner ear sense the relative motion. After a short period of time, the fluid catches up and the sense of motion stops. Without any other cues, the person no longer feels any movement, even if it's still there. The lag corresponds to the time it takes to get re-oriented. Once the fluid settles down, the world stops spinning.

There's also a threshold of detection—rotate slowly enough, and the inner ear won't detect it at all. Simple vertigo involves movement around one axis. It's equivalent to dizziness. The pilot feels movement in one direction. When the orientation of the head is changed suddenly while this is going on, however, the "Coriolis reaction" may set in. That's when two of the semicircular canals interact, and it is a truly violent sensation. The Coriolis reaction can happen when a pilot who's already disoriented and suffering from vertigo turns his or her head suddenly, for example while turning to reach into the back seat or pick up something off the floor.

No Escape

The experts say there's no way to avoid vertigo. It's simply a fact of life. However, it can be dealt with, and combating vertigo is given a lot of attention during the training for an instrument rating. The common wisdom is to immediately go on the gauges when one feels disoriented. The statistics indicate that this may work most of the time. In the FAA accident study previously mentioned, 85 percent of the pilots did not have instrument ratings. This suggests that being used to flying on instruments can help a pilot fight disorientation. But it is no guarantee.

Many pilots have never actually experienced vertigo. The FARs call for recovery from unusual attitudes and hood work but not for giving a student a taste of vertigo. Instructors who try to give their students experience with vertigo often are unsuccessful. The reason, according to CAMI's Valdez, could be that there are unwanted points of reference that can't be kept out of the cockpit—like the direction of sunlight falling on the panel (most student pilots, after all, typically train in good weather).

Exploring the Unknown

There's no way to assess how one will really react to vertigo unless it's actually experienced. Andrew Douglas, one of *Aviation Safety's* editors, gives this first hand account of an intentional experience with vertigo.

> I'm among the students who resisted their instructors' attempts to induce vertigo. As a 350-hour instrument pilot who routinely flies single-pilot IFR, I am well aware that if I do get badly disoriented in the cockpit, I may be in deep trouble.
>
> So, when another opportunity came up to experience vertigo, I jumped at the chance. I was anxious to explore my ability to handle an aircraft while in the throes of spatial disorientation. The opportunity was presented at an FAA safety seminar. It was an eye-opening experience, not what I expected at all.

The device used to induce disorientation was a very simple but highly effective contraption called a Barany chair. Basically, it's a typing chair with a seat belt and footrests. There's a set of opaque goggles with a box off the front end containing a pair of tiny blue lights and a joystick the subject uses to indicate the perceived direction of motion.

Strapped in with the goggles on (one sees only the interior of the box, with the two lights at the far end), I was asked to look down. The FAA safety program manager conducting the demonstration started spinning the chair. Having seen two others undergo the treatment, I knew what to expect: the feeling of rotation in the correct direction at first, but after several seconds a cessation of all sensation of rotation, followed by a sense of motion in the opposite direction.

Even though there were a couple of small light leaks in the goggles that provided some visual cues to the direction and speed the chair was moving, the sensation was utterly convincing. At that point, I was confident that, even though I felt odd, I could have handled an aircraft's controls safely.

BOTTOM DROPS OUT

Then, the FAA manager had me look over my shoulder. I felt as if somebody had kicked the chair over. I was tumbling and felt an instant (though mild) sensation of nausea. The goggles were pulled off, and I found that everything was swimming violently. I couldn't focus on anything, and my motor coordination was utterly scrambled. If I had been asked to put my finger on the tip of my nose, I probably would have poked an eye out. It was hard to think of anything except how screwed up everything was.

I am sure that if the same sensations ever struck me in the cockpit, I wouldn't have been able to even find the instruments, much less make sense of them. I'm not sure I would have been able to tell if I was moving a control wheel or not—I even lost track of the joystick I was holding in my hand.

That's the bad news. The good news is that everything settled down after only 15 or 20 seconds, and though I was a little tipsy walking away from the chair, I was all right.

It was an experience that words can't adequately describe. I highly recommend a demonstration to anyone who flies, especially those who have never experienced vertigo.

Where to Go

Demonstrations are offered at many FAA safety seminars. But there's a more sophisticated variant of the Barany chair, commonly called a Vertigon, that is often available at large air shows. It's an enclosed cockpit simulator with a full set of instruments for a more realistic experience.

Pilots also can go straight to the FAA for help. Many district offices have Barany chairs that are used at safety seminars, and a group of pilots may be able to arrange a special demonstration. Information can be obtained by calling your local GADO and asking for the accident prevention specialist.

Those interested in a more intensive course can contact CAMI for information on the FAA's Physiological Training Program. It's a one-day course held at military bases around the country and open to anyone with a valid medical certificate and who meet certain other minor criteria. In addition to a demonstration of spatial disorientation, the course includes some classroom instruction and a "ride" in an altitude chamber. The cost is only $20 but the wait is anywhere from three to six months. Applications can be obtained from the FAA Civil Aeromedical Institute, Airman Education Section, AAC-142, Oklahoma City, OK 73125. The phone number is (405) 680-4837.

The Bottom Line

We feel it's a good idea to experience true disorientation in a controlled environment to see how powerful an influence it really is. If a pilot can get it in a cockpit with an instructor, so much the better. But there's nothing wrong with the Barany chair or Vertigon, and they will *certainly* provide the experience, even if an in-cockpit demonstration won't.

The experience should help the pilot in the future. Part of the confusion that attends disorientation comes from the pilot's failure to recognize what is happening. "I think the demonstration does help," said FAA's Bob Martens. "It won't relieve the vertigo, itself, but it takes out the element of shock and surprise because you recognize vertigo for what it is."

If it happens for real, Charles Valdez advises that the pilot concentrate on the gauges. They can, and will provide the missing points of reference your brain needs to get re-oriented. But if the disorientation is truly debilitating (as was my experience with the Coriolis reaction) and the airplane is trimmed and flying at altitude, you might consider letting go of the controls for a moment. Most aircraft will fall off slowly one way or the other, but it's unlikely you'll get into more trouble that way than by miscontrolling the airplane, at least for the few seconds it takes your senses to become re-oriented.

Going on the gauges may do little good, however, if the pilot isn't sufficiently used to deriving information from them. Some hood work with an instructor can help, particularly for VFR pilots. The minimal amount of simulated instrument instruction most pilots get during basic training can theoretically get one out of the clouds, but the skills need to be polished regularly.

The Black Hole Explained

One of aviation's more interesting challenges is that of landing an airplane at night on a runway where there are no surrounding lights. This is the aviation "black hole," a thing into which pilots drop sometimes never to return.

Robbed of their normal visual cues, and presented with an unfamiliar set of indicators about their position in space, pilots facing the black hole have a demonstrated tendency to make excessively low approaches—some low enough to end up short of the runway. Research shows that this is a result of misperceiving the slant of the runway relative to the straight-ahead direction.

This misperception results from the absence of visual information from either side of the runway—information pilots normally use in constructing their view of runway reality. Deprived of the normal cues, the brain goes searching for something, and what it finds is the runway edge lights, from which the mind calculates where it thinks the runway is.

Unfortunately, using the narrower width of the runway edge lights leads to a very erroneous conclusion about approach positioning, which can leave the pilot low, slow and running out of options.

Research has shown a somewhat paradoxical finding that a runway whose visible length is diminished (by fog, for instance) will be safer, at least in terms of undershoots, than one whose full dimensions are in sight. Because the length-to-width ratio of the runway is less with the end obscured, the amount of slant misperception is less.

The black hole lesson can also extend to a daytime situation where terrain surrounding the runway is uniform and featureless.

It all comes down to the fact that humans are not very good at judging the slant of long, narrow rectangular surfaces. Since it's highly unlikely that runways will ever be built in anything but that shape, pilots must believe their instruments and not their eyes. That's an interesting thought about night flying—particularly for the non-instrument-rated pilot.

Distance Error Illusion

Science works in mysterious ways its wonder to perform, and thus it came to pass that a Canadian psychologist used a rubber doorstop and a coat hook to discover a new type of distance measurement illusion that could affect how long a pilot thinks the runway is.

The carefully prepared pilot, of course, *knows* how long the runway is, at least in terms of linear measurement. But when it comes to landing the airplane, each pilot literally sizes up the runway all the way through the approach. And therein could lie the problem.

For reasons he (perhaps wisely) chose not to state, psychologist Richard Hammersley one day found himself staring at a door with a coat hook on the back. He noticed that on an adjacent wall there was a rubber doorstop, intended to keep the coat hook from hitting the wall when the door was fully opened. Looking at it parallel to the wall with the door, Hammersley thought the coat hook and the door stop were at different distances from the corner where the two walls joined. But measurement showed they were exactly equal.

This led to the discovery that, as the title of his paper said, "Things are deeper than they are wide," at least in the mind's eye, even when they're in fact equal. To test the phenomenon, the investigator joined two file cards at a 90-degree angle. On one he placed a fixed dot, on the other a dot which could be moved using a slider. Seventy-two students were then asked to use various configurations of the apparatus and adjust the movable dot until it was as far from the corner as the fixed dot.

When the "walls" were at right angles, the measurements went wild. The fixed dot was in fact 100 millimeters from the corner. When the fixed dot was along the line of sight and the movable dot was at a 90-degree angle, underestimation was the rule. When they had to match the dot facing them to the dot along their line of sight, they overestimated. The magnitude of the error was about 30 percent, which is very high—in most visual illusions people misjudge by around 10 percent. When the two cards were placed side-by-side, so the dots were in the same plane, the estimates improved to an error of less than 10 percent.

Length viewed in depth, the study concludes, looks longer than length viewed in width. The runway sized up sideways while on downwind may seem much longer when viewed head-on during the final approach.

Dizziness: Meniere's Disease?

Any system, mechanical or biological, is subject to glitches, and the human body's ultra-complicated balance system can be severely affected by a variety of maladies. One of the most highly publicized is Meniere's disease, made "famous" by a couple of the original seven astronauts, otherwise prime physical specimens whose bouts with dizziness caused them a lot of problems.

One of our readers was understandably concerned about the FAA's position on his attempts to achieve pilot certification, and the possibility that he might suffer from something other than Meniere's disease. Here's his question, and an aviation physician's answer:

> I am a 59-year-old student pilot. I have been taking flying lessons for about 10 months, in spite of knowing I have (or have had) Meniere's Disease. I have been subjected to several exams, including an audio evaluation, an MRI scan of the head and an electronystagmography test. To the best of my knowledge, none of these indicated that a problem exists. I believe the diagnosis was made based upon the description of these attacks that I gave to my otolaryngologist.
>
> The fact remains, however, that I have had infrequent dizziness accompanied by stuffiness and ringing in my right ear. Subsequent audio evaluations have not shown that I have had a significant hearing loss as a result of recent attacks. I have never had an occurrence of dizziness or nausea while flying.
>
> I recently had an FAA physical. In addition to noting the dizzy spells, I reported taking diazepam (Valium) for the dizziness and nausea. My AME said he had never heard of the FAA issuing a medical certificate to someone with Meniere's Disease and that in his opinion I had little or no chance of getting a certificate.
>
> The FAA denial letter said, "We feel it only fair to advise you that as long as your condition requires medication for control, the chance of certification is not favorable." Since diazepam was prescribed, I have had slight nausea and ringing in the ear on two occasions. For about a month I have not taken the drug and have had no episodes.

In your opinion, should I pursue the matter of certification with the FAA or just forget it? If I pursue it, do you have any notion of how long the FAA might require me to be without dizziness in order for my application to be considered? What is the possibility that my problem is not Meniere's Disease but something with similar symptoms that might require different treatment?

THE DOCTOR'S ANSWER

Your last question is the most pertinent. You have a chronic disturbance of equilibrium. That is very serious, whether or not you are a pilot. For it to be undiagnosed, if in fact it is, should be totally unacceptable to you.

Yes, it certainly is possible you have Meniere's Disease, a condition that is poorly understood but which leads to attacks of frequently disabling vertigo. However, you could have one of a number of other medical problems that adversely affect the inner ear.

Your first and most important task is to find out, as definitely as possible, what is wrong. If you are not comfortable with the specialist you are seeing, find one who will make an exhaustive search for the cause of your problem and clearly and effectively communicate his or her findings to you.

I would say your chances of being certified while the problem remains, whether or not you are taking medication, are nil. Inner ear function is so critical to flying safety that any significant and uncontrolled disturbance of this mechanism is disqualifying, and for very good reason.

If you're interested in flying, the best step you can take is to get a definitive diagnosis. You may in fact have a condition that is more amenable to treatment than Meniere's, for which many things have been tried, but none have proved consistently curative without a concomitant loss of hearing or other substantial side effects.

Every Which Way But Up

Spatial disorientation. It's one of those things everyone hears about in pilot training, but rarely experiences. And until it happens, it remains something which is intellectually acknowledged but emotionally doubted. How, after all, could anyone really fail to know up from down?

Most pilots will, fortunately, never get to know what a full-blown case of spatial disorientation looks and feels like. Of those that do, even fewer will share the misfortune of being at the controls of a Boeing 747 when it happens.

For the pilot of China Airlines Flight 006, that misfortune became reality on February 19, 1985, on a flight from Taiwan to Los Angeles. The plane was about 300 miles northwest of San Francisco at FL 410 when, as the NTSB accident report calmly put it, "the airplane rolled to the right, nosed over, and entered an uncontrollable descent. The captain was unable to restore the airplane to stable flight until it had descended to 9,500 feet."

A close look at what happened, according to the flight recorders and the cockpit crew, provided a classic study in human factors and the ways in which a good flight can go bad in a hurry.

It was not, on the surface of it, an inept crew. The commander was a 55-year-old captain with 15,000 total hours and 3,700 in the B-747. The first officer, age 53, had 7,700 total hours and 4,500 in the jumbo jet. The flight engineer had 15,500 total hours, 4,300 in type. They were all current and competent—but at the instant of need, some were better able to cope than others.

If one cuts through a wealth of technical information about the machinery, the story is relatively simple: At about 9.5 hours into the flight (10:11 a.m. PST), the jet's No. 4 engine (which had logged a number of power loss problems previously) developed a "hung" condition (abnormal response to throttle movement). Within about a minute and a half, the engine flamed out. While attending to the problem, the captain allowed the sophisticated autopilot system to remain engaged, and mainly devoted his concern to the plane's airspeed, nudging the pitch control for minor adjustments. This was a serious error, since the autopilot had no way to employ the rudder, the critical control needed to deal with the loss of an outboard engine. Had anyone put his foot hard on the left rudder, or adjusted the rudder trim, nothing more exciting than an airstart of the No. 4 engine might have occurred.

The autopilot was slowly being overpowered, the ship rolling to the right, when the captain finally took control, and was immediately beset by several disorienting influences. The plane had now descended into clouds, it was rolling to the right but the yoke was deflected to the left in opposition to the roll, and the pilot was still concerned with the airspeed indicator.

The NTSB believes the captain suffered immediate spatial disorientation as he tried to interpret the attitude indicator while the huge plane rolled over on its back and dived. Indeed, when later interviewed, both the captain and copilot thought their attitude indicators had "malfunctioned."

The flight engineer was deemed to have handled his tasks fairly well, but he did forget to close the bleed air valve before attempting a restart of No. 4. And when one of the pilots apparently reacted to the upset by retarding the throttles, the engineer mistakenly announced that the other three engines had flamed out.

The copilot was not flying when the engine quit, so his main accomplishment was to request a lower altitude from ATC. The NTSB investigation revealed that the captain never detailed the first officer to either fly the plane or assist the flight engineer, both of which he was competent to do.

Off-duty crew in their bunks were called out, but wound up being glued to the cabin floor by the G forces of the two pullout attempts.

The captain stated he was unable to recover the airplane while it was in the clouds because he was uncertain of its roll attitude and was moving the control wheel left and right. Finally the plane began to decelerate. But it was a case of too much of a good thing as the big plane's speed dipped to between 80 and 100 knots. Fearful of a stall, the captain once again lowered the nose, and the plane again accelerated to a threatening airspeed. This time the captain and first officer together pulled on the control column, decelerated, lowered the nose and finally emerged from the clouds at around 11,000 feet. Finding the horizon, the captain regained control of his 747 at about 9,500 feet.

Later analysis showed the airplane had, without the captain's recognizing it, gone through a full 360-degree roll, among other maneuvers. Indeed, several of his control inputs had actually aggravated the situation. The plane had exceeded maximum operating speed (Vmo of 0.92 Mach) and had pulled some 4.8 and 5.1 Gs in the attempted pullouts.

There was substantial damage to the airplane (the wings were bent slightly and several large chunks of the horizontal tail were missing upon arrival in San Francisco), and there were some injuries to passengers and crew.

What had happened? According to the crew, they'd experienced a total failure of their attitude indicators and that had precipitated the upset. The 747 was equipped with redundant attitude indicators installed at both the pilot and first officer's position. The NTSB says the crew's view of what happened was "not substantiated by the facts. It is most likely that the flight crew became spatially disoriented during the upset. They were unable to believe the information displayed on the ADIs, did not recognize the unusual attitude of the airplane, and were unable to take the correct action to recover the airplane until it began to emerge from the clouds."

Not satisfied with knowing the crew had suffered spatial disorientation, the Safety Board wanted to know why. Among the factors they considered were overdependence on the automated flight controls, boredom, fatigue, and other factors relating to changes in time zones and sleep patterns. Each of these was found to have played a role.

For about three minutes and forty seconds after the plane started to decelerate following the engine failure, the pilot left the flying to the autopilot—which did what it could. "When the autopilot was disengaged," the Safety Board found, "the airplane's excursion from the stabilized condition was well advanced and at the point where immediate and proper corrective action was required if the situation was to be remedied safely.

"The captain was not only unable to assess the situation properly, he was confused by it; therefore, he was unable to take the necessary action to correct the situation."

How can a 15,000-hour 747 captain roll his airplane? By not hand-flying as soon as the situation got unusual, the captain chose to remain "out of the loop" and thus lost the opportunity to "feel" where the airplane was going. The Board notes that airline crews have consistently displayed reluctance to take control even when the autopilot is well on its way to doing things a student pilot would recognize as unusual. What "George" then handed to the captain was a situation very similar to the unusual attitude exercise every student experiences.

The Board also recognized the possibility the captain was suffering from the effects of a long flight (10 hours) across several time zones. Although he'd had a five-hour break (including about two hours of sleep) earlier in the flight, the captain was "out of synch" physiologically and the Board pointed out that the crew was "performing in a time spectrum that was later than their typical sleep periods."

When it came time to reach conclusions, however, the Board decided that after all was said and done, the captain was simply suffering from spatial disorientation. Unfortunately, it happened to him while flying a 747.

An "Illusion" of Sorts

We've been discussing various conflicts of the senses, mostly those that occur when a pilot sees something that doesn't agree with what he feels. There's yet another area of human factors that falls generally into this category of problem areas, but the resultant upset is always centered in the old solar plexus; we're talking about cookie-tossing, barfing, mal-de-air, or just plain airsickness. As long as humans fly, some of them will suffer the nausea that results from moving in a manner to which they're not accustomed.

If you are one of those extremely lucky persons who has never dealt with airsickness, or one who has fought the battle and overcome, at least pay attention to this information for the sake of your passengers. It will not only help them to feel better, it saves cabin-cleaning bills.

Keeping It Down

The search goes on, among those who fly or sail, for the perfect drug, device or technique to combat motion sickness.

It hasn't been found, but there has been progress. The latest step appears to be the discovery that a category of drugs known as calcium antagonists provides excellent relief without many of the well-known side effects which often make people sick of taking the drugs that are supposed to keep them from getting sick.

Researchers gave volunteers either 10- or 30-milligram doses of the drug flunarizine or a placebo. They were tested in a spatial disorientation trainer, which was accelerated to 17 rpm and then stopped suddenly. Involuntary movement of the eyes (nystagmus) was recorded, providing a measure of the degree to which a person was suffering what's known in the trade as "the somatogyral illusion." Pilots know it as something that makes them sick.

When the results were tallied, the calcium antagonist was found to be a powerful suppressant of unwanted sensations of motion in the inner ear. This is thought to occur because calcium ions are present in the fluid through which the motion message is delivered; the calcium antagonist probably slows down, or blocks, transmission of the message that the body is moving in unpleasant ways.

The next step will be actual motion sickness tests of the drug. At this time, researchers feel that flunarizine "offers potential as an anti-motion sickness drug." They intend to keep testing, so hold on to your sick sack. Help is on the way.

Patch Problems

Pilots and sailors have been using the scopolamine patch for motion sickness since it became available. Many skippers have found that people who react with psychosis to the patch are those who are sensitive to other drugs as well.

A common side effect is the dilated pupils that occur in bright light, or an inability to focus in low light levels. That's not all bad for sailors, but pilots must think twice, and know their personal reactions before using this medication while flying. This is another of those situations in which people react quite differently to the same thing.

Anyone who uses a patch should follow the directions very carefully. Wash your hands after applying it and beware of getting the drug in your eyes; scopolamine will definitely affect your eyes if it's introduced directly. You might consider putting a Band-Aid over the patch as a reminder that it's there so you won't inadvertently scratch it off.

To be effective, the patch must be applied quite some time before encountering the motion which is causing the nausea problem, so in most cases it's not going to be a good solution for pilots—we rarely enjoy the luxury of a wholly accurate forecast about the intensity and extent of unpleasant turbulence.

However, if you are taking along a passenger with a known predisposition to motion sickness under even mild conditions, I think the patch is worth a try as a preventive measure.

Plugging Up Motion Sickness

In a flight safety seminar put on by the FAA a few years back, a flight surgeon offered this tip: "About 80 percent of those susceptible to airsickness can be relieved with ordinary earplugs. No medical or scientific basis exists, but they work in aircraft, boats and autos."

Does it work? One of our readers tried it on a friend who gets sick on airliners and queasy on the second rung of a stepladder. He plugged his ears and went flying in a light airplane on a day with light chop; the report came back "no discomfort, and we enjoyed a fine dinner between flights. This works on my children, too."

It seems we're always learning new things, some of which haven't exactly been given a full scientific trial. While most of us are generally wary of "cures" that haven't been proved other than by anecdotal evidence, this one has the benefit of being entirely benign and utterly inexpensive. That's a hard combination to resist, and since motion sickness is such a miserable matter for so many, you might consider having an airsick-prone person try the earplug cure before he starts taking drugs to try to control the problem.

Earplugs may work by some bizarre mechanism related to acu-puncture of the ear, which may not be as effective, but they also have no known side effects, which is more than can be said for virtually all the widely dispensed motion sickness medications. And the use of earplugs is not only compatible with PIC duties, it may even improve *your* performance.

9 | Alcohol, Drugs, and Medications

Just in case you've forgotten, FAR 91.17, Alcohol or Drugs, says, "No person may act or attempt to act as a crew member of a civil aircraft (1) within 8 hours after the consumption of any alcoholic beverage; (2) while under the influence of alcohol; (3) while using any drug that affects the person's faculties in any way contrary to safety; or (4) while having .04 percent by weight or more alcohol in the blood.

So saith the regulations with regard to FWI—Flying While Intoxicated. A relatively recent change, the "new" alcohol and drug rules put the cards right on the table; and it's about time, because until the advent of FAR 91.17, no one had a firm basis on which to evaluate a pilot who appeared to be in violation. The regulation also requires that pilots submit to a blood alcohol test when asked to do so by a law enforcement officer.

The quantitative portion of the rule, .04-percent blood alcohol, raises questions regarding the choice of that number. As might be expected, .04 percent was not selected by throwing darts at a list of numbers on the wall; some serious studies were conducted before 91.17 was published.

On-going research points to serious impairment of pilot performance at levels of alcohol even below the new limit. Certain studies have shown that in experimental situations not involving the added element of actual risk of a crash, pilots flying at the .04-percent blood alcohol content (BAC) standard would actually be dangerously impaired. In some cases, despite being in the safety of a simulation laboratory, while "flying" a non-motion simulator, licensed pilots have actually "crashed" when, according to the .04 BAC rule, they could well have passed breath and blood tests.

Selecting a Limit

For decades prior to adoption of the new rule in 1985, pilots were governed by the eight-hour "bottle to throttle" rule. Whereas many states had adopted a BAC limit for auto drivers—typically .10 percent—federal rules for pilots did not specify any particular BAC.

The inadequacy of the eight-hour "bottle to throttle" rule was obvious for some time prior to the FAA's recent additions to Part 91 regulations dealing with alcohol use. One problem was that the letter of the rule could be met while the individual was still affected by alcohol to a very dangerous degree. Another was that it gave a false sense of security to some who unwisely assumed that they could safely fly eight hours after consuming any quantity of alcohol.

Following the urging of the NTSB, which recommended that a BAC limit be set "at the lowest possible level consistent with the capability of testing equipment to measure any ingested alcohol," the FAA added the 1985 rule that no one with a BAC of .04 percent or higher could act or attempt to act as a crew member of a civil aircraft.

Since the rule was adopted, the .04-percent BAC value has become widely known as the definition of intoxication for aircraft crew members. Reports of alcohol involvement in aviation accidents now are often presented as the percentage of deceased pilots who were found to have a BAC above that value.

Does the .04-percent rule still permit flight with a dangerous amount of alcohol in the bloodstream, and is the impression being given that it is safe to fly with alcohol levels of that value and lower? Is it possible to compensate for low blood alcohol levels by concentrating on the piloting task at hand, and does experience protect a pilot to some degree from the effects of low alcohol levels? The answers to these questions have important implications for aviation safety.

It's not just a matter of obeying a given rule. Anyone with respect for the demanding nature of safe flight realizes the danger of flying while intoxicated. Those very few who do fly when intoxicated are at a very high risk for accidents and are generally apart from the vast majority of the aviation community who work toward making flying as safe as possible. To the extent that questions still exist regarding alcohol use and flying, they concern the effects of low blood alcohol levels on flight performance.

For one pilot, an "innocent" drink or two before a flight—clearly not enough to put him over the limit—may seem acceptable. And for another, flying with a moderate to severe hangover, or alcohol still in his system from a heavy drinking session the night before, may not seem unduly risky. But in fact, either of these actions could be dangerous.

Is a Little Alcohol Too Much?

A pilot and a business friend flew in a Piper Warrior to the Playboy Airport at Lake Geneva, Wisconsin, to sample the night life there. Sampling completed, they departed at about midnight, headed for their home base, Schaumburg, Illinois.

According to the pilot's statement made a day later, he had arranged for the runway lights to be on at Schaumburg when he returned, but he arrived in the area and "could not find the airport," possibly because the lights were off. So, he explained, he diverted to DuPage Airport.

However, the explanation doesn't exactly fit the facts. The evidence suggests that the pilot did attempt a landing at Schaumburg and botched it, since two runway lights were wrecked that night and the pilot later paid for them. He later told investigators he had attempted a landing at an "unknown" airport and later found out it was Schaumburg.

In any event, the pilot further stated that when he got to DuPage the tower was closed, so he talked to the FSS, which advised of wind information and advised that the active runway was up to the pilot's discretion.

The pilot in his written statement claimed he chose runway 15. But in a telephone conversation with an FAA inspector, he said he actually thought he was landing on runway 28. DuPage doesn't have a runway 28; the runway in question was 22.

The Warrior made a landing, but only after striking a tree a quarter-mile short of the runway. The pilot stated that he taxied up to the tower and notified the FSS of the accident.

However, the runway lights and the tree apparently had not been the end of the evening's encounters for the Warrior. Investigators also found evidence at a nearby fueling ramp (one pump knocked over, another scratched, a nav light lens knocked off the wing) that the plane apparently whacked a wingtip there on the way past while taxiing in the dark.

Why was it in the dark? Well, the pilot stated that when landing at DuPage, he discovered that his landing light was not operative. Later, he conceded that he found it inoperative when he landed at Lake Geneva.

The pilot and his friend later admitted to investigators that each had had a "couple" of gin-and-tonics while at Lake Geneva. The airport security officer, who was the first to talk with the pilot after the accident, said he appeared "scared but not drunk."

The Evidence Grows

The NTSB's position is quite clear with respect to the safety of low blood alcohol levels. In a 1984 statistical review of alcohol-involved aviation accidents it stated, "the Safety Board believes that the presence of any alcohol in a pilot's blood jeopardizes safety." The degree to which pilots generally accept this statement is unclear, but probably some pilots do not. Certainly there is a great deal of evidence indicating that motorists believe that as long as they are below a .10-percent BAC—the value that defines driving while intoxicated in most states—they are safe from both DWI charges and alcohol-induced accidents.

This is in contrast to the opinions of safety experts. A commonly published chart from the National Highway Traffic Administration defines the .05- to .09-percent range as a "driving impaired" zone, and BAC values up to .05 percent as representing a condition where one must be careful driving. Research data support these cautions and make it clear that the .10-percent BAC figure is more a reflection of political realities than a rationally derived value based on research evidence. Most European countries have adopted lower values to define the intoxicated use of motor vehicles.

If expert opinion indicates that blood alcohol levels in the .05-percent range can be dangerous when driving, common sense suggests that flying with a .04 percent BAC could be quite dangerous.

Research: Airplane and Simulator

In fact, a number of studies have investigated the effects of a low BAC on pilots' performance. The most comprehensive of these, and the only study cited by the FAA in proposing the .04 percent rule, was carried out in the late 1960s and early 1970s at Ohio State University by C.F. Billings and associates under FAA sponsorship.

This study is notable in that it examined the effects of alcohol in an actual flight situation, with instrument-rated pilots flying a Cessna 172 at night on simulated ILS approaches. Four BAC values of zero, .04 percent, .08 percent and .12 percent were used.

The 16 volunteers all were instrument-rated. They comprised a group of eight highly experienced pilots (median number of hours, 9,500; instrument hours, 1,125) and eight relatively inexperienced pilots (median number of hours, 548; instrument hours, 73).

The Cessna 172 was outfitted with sensors to record the flight control movements as well as deflections in the localizer and glideslope needles, etc. An experienced safety pilot was in the right front seat, and a medical observer sat in the rear seat. The subject pilot was responsible for radio calls, except calls of other traffic, to which the safety pilot would respond.

The 16 pilots each conducted two night simulated instrument flights while under the influence of each of the four BAC levels. Each flight included four ILS approaches to minimums. A landing was made after the first and fourth approaches, and missed approach procedures were conducted after the second and third approaches.

The pilots were dosed before the flight with measured amounts of alcohol in the form of vodka in orange juice (i.e., a "screwdriver") and were given "maintenance doses" during each session according to a pre-determined metabolic rate, to keep them at the required BAC.

In summary, the experienced pilots showed significant alcohol effects on glideslope control with the higher BAC values. For the less-experienced pilots, both lateral and vertical control suffered. At the highest BAC level, the subjects lost control of the airplane entirely on 16 occasions among 30 flights. It's not surprising that very intoxicated pilots would crash.

Of perhaps greater importance was the finding that major procedural errors occurred in a regularly increasing number as each pilot's BAC increased. These errors included taking off with full flaps, flying without lights, taking off with carburetor heat on, turning the wrong way in response to instructions from ATC, and attempting to fly the approach while tuned to the wrong ILS frequency.

While inexperienced pilots made more such errors than experienced pilots, both groups showed similar increases in errors as their BAC increased, and even experienced pilots made a considerable number of errors even with the lowest BAC, .04 percent. The Ohio State investigators pointed out that while the pilots were able to do fairly well with ILS lateral and vertical control after drinking, they did so at the expense of other tasks necessary for safe flight.

"It must be borne in mind that the Cessna 172 is perhaps the simplest, most forgiving airplane in the general aviation fleet. We believe that similar experiments in more complex, faster aircraft would show substantially greater decrements at low blood alcohol levels," the researchers commented.

Several studies have looked at the effects of alcohol on pilots' simulator flight performance. While it would be preferable to investigate alcohol's effects during actual flying, such studies would be difficult to carry out today in view of the current rules and procedures that protect the safety of humans used in experiments. Further, instrumenting an actual aircraft to obtain the quantified flight information that is available from simulators is difficult and costly.

Some Inconsistencies

A variety of tasks have been used in simulators to investigate alcohol's effects, from air work maneuvers while flying different courses or cross-country flights, to holding patterns and ILS approaches. The studies have not always yielded consistent results.

Given the variety of procedures and tasks used, it is not too surprising that the effects of low blood alcohol levels sometimes have appeared inconsistent. In many of the studies, however, performance decrements have occurred, and most authors have concluded that low BAC levels can seriously affect flight performance. "One must be prepared for a lower ability to perform with a .02-percent BAC," wrote one early investigator in summarizing his results.

Attend to One Thing, Ignore Another

One reason that the results of simulator experiments have not been more consistent may be that some of the studies did not investigate a wide enough range of pilot responses. In research on auto driving, a common finding is that alcohol reduces one's ability to divide attention and attend to multiple tasks. This focusing of attention visually is characterized as a "narrowing of the functional visual field." Such a process can, of course, result in ignoring information or tasks that are not the focus of attention.

This concept fits well with the results of some of the studies of alcohol's effects on pilot performance. The procedural errors reported in the Ohio State study were probably the result of such a process. Similarly, a recent simulator study carried out at the University of Wisconsin found some effects of a .04-percent BAC on straight and level flight, but the most potentially dangerous alcohol effects came when the pilot was given a secondary task and then required to cope with an unusual aircraft attitude.

The study involved 32 males, half of which were licensed private pilots and half with no flying experience. The pilots ranged in experience from 40 to 530 hours with a median of 100 hours. None had any significant amount of IFR training or an instrument rating.

The simulator was a highly modified ATC 610 procedures trainer. Monitor screens in front and at each side of the subject gave a visual horizon reference and allowed researchers to display aircraft silhouette targets. The subject could acknowledge the target by pressing a button on the left control yoke.

The simulator also was modified to include rudder pedals that could be adjusted to the subject's feet, backlighted instruments, and changes in many of the electronic components for higher precision. In addition, the subject wore a head movement device allowing measurements to one-degree accuracy.

Half the subjects in each group were "blind" as to their alcohol condition—not aware of whether they really were being given significant amounts of alcohol. The other half were correctly informed. The alcohol dose, carefully calculated according to the subject's body weight to result in .04-percent BAC, was again in the form of a "screwdriver." For placebo doses, a very small amount of alcohol was floated on top of the orange juice.

All the subjects were given familiarization training in the simulator on the first day of their three-day session. On the second and third days they would "fly," in 20-minute flights for the non-pilots and 25-minute flights for the pilots. On one of his "flying" days, each subject would fly sober, while on the other, he would be at .04-percent BAC. The non-pilots were merely asked to maintain straight and level flight under light or moderate turbulence conditions while scanning the three screens for target airplanes appearing at irregular intervals.

The private pilots were given the same task, but also had a five-minute flight segment in which they were asked to descend from 3,500 feet to 3,000 feet while turning right 90 degrees. At this point, they were then required to (a) copy weather information for their destination airport, or (b) make comm and nav frequency changes, center the course deviation needle, change the transponder code and check the fuel supply.

While these tasks were being conducted, the simulator's instruments and the visual displays were gradually sneaked into a steeply banked climb or descent over a five-second period. The subject was expected to recognize and recover from the unusual attitude.

The non-pilots were surprisingly good at maintaining straight and level flight, but they showed a number of significant alcohol effects. They were measurably less inclined to make horizontal head movements in scanning for traffic when under the influence of .04-percent BAC, and were significantly slower in detecting targets.

Among those who received alcohol on the second "flying" day, there was a slight improvement in performance in the higher level of turbulence, compared with those who received alcohol on the first "flying" day.

Computer sampling of flight control responses was conducted. Among other measures, the computer counted the number of times the plane deviated at least 10 degrees in bank from level flight, as well as the associated yoke inputs; heading changes of 10 degrees from the assigned heading; and altitude deviations of more than 100 feet.

Measures of pitch response, altitude deviations and heading deviations did not turn up significant differences with and without alcohol, but the number of roll deviations and control inputs were both significantly increased for the non-pilots with alcohol.

Pilots Try It

Among the pilots, there was a significant tendency to perform fewer traffic-scanning head movements when under the influence. In a surprising result, however, the pilots' speed in detecting displayed targets was slowed significantly in light turbulence, but not in moderate turbulence. The pilots generally maintained straight and level flight less well with alcohol, but interestingly, the statistically significant effects were tied to those pilots who had been informed they were receiving alcohol.

To quote from the study: "In general, it appears that the effects of alcohol were somewhat less consistent for pilots than for non-pilots. While alcohol effects on traffic scanning were found on both groups, the alcohol effects on the straight and level flight performance of pilots often interacted with other variables, with the roll control input and 10-degree heading deviation measures both showing alcohol effects only when the pilots had been informed that they had been given alcohol. It is possible that these information-alcohol interactions reflect overcompensation efforts by the pilots, especially since it is relatively easy to overcontrol an ATC 610 procedures trainer and non-pilots did not show such effects. Heading deviations did, however, show the expected pattern, with alcohol negatively affecting performance under moderate turbulence but not under low turbulence conditions."

Attitude Adjustments

Perhaps the most interesting alcohol effects were found when the pilots were given secondary tasks and then led into unusual attitudes. Prior to data examination, it was decided by the researchers that a pitch of plus or minus 7.5 degrees from level was acceptable as within a normal flight regime. The time to return to within this value from the excessive climb or dive was then assessed. With alcohol the subjects lost or gained more altitude and took longer to recover from their "unusual attitudes."

On the average, the subjects lost or gained about 750 feet with alcohol, versus 430 feet without. More strikingly, the average time to recognize and recover from the unusual attitude was about 24 seconds for the alcohol-affected pilots, versus about 10 seconds for the sober ones. Two pilots with a .04-percent BAC "crashed" the simulator, although none of the pilots showed serious problems in recovering to straight and level flight when they had not been given alcohol.

One of the "crash" pilots descended more than 2,500 feet and reached terminal simulator airspeed before recovery. Another pilot—with more than 300 hours logged—entered a stall and continued a series of stalls to zero altitude. He was apparently aware of the problem, but unable to respond appropriately to recover.

Again quoting from the study: "While the data indicate alcohol results in a longer time to respond to indications of an unusual attitude, and in some cases confusion over how to respond, another aspect of the unusual attitude data is of some interest. It was expected that after alcohol ingestion pilots might take longer to respond, but when they did respond it would be vigorously, perhaps in a manner that could overstress an actual aircraft. What was found in examining a number of records, however, was a series of control inputs that individually were insufficient in amplitude to result in recovery. This raises the interesting possibility that the effect of a low BAC on some pilots may be a lack of decisive responses to potentially dangerous situations. Certainly any increase in indecision and/or the occurrence of inadequate corrective responses may result in an increased probability of an accident during flight."

More Distractions

In another Wisconsin study with low-time pilots on the same simulator, performance on what was seen by the pilot as the primary task in a flight segment was sometimes unaffected by a .04-percent BAC, but other flight performance aspects simultaneously showed significant decrements.

For example, keeping the CDI centered while tracking a VOR radial could be done almost as well with alcohol, but altitude control was significantly poorer than without alcohol.

In the simulation, a controller would call traffic and then aircraft silhouette targets were displayed as "looming at" the pilots from the side screens, with the controller calling for a climb or dive as the collision avoidance maneuver.

Although there was no statistically significant result in the collision avoidance data, in all instances the subject's response was poorer with alcohol. Interestingly, there were five cases in which the subjects made mistakes when responding to a looming target—three who failed to respond and two who made the wrong altitude change.

The strong suggestion from these findings is that in some cases it may be possible to partly compensate for the effects of alcohol by concentrating on a task, but that this may be at the expense of reacting properly to other information or overlooking other tasks that should be performed.

Disorientation Danger

Another danger is focusing on a secondary task or problem that arises, at the expense of the primary task of controlling the aircraft. Distraction may be more of a serious problem when even small amounts of alcohol are involved.

Other effects of alcohol that could affect flight safety have not been studied to any great extent. For example, alcohol in the bloodstream may increase susceptibility to disorientation and confusion. Following publication of an article on alcohol and flying, the writer of a letter to the editor of a national aviation magazine reported that both he and his friend became disorientated after a nighttime departure 90 minutes after each had drunk a glass of wine.

This is not an unexpected or uncommon event. The inner ear is especially susceptible to the effects of alcohol and it is quite possible that even small amounts of alcohol can greatly increase the probability of disorientation occurring.

Another question that remains to be addressed is the degree and manner in which decision-making is affected by alcohol. Anecdotal evidence suggests alcohol can affect a person's judgment, but research on this topic is only in its early stages. Because flight conditions are often such as to make disorientation possible, and mental alertness is required to maintain orientation and proper control of the aircraft, any factor that can decrease mental alertness or contribute to confusion is a potential threat to safety. Even a small amount of alcohol in the bloodstream clearly is one such factor.

Experience Counts, But Not That Much

A variant of the "it can't happen to me" syndrome is the notion that while low alcohol levels could have an effect on performance, one can overcome them by experience. The 2,000-hour pilot may be convinced that he or she is skilled enough to fly perfectly well after consuming some alcohol, and indeed it could be the case that performance decrements would not be detected during a flight that involved no unusual or complicated demands.

The evidence is compelling, however, that although there might not be visible effects, the margin of safety in such a situation has been reduced. Consider the Ohio State study. While experienced pilots made fewer errors than inexperienced pilots, they too made an appreciable number of major errors even with a .04-percent BAC. Further, the rate of increase in procedural errors with increasing BAC was no less for experienced than for less experienced pilots—and this with a Cessna 172 flying uncomplicated ILS approaches.

It's worth remembering that experienced pilots are also more likely to be flying in more demanding situations—exactly the kind of situation where alcohol effects are most likely to be dangerous.

An NTSB analysis of alcohol-related accidents from 1975-1981 gives no comfort to those who think experience can protect them from alcohol's effects. Pilots with 2,500 or more flight hours were involved in only three percent of the fatal general aviation accidents during that period, but accounted for 18 percent of alcohol-involved fatal accidents. This was the only flight-hours category where the fatal accident percentage was less than the alcohol-involved percentage, except for the case of pilots who had less than 99 hours.

During the years from 1975-1981, there were 19 pilots with more than 10,000 hours in alcohol-involved accidents; 30 percent of pilots in such accidents had 1,500 or more hours. Clearly, as the NTSB states, "...experience cannot compensate for the effects of alcohol."

Over several recent years, the percentage of fatal accidents in which alcohol was involved declined dramatically. The percentage of deceased pilots found with BACs above .04 percent decreased from 10.9 percent in the period 1968-1970, down to 4.8 percent in 1984 and 4.9 percent in 1985.

Assuming these results are accurate (given recent questions raised about the accuracy of blood testing by the Civil Aeromedical Institute's blood testing laboratory), they demonstrate an increasing pilot awareness of alcohol's dangers. This may be due to publicity given the danger of drinking and flying by the aviation press, and the educational activities of the FAA. Whether federal rulemakers see fit to change the current regulation or not, it is to be hoped that the .04-percent rule will not suggest that a small amount of alcohol is without significant danger.

The only position that may reasonably be taken is that any alcohol in the bloodstream can seriously compromise flight safety.

How About a Lot of Alcohol?

Funny thing about alcohol: Some people think that a snort or two helps them do better, while still others apparently believe that their capabilities are unaffected no matter how much they drink.

Witness the experience of a Michigan pilot who almost made it; unfortunately, "close" counts only when you're playing horseshoes or hand grenades.

> The Bellanca Viking circled over the town of Hessel, Michigan, for about 30 minutes waiting for a thunderstorm to depart the area, then made a pass at the local airport. It crashed after overflying the field, killing the two persons aboard. Investigators said the pilot had a blood alcohol content of .168 percent, according to toxicology reports. In many states, a content of .10 is sufficient to consider an automobile driver intoxicated.
>
> According to the NTSB, the pilot had a private license and instrument rating, but did not make any arrangements for his intended landing at the 2,800-foot unlighted and unattended airport, even though the passenger had called his wife and arranged to have a car meet him at the field.
>
> After observing the Viking circling the town, the local sheriff and his deputies surmised the plane was looking for the unlighted airport; they drove to the field and shined their car headlights on the runway. As luck would have it, the driver positioned at the approach end pulled his car off the runway when the plane came near, leaving it unlighted. The Viking flew low over the airport, made a shallow turn and struck 60-foot trees, demolishing the aircraft.

Bad Habits May Transfer

Researchers frequently make comparisons between automobile DWI and the effects of alcohol on fliers, and even though the problems are considerably less for a person operating in only two dimensions, there may well be a correlation when it comes to personal attitudes. The FAA has ruffled more than a few feathers with its policy of sharing computer data to find out which pilots have alcohol-related problems in their auto-driving histories, and we may see the day when a highway offense of this nature will impact one's flying privileges.

An apparent disregard for (or inability to cope with) the problems of intoxication may be a personality trait. Here's the case of a student pilot who was killed early one morning (or very late; take your pick) when his Piper Archer flew into the ground at a steep angle in a remote area of Florida's Everglades National Park.

Preliminary reports indicate a blood alcohol level in the pilot's body of .25 percent. In many states, an automobile driver is considered driving under the influence at a level of .10 percent. The pilot, with an estimated 60 total hours, had embarked from a small airport near Tampa on a student cross-country to Key West, where he had arrived safely. His instructor told investigators he had been scheduled to make the return flight, in day VFR conditions, the day prior to the accident, but had not done so for reasons unknown.

At about 3 a.m. the morning of the accident, the pilot was picked up by cab in downtown Key West and driven to Key West International Airport. Upon arrival, the pilot fumbled for money and attempted to pay the cab driver with matchbooks. When the pilot said he had no money, the driver used his cab radio to summon police. The officer who responded noted that the pilot appeared drunk, but had no reason to believe he might fly an airplane. After making arrangements for the pilot to settle the cab fare by mail, the policeman left.

An airport security guard next noticed the pilot, sitting in the Archer's cockpit with the cabin lights on. When the guard approached, the pilot slouched in the seat as though attempting not to be seen. The guard asked the pilot's intention and was told in slurred speech that he intended to depart. After suggesting that the pilot might want to remove the tiedown ropes, the guard went to a phone and called police. The same officer who had settled the previous altercation arrived, but the Archer had taken off, without nav or landing lights.

The crash site was nearly 100 miles from Key West, along a route consistent with an attempt by the pilot to return to his home airport.

Investigators discovered the pilot had a history of driver's license suspensions and revocations for DWI (or refusal to take an alcohol test), dating back several years, and extending to a one-year suspension of driving privileges just two years prior to the accident.

The Hair of the Dog

According to the FARs, a pilot may not fly within eight hours of consuming any alcoholic beverage (or with more than .04-percent blood alcohol content). The goal is to prevent pilots whose mental functioning might be impaired from being in the air.

There has been little evidence, however, of how pilots perform the morning after. That is, at 8.1 hours after the last drink, is a pilot who drank a lot really fit to fly? While empirical evidence suggests he's not particularly safe, a clinical answer to the question has turned up a surprising result.

Taking the question to the lab, two FAA investigators recruited 11 pilots and set out to see what would happen when these pilots were asked to drink and then perform complex flying tasks both immediately after drinking and then again eight hours later. The subjects were between the ages of 22 and 55, and all were light to moderate drinkers who said they could handle five or so drinks in the course of an evening. Their average total time was almost 4,400 hours; some were flight instructors, some held commercial certificates.

Over the course of several weeks the volunteers spent one day a week, from 5 p.m. until noon the next day, at the lab where they were given either bourbon, vodka, or a placebo disguised to look like booze. Each person got a different mixture on different nights, and never knew which one was which (the placebo had a few drops of rum extract, to make it smell like alcohol).

Each person got 3.25 milliliters of booze drink per kilogram of body weight—four large drinks. This produced an average Breathalyzer reading of .093 percent, just a fraction under the level at which most states deem a driver to be legally drunk. In two instances the alcohol was incapacitating to the point where the people couldn't participate in the evening's testing.

Immediately after the drinking was finished (about midnight) and again the next morning (8 a.m.), the pilots were subjected to a wide battery of tests designed to gauge their mental and physiological responses to the alcohol. The tests included flying a laboratory glideslope, monitoring four meters whose pointers were moving, doing mental arithmetic, and detecting warning lights.

The high fliers were asked to rate their ethanol-induced degree of drunkeness on a 0-4 scale, and in the morning were asked to rate their hangover symptoms on a 0-3 scale. The average drunkeness rating at midnight was 2.36 on bourbon and 2.09 on vodka, though everyone claimed to be sober by morning with the exception of two instances when people who'd been given real booze reported a "1" the next day.

There was significant impairment of almost all the skills tested immediately after people had been given alcohol, confirming the notion that drinking and flying don't mix.

The morning sessions, however, produced no significant impairments due to alcohol. Which is not to say everyone felt great. The subjects, according to investigators, "reported significant hangover symptoms, increased anxiety, greater fatigue and less vigor." They did not, however, perform worse—at least in any statistically significant and detectable way.

The researchers point out that the addition of noise, altitude and other sources of stress could have an effect on people's performance, as could an even slightly higher blood alcohol level.

Guilty as Charged

There's the evidence, a wealth of rather solid research and real-world experience that indicates what we've all known for years—alcohol and flying simply don't go together well.

Side Effects of Harmless (?) Drugs

Splitting headache? Could be the altitude, of course. Or maybe the hectic day at the office. Then again, it just could be a prescription medication. A number of drugs, including those which are permissible for pilots to take while performing flight duties, can cause side effects involving the nervous system. Such side effects range from the relatively minor and annoying, such as headache, to the potential serious and life-threatening, such as seizures.

Among drugs known to cause headaches, sometimes severe, are the painkiller/anti-inflammatory agents ibuprofen, indomethacin and naproxen, and the high-blood pressure medications clinidine, prazosin and propranolol. Propranolol is also a heart drug.

Perhaps more threatening to the pilot are drugs whose side effects can include eye problems. Once again, ibuprofen and indomethacin appear on the list, along with the diuretics acetazolamide, furosemide and hydrochlorothiazide.

Hearing can be affected, on both a short- and long-term basis, by many antibiotics including streptomycin, tobramycin, gentamicin, neomycin, ampicillin, erythromycin and polymyxin B.

Seizures are a relatively rare drug side effect, but obviously represent a substantial threat to pilot-patients. Among the drugs for which there is substantial evidence of the ability to cause convulsions are several of the penicillins, isoniazid, theophylline (used by asthmatics), and several of the contrast media used for X-rays of the bowel and other internal soft-tissue parts.

Women pilots might keep in mind the heightened risk of stroke caused by contraceptive pills. This risk seems correlated with the estrogen content of the pills, and can be minimized by taking one of the newer low-dose or multi-phasic pills.

Aspirin could end your flying career. So could a lot of other substances you think are entirely safe. Some might put you on the ground for a few hours or a couple of days, and others can put you either on—or in—the ground forever.

When the FAA medical form asks if you're taking any "medications," it's asking the wrong question. It should ask if you're taking any drugs, and disqualify anyone who answers "no." Why? Because everyone is taking something, although lots of pilots don't know it.

Most people probably know that antihistamines cause drowsiness, so they don't fly while taking cold medications. And they may know that anything powerful enough to be dispensed by prescription could call for staying on the ground, or at least asking a few questions of the doctor about the known side effects. These are things we think of as medicines. They're visible drugs, and while most pilots know that caution is in order, many don't recognize the catastrophic consequences that can come from taking what appear to be "safe" remedies for conditions that seem to have nothing to do with any of the skills involved in flying.

But an even greater danger lies in wait for the uninformed pilot who, though he may avoid running afoul of visible medications, could be impaired and perhaps grounded by either the short- or the long-term effects of dozens of substances we don't normally think of as drugs. These chemicals are hidden drugs. They're concealed not because of anyone's effort to mislead, but by our own failure to understand what drugs really are and how they can act on the body.

Both visible and hidden drugs represent real, significant and very frequently overlooked dangers for the pilot. The pilot's drug dilemma can be summed up in two rules:

Rule 1: Everybody takes something sometimes.

Rule 2: Every drug can cause trouble sometimes.

Did you take a vitamin this morning? Vitamins are drugs, and they can interact with other drugs or act on their own to cause a wide range of unwanted and unexpected effects. Perhaps you used some nose spray or took a cold pill for a bit of stuffiness? The decongestants it contains are drugs, and one of the most widely-used decongestant ingredients has recently been linked to serious and sometimes life-threatening side effects.

Remember the sun screen you rubbed on while washing the wings of your flying machine last weekend? Sun screens are drugs with a surprise side effect that could suddenly make you a very uncomfortable and incapable airman. If you're a woman pilot taking birth control pills, they've become so familiar you may long ago have ceased thinking of them as drugs. Think again, because over the long haul they have numerous subtle effects on your system that could lead to the Aviation Medical Examiner one day picking up your ticket.

Deodorant soaps, shampoos and hair rinses don't seem like drugs, but they all contain compounds that can render you useless as a pilot every time the sun shines! And then there's good old common table salt. Salt? A drug? You bet it is, and for pilots it can be a very dangerous one. A certain percentage of the population is salt-sensitive. These people have a genetic predisposition towards high blood pressure, and for them salt is a trigger every bit as dangerous as the one on a gun. Pull it and it shoots a hole in your pilot's license.

There's no way, at present, to predict who these salt-sensitive people are, but you can predict one thing—they can't remain pilots, at least not for long. High blood pressure is one of the swiftest and surest medical disqualifiers. When it comes to heart and blood vessel problems, the FAA has no heart. Show up for your physical with high blood pressure and kiss your flight privileges good-bye unless you can bring the problem under control without using drugs.

It's also possible for a "safe" drug to cause a problem which, while not directly disqualifying, leads to another problem that does mean getting your wings clipped. Or the second problem may require taking a medication that puts you on the ground for anywhere from a short time to forever. The high-powered Captain of Industry, gulping antacids (a drug) can wind up with either an ulcer (because some antacids actually stimulate stomach acid production) or kidney stones (because of the high calcium content of certain antacids). And many antacids contain high levels of salt, which leads us (or the unwary Captain of Industry) back to the blood pressure problem.

It's a vicious circle, with the pilot caught in the middle. In order to stay out of there, he needs to know what a drug is, and the likelihood that any given drug can or will cause him difficulty.

Just because a drug can cause a reaction doesn't mean it will, but it does mean you can't afford to completely ignore the possibility. Most drugs cause some adverse reaction in two to ten percent of the people taking them, though this figure can go as high as 40 percent. Several studies show that around ten percent of the people receiving drugs in the hospital will suffer some kind of adverse reaction, so that's not a bad estimate of the chances a pilot will feel something other than cured whenever he takes a drug.

The question is not whether you will take drugs, but when. The real question is whether you will be prepared to make a smart decision about what you take, with full knowledge of what the odds are that drug can or will cause you problems.

What is a Drug?

A drug, by Food and Drug Administration definition, is anything that can alter the function of the body. The reason we often don't recognize a drug as a drug is that lots of things alter the function of the body as a secondary, rather than a primary, effect. You take salt to change the taste of something, not out of a desire to raise your blood pressure. The salt, of course, doesn't know that.

The most important thing to understand is that there are no absolutely safe drugs. There is no drug you can take which doesn't have attached to it some risk—however small—of causing an adverse reaction. As one leading pharmacology text puts it, "No drug escapes the stigma of causing disease." One study found that 18 percent of the hospital admissions were attributable to the effects of non-prescription drugs. When you consider that these drugs are less powerful than their prescription-only counterparts, the magnitude of the problem becomes evident.

Let's take a look at some of the most common drug actions and reactions in order to see which ones could affect your flying:

The Nose Never Knows What's Good For It

Lots of pilots fly with an allergy or cold. Some do it because they have to, others because they want to. Many of them take something to keep their sinuses and eustachian tubes at least partially cleared out. This is one of the greatest and most frequently overlooked hazard areas, because virtually every medication that can have any effect on the symptoms of a cold or allergy causes some degradation in skills critical to piloting. How much degradation, and which skills are affected, varies with the drug and the person.

Histamine is a substance released by your body to fight what it perceives as an invader. Histamines cause the itching and swollen tissues we associate with a cold or hay fever. An antihistamine, as its name implies, works to block the action of a histamine and thus relieve the symptoms. It would all be quite simple except that most antihistamines cause their own set of symptoms, some or all of which can have a significant effect on your ability to fly.

The most well-known problem is drowsiness. In fact, some antihistamines are so effective in producing sleep that they're the major ingredients in over-the-counter sedatives. Benadryl (dephenylhydramine hydrochloride) is one. Other antihistamines noted for their soporific effects are Phenergan, Pyribenzamine and demenhydrinate, which you'll recognize better when called by its trade name—Dramamine.

PPA (or phenylpropanolamine, if you'd like to try wrapping your tongue around the full word) appears not only as a decongestant, but also as the primary ingredient in many diet pills and "pick-me-up" stimulant potions. It turns up, in fact, in more than 75 over-the-counter medications, not to mention most of the semi-licit "look-alike" stimulant pills being peddled in many areas.

Reports in medical journals describe some of the reactions to PPA. An 18-year-old woman took two Comtrex tablets for "congestion." Two-and-a-half hours later she showed up at her doctor's office complaining of a severe headache, nausea, blurred vision and shakiness. By the time she got to the hospital, the woman was disoriented and lethargic, and minutes later she suffered a grand mal seizure. (Think how much fun all that would be while flying.) In four hours her blood pressure, which had soared to 148/98, returned to a normal range (118/80); within 12 hours she'd once again become oriented.

One of the things PPA does quite well is cause a rise in blood pressure. One researcher said that an "important and sometimes potentially dangerous rise in blood pressure may occur even after ingestion of a single capsule of a preparation containing PPA." Two capsules proved fatal for a 17-year-old who suffered a massive cerebral hemorrhage. A 37-year-old woman also suffered a cerebral hemorrhage after taking two diet capsules containing PPA.

In addition to the blood pressure problem, PPA can have a profound effect on the central nervous system. Effects reported in the medical literature include restlessness, headache, dizziness, disorientation, confusion, agitation, and even hallucinations. (Not what you'd want for cabin company, we'd imagine.)

If the NTSB had had a better understanding of PPA, perhaps they'd have reached a different conclusion on the probable cause of a crash involving a student and instructor in a Piper Tomahawk. The instructor was reported to be above average in his skills and meticulous in his preparation. The "student" was a newcomer (third lesson) to fixed-wing flying but he'd been an Army helicopter pilot, and held a commercial helicopter ticket with an instrument rating.

The plane was reported by observers to have been flying level in CAVU conditions when it entered a spin and descended until striking the ground. The aircraft was destroyed and both pilots were killed. An inspection of the wreckage yielded no structural failure not attributable to the impact, and the engine teardown revealed nothing out of line. At the autopsy the medical examiner said "no medical cause for incapacitation could be confirmed." Toxicology tests were negative for alcohol, carbon monoxide, and all drugs except one: they found PPA in the instructor's urine.

Now Ear This—If You Can

In lieu of a full-fledged audiometer test, an aviation medical examiner may whisper in your ear. If he has to speak up to make himself heard, it will be to tell you that you aren't going to get a medical certificate. Whether you hear him or not might depend on what drugs you've taken in what quantities. Drugs that damage the ear and cause loss of hearing or problems with balance and motion are referred to as ototoxic.

In order to qualify for a third-class medical, you must be able to hear a whispered voice from three feet away. For a second-class ticket you must be able to hear that same whisper eight feet away, in each ear separately. The first-class certificate seems most easily available to a bat—you have to be able to hear that whisper at 20 feet in each ear. What could keep you from hearing those whispered words? One thing that might do it is aspirin.

Aspirin is one of the most widely used and readily available drugs. Millions of doses are taken by pilots every year to ease everything from a headache to stiff muscles from holding too much right rudder. It has long been known, however, that in large enough doses, aspirin can lead to ringing in the ears (tinnitus), vertigo, and partial or total loss of hearing.

You won't go deaf from taking two aspirin for a headache, but those who suffer from arthritis and use a large daily dose of aspirin to control the inflammation are at greater risk of impaired hearing. The same would apply to a pilot who takes a lot of aspirin during the course of an illness or while recovering from an injury. And it might come as a surprise to learn that the Vitamin C you've been taking in megadoses to keep you from getting a cold has the effect of slowing the rate at which the body excretes aspirin, thus piling the stuff up in your body and exposing you to higher levels than you might guess.

There's a wide variation in how rapidly people's bodies deal with aspirin, so one person's safe level can be another person's loss—of hearing. As much as a fivefold difference has been shown in the blood level of aspirin by-products when the same amount of aspirin was administered to people of equal weight. The kidneys are critical in the elimination of aspirin, so if you have any kidney problems—detected or otherwise—the risk of ear damage from aspirin escalates.

Streptomycin, a familiar antibiotic, is a drug that can literally throw you off balance. Up to 15 percent of the people who receive one gram or more daily for more than a week develop measurable hearing loss. This usually happens a week to 10 days after the drug has been given. With that hearing loss goes damage to the vestibular structures—those delicate ear structures responsible for keeping pilots and planes upright. While vertigo and balance difficulties are usually temporary, they can become permanent if the problem isn't detected and the drug stopped promptly.

Neomycin is another familiar antibiotic that can lead to problems. In fact, it's the most damaging of drugs to the Organ of Corti, which houses the special and irreplaceable hair cells that make hearing possible. Other drugs that can lead to problems with the mechanisms of hearing and balance include kanamycin, vancomycin, and gentamicin. These last three normally only see duty in a hospital setting, but if you find one being drained into your arm, muster enough strength to remind the doctor that you're concerned about any hearing loss. Then listen closely for an answer.

Another category of drug that's a problem-causer is the antimalarials, which might well be prescribed should you find yourself vacationing or working in a tropical area. Quinine, chloroquine and hydroxychloraquine can all cause hearing loss. In most, but not all cases, the loss is temporary and reverses upon cessation of drug use.

Your first tip-off that a drug could be leading to hearing or balance damage is tinnitus—ringing in the ears. If you're taking a drug and experience tinnitus, run, don't walk to the doctor.

Here Comes the Sun

You'd been using good old Caladryl to slosh over those pesky, itching mosquito bites while remarking to your camping partners how great it was to have a floatplane that could carry everyone to such a remote place. Unfortunately, you aren't able to fly them out again because you've broken out in great, weeping sores.

What happened? Caladryl contains a substance called diphenhydramine hydrochloride, also known as Benadryl. It's capable of causing skin irritation just from contact, and the effects are magnified by exposure to the sun.

A skin reaction upon exposure to sunlight—photodermatitis—is the hidden side of many medications. Skin reactions can result when sunlight converts a nontoxic substance into a toxic one, or when the sunshine transforms a drug from one form, to which you're not allergic, to another, which does produce an allergic reaction. While most people won't be affected by most things, for those who are affected, a romp in the sun after taking a sensitizing drug can turn into a disabling disaster.

Among the drugs that can cause skin reactions when the user is exposed to sun are antibiotics such as tetracycline and sulfonamides; sunscreens; salicylates (aspirin); dandruff shampoos; antibiotics and antiseptics in soaps, hair rinses, and creams; and several oils which could turn up as flavoring and/or scent agents in things you swallow or rub on your body.

Other medications can wreak havoc on your skin without benefit of the sun. Among these is benzocaine, a common pain-relieving ingredient that appears in more than 700 different products ranging from sunburn preparations to hemorrhoid, poison ivy, athlete's foot and toothache concoctions. Its widespread use might imply total safety, but benzocaine is a powerful sensitizer, and the resulting reaction can be disabling.

Interestingly, some drugs will produce no reaction when taken internally but are known to be powerful sensitizers when applied directly to the skin. Among these are Vitamin E and nitroglycerin.

For Women Only

Women pilots face some drug effects the men don't have to deal with. It may not be fair, but it's definitely there.

Oral contraceptives are a subject of much debate. Recent evidence tends to absolve them of being a major risk factor for most types of

cancer in most women, and in some cases they even seem to offer protection against certain cancers. However, women smokers do face a greater risk of blood clots, which could lead to a stroke or heart attack. You should also note that some oral contraceptives can cause skin eruptions when you spend a lot of time in the sun.

Almost every woman will at some time or another suffer a vaginal infection, and for trichomonal and often for bacterial infections, the drug the doctor reaches for is Flagyl. What he may forget to tell you is that there's often a powerful interaction between Flagyl and alcohol that leads to nausea, stomach cramps and headaches. That one drink you have the night before flying could mean staying uncomfortably stuck on the ground the next day, if you're taking Flagyl.

The third drug group women will often face is nonsteroidal anti-inflammatory drugs—NSAIDs. Perhaps more familiar as Naprosyn, Indocin and Motrin, these drugs have given millions of women a good deal of relief from otherwise debilitating menstrual cramps. However, be aware that recent research points toward an uncomfortably high number of kidney problems. And because NSAIDs work by suppressing the production of a substance in the body that works to excrete salt, it's possible that these drugs could aggravate any tendency you might have towards high blood pressure.

Staying Alive

If you can keep your body operating faultlessly for the rest of your life and require no drugs of any kind at any time, you don't need an airplane in order to cross either land or water. For the rest of us, drugs are everywhere, and a pilot must factor them into his decision on whether to go or stay on a particular day.

Like most other aviation decisions, this one is entirely self-policing. You're going to have to be your own pharmacist. By being aware that all drugs—visible and hidden—have some side effects for some people, you can ask reasonable questions about how, where, when and why a drug acts on you and thus assess the risk it might pose for your flying on a given day.

A pharmacist or aviation-trained doctor can help you make this decision, by providing information about drug actions, interactions, and known side effects. Just because a side effect has been reported doesn't mean that it will affect you, of course.

On the other hand, if you've never taken the drug before, you're really running a mini-medical experiment. If the side effect might be

uncomfortable but not disabling, that could lead to a different decision than if the known effects were to cause dizziness and vertigo.

No-Nod Allergy Relief

Pilots seem to be an allergic bunch. They're allergic to being on the ground, they're allergic to excessive rules and restrictions, and they're often allergic to all sorts of growing things.

Spring and fall are prime allergy time, as a variety of trees and plants rush to put out pollen while the putting is good. What's good for the plant is often bad for the aviator, and until now there has been no medication which offered relief without also putting a dangerous damper on a person's ability to stay awake. Since most pilots prefer to fly wide awake, antihistamines have long been a forbidden fruit, though it's one many pilots eat on occasion.

Now there may be relief, in more ways than one. The Food and Drug Administration has given approval to a new antihistamine, terfenadine, which seems to lack the noxious tendency to make a person drowsy. Sold by prescription only, under the brand name Seldane, the drug has had extensive use in Europe and thorough testing here, and the reports are consistent in saying it produces neither drowsiness nor the dry mouth and dry eyes which are also typical of most antihistamines.

Pilots suffering from seasonal bouts with allergies would do well to have a talk with their AME, with a thought to giving the new drug a try. Despite the optimistic reports, this medication (like any medication) should be test flown on the ground before anyone bets his or her life on it.

Pilot, Know Thyself

In the best of all possible worlds there would be a friendly, handy, non-judgmental pharmaceutical advisor on hand to consult when requested before each flight. In a sense there is—you're both advisor and advisee.

It's rare that a drug reaction will incapacitate in seconds. But by being aware that adverse drug reactions can and do exist, the pilot adds an alarm system to his flying skills, and thus minimizes the danger of flying past the first symptoms of a drug reaction. This early warning system, combined with thoughtful consideration of what he's taking, should enable a pilot to successfully avoid drugs which will negatively affect his flying.

Marijuana: A Touchy Social Problem

Pilots are not supposed to smoke dope, but some of them do—even some of those at the top of the professional ladder. Traces of marijuana turn up all too often in the blood of those killed in accidents, and there's reason to believe that marijuana has a negative effect on piloting skills long after the sense of being high has gone.

This potentially fatal prolonged effect was revealed in a research study of 10 experienced private pilots. Their mean age was 29, and they had an average of 303 hours total time. All the volunteer subjects were experienced marijuana smokers, though each used it less than daily and agreed not to smoke dope or take other drugs during the period of the experiment except for what was provided as part of the testing procedure.

Each person received eight hours of training on a visual simulator set up to mimic a Cessna 172. The simulator was heavily instrumented, with all data being fed into computers for later analysis. Measurements were taken of every control yoke and throttle movement as well as data determining where the "plane" was at certain critical portions of the flight.

The test agenda called for a takeoff, climb to 700 feet, two turns, descent and landing. Pilots were instructed to treat the task as though it were an FAA check flight. On the day of testing each person first took two practice flights, which weren't recorded, and then one baseline flight which was recorded. They then smoked an official National Institute of Drug Abuse "joint," with a known amount (19 mg) of THC, the active ingredient in marijuana. This amount of THC was rated by the investigators as "probably the equivalent of a strong social dose."

The test pilots then re-flew the profile twice, once one hour after smoking the marijuana and again three hours later. They returned the next morning, again took two practice flights, and then flew a recorded flight 24 hours after they'd smoked.

The results were startling. A day after smoking marijuana the pilots reported no feeling of being high, nor of being less alert, more anxious or more happy. They were, they felt, quite normal.

And therein lies the problem, because their performance certainly wasn't normal. On the baseline flight, they landed an average of 12 feet off the centerline of the runway. That increased to 32 feet an hour after marijuana ingestion, and was 24 feet—double the baseline measurement—a day later. One pilot landed completely off the runway on his day-after flight.

There were considerable degradations of all piloting skills right after smoking marijuana, and these persisted for 24 hours—long after the time in which a pilot perceived there was any effect from his chemical trip.

"The difficulty the subjects experienced in aligning and landing precisely at the center of the runway is a particular cause for concern," wrote the investigators. "It is important to note that the near-doubling of lateral deviation on a landing after 24 hours may be an extremely serious error." In actual flight, where there is wind and turbulence, such errors can easily lead to crashes.

"These results suggest a need for concern about the performance of those entrusted with complex behavioral and cognitive tasks within 24 hours after smoking marijuana," the researchers stated.

Even Good Old Coffee Isn't Above Suspicion

Several years back, coffee was fingered as a possible cancer-causing agent. This made many people think that any coffee, no matter how it tasted, was bad coffee; then further research indicated there really wasn't an elevated risk for most coffee drinkers. To the caffeine addicts of the world, that confirmed that good coffee was indeed good coffee.

Now it's possible that even good coffee is bad coffee, at least for those who have a familial predisposition towards high blood pressure. In a study of 34 normal young men, researchers found that for those in the study who had a family history of hypertension, the combination of caffeine and mental stress caused a significant elevation in the level of cortisol, a hormone that can lead to sodium retention and thus aggravate high blood pressure problems—especially for that subset of the population who are salt sensitive.

While cortisol levels climbed in the "at risk" group, the control group showed no such elevation, suggesting that those with a history of high blood pressure in the family may be much more likely to be caffeine reactors.

The ultimate role of coffee and/or caffeine in high blood pressure and other cardiovascular problems remains ambiguous, at best. While current evidence suggests that a cup or two a day represents no substantial increase in risk, those with additional risk factors might want to think twice about downing a dose from the hangar pot.

Pilot Error

We've been looking for years for an accident report which absolutely, totally absolves any pilot, mechanic, controller or aircraft designer of any responsibility. This may be the one: The 3,200-hour commercial pilot fired up his Piper Comanche 260 and started out onto the taxiway at California's Santa Paula Airport on July 28, 1980. He intended to practice some touch-and-goes.

He had gone no more than 50 feet when the taxiway surface gave way, dropping his nosegear into a five-foot hole. The pilot emerged uninjured, but the plane suffered an estimated $18,000 worth of damage. Apparently, recent rains and a swollen nearby creek had undermined the taxiway.

Of the more than 20,000 probable cause reports that we've reviewed over the years, that one comes closest to completely absolving the parties normally charged with causation; it's good for a chuckle, but it sheds no light on the ongoing problem of pilots being responsible for most aircraft mishaps. In most aviation accidents or incidents, the pilot is reasonably intelligent, fairly well trained, and possessed of a strong desire to do things right...nobody wants to arrive at the scene of an accident as the person in charge.

Yet strange things happen, things which can be post-mortemed to a fare-thee-well, but the fact remains that when something goes badly wrong, there's a system failure at the heart of the trouble. And the system which is most complicated and therefore most susceptible to failure is The Human.

In this section of our Human Factors volume, we'll look at a number of situations in which the human system broke down. In short, this is a look at pilot errors or pilot failure. We present them as a broad scenario of events which may help you to recognize and cope with similar occurrences in your aviation experiences.

The Failing Aviator Syndrome

"You could see it coming." Too often that's the sad-but-true pronouncement of friends and colleagues about a pilot involved in an incident. With hindsight, you could see it coming.

And with a bit of foresight, suggests a Naval doctor, it just might be possible to see it coming and know what you're seeing—in time to try and do something about it.

As every reader of _Aviation Safety_ knows, most accidents are eventually ruled "pilot error." It's the human factor, not the airplane factor, that brings too many flying machines and their contents to an untimely end.

The pilot in peril, says naval medico Victoria Voge, is the one suffering from failing aviator syndrome. It's a good term for a bad condition in which situational factors pile up to create a highly stressed individual who, absent a means of relieving the stress, falls victim to it. In the case of a pilot, the fall is too often literally just that.

In its more obvious forms, the condition takes the form of a person who has suffered a number of personal life changes—good or bad—within a relatively short period of time. It may be a divorce or other marital problem, the birth of a child, or a recent substantial career move. Whatever the cause, the effect is stress. For most people, there are sufficient outlets to relieve the stress. For the failing aviator, there aren't.

Researchers have devised a checklist of characteristics that provide early warning signs that a pilot is in failure mode. These include:

• Excessive risk taking, including excessive aggressiveness or impulsivity.

• Excessive drinking.

• False association of flying ability and a masculine image model.

• Feels above ordinary mortals—lives (and dies) by his own rules.

• Acts out the role of the "hot" pilot.

• Resents authority.

• Harbors deeply ingrained rebellion against those in authority.

• Action oriented, working out frustrations by action, not words.

• Overly sensitive to criticism of his flying ability.

• Defensive about his flying ability.

• Feels he can do no wrong (the "golden boy" syndrome).

• Difficulty with interpersonal relations.

• No sense of his own limitations.

• Recent changes in personality.

• Recent marriage or career change.

• Takes unnecessary risk, often escalating and getting closer to the edge with each repeated action.

• Strong pattern of denial; denies he's aging, mortal, or not great at everything.

• Strict moral/religious background resulting in a strong drive for independence.

Initially, the failing aviator may exhibit some of these traits some of the time. As the situation worsens, and the fall becomes more imminent, there's an acceleration. More and more items tend to appear, and the gravity of the excursions tends to grow. Sometimes there are seemingly deliberate incidents ("How could he think he was going to get away with that?") that are disguised pleas for help. If unrecognized, the aviator will continue his free fall descent.

One of the best clues to a falling aviator may be a series of flying errors from a normally-competent pilot. "If an aviator is experiencing an abnormal burst of errors," writes the naval researcher, "even in social or non-flying activities, he may be past the mishap threshold."

Because the changes involved are often gradual and subtle, those best able to detect them are those closest to the pilot—family, close friends, and those who fly with the affected person. Once detected, failing aviator syndrome needs treatment. To do otherwise exposes the pilot, and any passengers he or she might carry, to an unacceptable level of risk.

Probing for Boredom

Pilots love to fly, and one rarely thinks of keeping an airplane shiny side up as being boring. But there are those moments—sometimes hours of them—when the trim is trimmed, the throttle throttled, and the autopilot piloting. That's when boredom can set in, and the result of such mental inattention is sometimes fatal.

Ironically, the problem is much greater for those with sophisticated airplanes. While the Cessna 152 pilot is constantly busy twiddling and fiddling, the Boeing 747 commander can let George the Autopilot take a few hundred people across the country without touching a thing, should he choose. The only thing the autopilot can't presently do is figure out when the human brains of the operation have gone vacant, endangering plane, passengers, crew *and* autopilot.

In a search for ways of knowing when a person is bored, Russian researchers monitored a particular set of brainwaves seeking signs that the owner had mentally checked out. Each lucky subject was put before a computer screen on which there appeared continuous "noise" and an occasional geometric figure. The task was to find the figure when it appeared.

The researchers found that certain slow oscillations of both the brain and heart waves correlated well with the degree to which their subjects were taking care of business.

In the future it may be possible to hook the pilot to the autopilot, and the autopilot to the plane. The autopilot can then watch the pilot, along with the ailerons, and tweak either should they get out of trim.

Oops! Wrong Airport!

Landing at the wrong airport is not only the nightmare of every student pilot but the dubious achievement every year of more than a few experienced pilots—occasionally including a fly-for-pay jet captain. Not long ago, a hapless pilot searching for a small nearby airport plunked himself down in front of the media, the U.S. Air Force, the FAA and everyone else who was awaiting the unveiling of the stealth bomber at the restricted Palmdale Airport in California.

This "geographic disorientation," as it is politely referred to in the official literature, is probably the ultimate human factors failure. As one group of researchers wrote, in a rather classic understatement, landing at the wrong airport is "an unpleasant experience for aircrew members." Sometimes the explanation for such an incident is both simple and obvious: two airports, close together, with single runways oriented in the same direction. Add a pilot who's unfamiliar with the territory and it's easy to see where one can become another "Wrong-Way" Corrigan.

On the other hand, many incidents are seemingly inexplicable. How does a professional pilot take a large turbine airplane and plant it at an airport that's miles—sometimes *many* miles—from the intended destination?

Researchers at Wright State University's School of Medicine examined 75 incident reports submitted by air carrier pilots to NASA's Aviation Safety Reporting System between 1982 and 1987. They also studied 16 general aviation accidents in which pilots landed at wrong airports from 1983 to 1985.

For the air carrier pilots, the bad news is that things are getting worse, at least in terms of getting to the right airport. In 1982, five heavy iron operators found themselves displaced in space. By 1987, the roll of red faces rose to 20. Interestingly enough, there's a strong seasonal peak during the summer, with July the worst month by far for such happenings. August and September are next in line.

The air carrier people committed 83 percent of their goofs in VFR weather conditions, while another 15 percent were under "mixed" (VFR/IFR) conditions. One interesting tidbit was that daylight was prime time for such events, with 77 percent of the pilots going astray while the sun was still up. The same held true for the GA pilots who went astray and had accidents. Only four of the 16 accidents examined in this study occurred at night.

The GA data also revealed that experience is no guarantee of immunity from landing in the wrong place. Total flight times of the 16 pilots ranged from 89 to 12,000 hours. Of the 16, 11 had 300 hours or more. When it came time to sort out what really happened, the researchers found that problems fell into three categories: aircrew; operational; and environmental.

Under the aircrew rubric fell such problems as illness, emotional upset, fatigue and self-imposed stressors. These factors have a demonstrated adverse impact on pilot performance. Aircrew psychological factors included cognitive dissonance (a discrepancy between what a pilot expects and what he or she is seeing), individual judgments of navigation and orientation, and human limitations in decision making.

Operational upsets included inadequate preflight planning, improper in-flight management, incorrect in-flight decisions based on inadequate information, inadequate utilization of cockpit resources, intrusive in-flight distractions and inadequate aircrew coordination and communication.

Environmental factors, which might appear the most obvious explanation, were in fact fairly limited in number and scope. They included reduced visibility due to rain, smoke, haze, etc.; similarity of airports; and presence of confusing lights during night approaches—though, as noted earlier, night approaches were involved in relatively few incidents.

"Geographic disorientation is potentially disastrous to both airline and general aviation operations," they stated. "At the present time, incidents rather than accidents characterize airline aircraft that have landed at the wrong airport. In some of these incidents, the pilot's ability to handle a short runway landing, once committed, was the only factor that prevented an over-run accident." The general aviation pilots were not so fortunate: All of the wrong-airport mishaps involved accidents.

To avoid the embarrassment and danger of a wrong-airport landing, the researchers suggest:

• Aircrew members must be aware of the detrimental effects on overall performance of self-imposed stressors and should avoid them. Such stressors include visual fatigue, general fatigue from sleep deprivation, alcohol abuse and use of other addictive substances.

• Aircrew must be aware that emotional upsets, preoccupations and other disconcerting psychological processes interfere with pyschophysiological performance.

• Pilots should be aware that the phenomenon of cognitive dissonance may underlie geographic disorientation. This concerns the development of a mismatch between the cognitively developed "model" of the world and the actual airplane path and location in flight.

• Adequate preflight planning together with the use of all available cockpit resources (especially navigation instrumentation and flight documents) are the prime means for preventing geographic disorientation.

• Correct identification of the airport in sight prior to initiating a visual approach is a major priority.

• Approaches under visual meteorological conditions should be cross-checked by appropriate navigation instruments until a definite identification of the airport in view has been made.

UNBELIEVABLE TALENT

A casual look at the 18-year-old student pilot only a few months before his accident would give the impression that the young man had it made. He was a member of his high school varsity basketball team and was described by friends as popular. A reputed expert with radio-controlled aircraft, the youngster had recently begun taking flying lessons in his grandfather's Piper Super Cub.

He earned his sign-off to fly solo after 14 hours of instruction. But his CFI was not always available when he desired dual instruction and, clearly impatient to progress in his new avocation, he had engaged a new instructor. After a few hours of dual, the new instructor described the student as methodical and as having good skills for his experience level.

On the surface, it would have appeared the student pilot had a lot going for him. But a closer examination would have revealed a young man who was very troubled—and heading for trouble. One acquaintance would later describe him as "a kid who had everything, loved to show off and was good at it." Another would say he "bottled his emotions and would occasionally explode."

PROPHECY

Perhaps the most disturbing clues to the student's inner turmoil were contained in a letter he wrote to a former girlfriend, in which he disclosed that his relationships with family and friends had deteriorated. He had quit the basketball team.

He also wrote in length about flying, professing an "unbelievable talent for flying" and an affinity for "being close to death only in airplanes." He said that he had taken a friend flying even though he knew it was illegal to do so. It was quite a flight. The student pilot claimed to have flown only three feet over a lake bed at full throttle and to have performed spins and hammerheads. Recovery from one of the hammerheads had been especially harrowing: "When I went to pull out, we were going about 150 mph and with one hand I could not pull us out. It took both hands." He said it was "the most fun thing I have ever done in my life" and wondered "why I did not die that day."

After relating his flight experiences, the student wrote, "I feel you should know this so in case anything ever happens, you will understand." It was prophetic. A month after writing the letter, the young man died, alone, in his grandfather's Super Cub.

The accident occurred in Brighton, Colorado, shortly after nightfall. Witnesses had seen the Super Cub repeatedly buzz the high school and an open, snow-covered field near the school. But descriptions of the accident by two eyewitnesses varied substantially. One witness, a commercial pilot, was in his home when he was distracted by the sound of the low-flying aircraft. He recalled seeing the Super Cub climb nearly straight up to about 500 feet and begin turning. He then lost sight of the aircraft.

POWER DIVE

Another witness, an eye doctor who was walking his dog at the time, said the Cub skimmed an open field at an altitude of about five feet before beginning a circling climb that lasted about seven minutes. He estimated that the aircraft reached 10,000 feet before entering a power dive.

"I watched as it came down, because it was really gaining tremendous speed," he said. "You could hear the engine, and it sounded to me like it was at full tilt." The witness said at no time did it appear that the aircraft attempted to recover from the dive.

Investigators determined that the Super Cub hit the frozen field in a near-vertical, nose-down attitude. Though the statements of the second witness might lead one to suspect a suicide, NTSB decided the evidence shows the student pilot most likely lost control of the Super Cub while performing an aerobatic maneuver at high altitude and then was unable to regain control of the aircraft during the descent.

The Board determined that aerobatics and improper use of flight controls were the probable causes, with overconfidence and lack of experience as contributing factors.

Deja Do, or Didn't Ja?

With great regularity, accident reports show discrepancies between what the pilot says happened and the tales the ground observers, passengers and physical evidence have to tell. In some cases it's a fairly transparent attempt on the part of a pilot to cover a goof. In other cases, though, the pilot really is convinced he or she switched tanks, or called for a clearance, or put the gear down.

The twilight zone between reality and fantasy can be quite substantial, and learning a bit about it may help everyone separate more clearly what really happened from what someone thinks happened when there's an incident. With that in mind, a Canadian researcher went in search of what people think they did.

She subjected a group of people to five experiments designed to see how well they could separate what they had really done from what they thought they might have done. One of the tests, for example, involved showing people a drawing and having them either just look at it, trace it or imagine tracing it. After 15 minutes they were tested on their ability to recognize the item and tell whether they had looked at it, traced it or imagined tracing it.

One of the most interesting findings to emerge was that there's a strong tendency for people to adopt the "I'd know it if I did it" theory. The problem is, they often didn't know it when they'd done it.

"Memories of doing are readily confused with memories of imagining doing," writes investigator Rita Anderson. "The present experiments and those on reality monitoring have shown that memories of simple actions and those of perceptions are easily confused with memories of imaginal actions and those of thoughts.

"The ability to use the mind as a mental laboratory, where plans and actions can be contemplated without the expenditure of physical effort, is an important human asset. For this mental laboratory to be maximally useful, imagined actions and thoughts must be memorable, and those memories must be discriminable from memories of overt actions and those of perceptions."

The mental playground is vast, and apparently so realistic that we can't always distinguish well between games played there and those played in the real world. The pilot who has put the same gear down on the same plane one hundred times, both in reality and in imagination, is quite certain he did it on the hundred and first time. Perhaps. But it could also have all been in his mind, though that will seem quite real.

Unsterile Cockpit

There's a rule in FAR 121 that requires airline pilots to concentrate on the safe operation of their aircraft during critical phases of flight. In the vernacular, it's called the "sterile cockpit" and it means no idle chitchat, company paperwork or other extraneous endeavors are allowed during taxi, takeoff and landing or in other than cruise flight below 10,000 feet.

Of course, with two or three pilots in the cockpit, there has to be some way of ensuring that everyone is minding the store when they're supposed to be. Until recently, captains were left pretty much alone to run their cockpits as they saw fit. Now, most airlines train their pilots in the techniques of cockpit resource management. Essentially, CRM defines the responsibilities of each flight crew member and provides a framework for working together as an effective team.

A couple of years ago, Delta Air Lines was in the process of setting up CRM training for its pilots when one of its Boeing 727s crashed on takeoff from Dallas-Fort Worth International Airport. According to NTSB, the flight crew had not deployed the flaps and slats properly for takeoff. The Board concluded that the oversight was caused, in part, by failure of the captain and first officer to mind the store while awaiting their departure clearance. A backup system, which should have warned the pilots about the oversight, also didn't do its job.

THE CAPTAIN'S LEG

The first officer (FO) had flown the first leg, a red-eye to DFW from Jackson, Mississippi. The 36-year-old, 6,500-hour pilot had been with Delta for 10 years and had upgraded from flight engineer to FO nine months earlier. The captain, who had 17,000 hours and nine years' experience in the left seats of 727s, would fly the next leg to Salt Lake City. It was a nice morning, with clear weather and calm winds.

The aircraft was pushed back from its gate at 8:30 a.m. and the taxi checklist was begun, with the flight engineer (FE) calling out the checklist items and the FO responding. They didn't complete the checklist, however. They paused after being informed by ATC of a departure delay, and shut down the number three engine to help conserve fuel during the wait.

According to the NTSB, the cockpit voice recorder picked up several nonpertinent conversations, including an extended chat between the FO and a flight attendant, during the 20 minutes it took the 727 to taxi out to DFW's Runway 18L. The number three engine was restarted when the 727 was fourth in line for takeoff, and the FE, a recent-hire with an ATP and 3,000 hours, resumed the taxi checklist.

With takeoff weight computed at 157,683 pounds, the

crew planned to use 15 degrees of flap and reduced thrust for takeoff from the 11,400-foot runway. Though the cockpit voice recorder picked up the FE's challenge of "flaps" and the FO's correct response of "15, 15, green light" (which should have come from reading needle positions in the inboard and outboard flap-position indicators and noting illumination of the leading-edge flaps and slats annunciator), the NTSB concluded that the flaps were not extended.

ROTE RECITAL

The Board said the voice tape indicates the pilots hurried to complete the taxi checklist. "The time between the checklist challenges and responses was less than one second, with little time to accomplish actions required to satisfy the proper response." The Board believes the FO may not actually have checked the flap indicators carefully. "It is very easy for crew members to fall in a habit of reciting checklist challenge and response items by rote and providing a response to a challenge on the basis of what should be the proper response rather than the actual condition of the system that was queried," it said.

The 727 accelerated normally to its rotation speed of 131 knots, but lifted off the runway at 158 knots and a 10-degree pitch attitude—14 knots and 1.4 degrees higher than normal. The tail skid struck the runway, and the aircraft rolled to the right, hitting the runway with its wing tip.

The aircraft gained only 20 feet of altitude before colliding with an ILS localizer antenna array, sliding about a quarter mile over the ground, jumping a ditch and erupting in flames. Twelve passengers and two flight attendants were killed; 21 passengers, the captain, FO and two other flight attendants were seriously injured. The FE and 49 passengers escaped with minor injuries.

The flap selector handle—which controls the inboard and outboard trailing-edge flaps as well as the three inboard leading-edge flaps and four outboard leading-edge slats on both wings—was found in its zero detent. Tests revealed that the takeoff warning system, which is supposed to activate when thrust is advanced and the outboard trailing-edge flaps are extended less than five degrees, was malfunctioning.

It is ironic that a similar accident had occurred a year

earlier, when a Northwest Airlines DC-9 crashed on takeoff from Detroit. The flaps and slats had not been extended, and an electrical malfunction had disabled the takeoff warning system. The FAA issued a bulletin directing its inspectors to check these systems, but the bulletin did not reach the field office responsible for Delta Air Lines until the day before the 727 crashed at DFW.

INADEQUATE DISCIPLINE

The captain's and FO's failure to maintain a sterile cockpit before takeoff, which resulted in their attempt to take off without the flaps and slats properly configured, and failure of the takeoff warning system to alert the crew of the improper configuration were the probable causes of the accident, the NTSB concluded.

The Board noted, however, that even with a clean wing the 727 might not have hit the ground if maximum thrust had been applied and the nose lowered. Increasing power from 34,500 to 43,000 pounds of thrust and decreasing the angle of attack would have allowed the aircraft to gain 20 knots of airspeed and over 200 feet of altitude, according to the NTSB.

Dumb Stunts: A Veteran Test Pilot Confesses

No matter how you cook it, airplanes can be dangerous. They don't have to be. Look at the safety record of the major airlines, and of the big corporate flight operations. Those are the safest ways to travel. The most dangerous portion of an airline trip is the drive to the airport.

You can't really make a sweeping statement that "General Aviation isn't safe." The corporate operations fall under GA. And lots of the 135 operations carrying people or cargo also fall under GA. The break seems to come between "professional pilots" and "non-professionals." The professionals, even though often lighter on total years and flight hours than many of the "amateurs," have an overall better safety record.

There's a connection in here somewhere, between "professionalism" and "amateurism." There are too many private, commercial and ATP pilots out there without the professionalism needed to conduct repetitive safe flights. We may have the pilot's license of an airline driver, but based on some of the goofy crashes that happen, lots of us are less proficient, and display worse judgment than a student pilot who's halfway to the private ticket!

In l950, I did what I would call my first real dumb stunt. I was going to pick up my mother. I had flown, in December in my Cessna 140, from Maryland to Pittsburgh, then on to Buffalo via Erie. Just short of Buffalo, and contrary to the weather briefing in Pennsylvania, snow started to fall. I could have landed right then (there were several airports nearby) or I could have returned to Erie. I didn't—I continued. The snow got heavier. The little Cessna I was flying started to ice. The ceiling and visibility went to zero, and the indicated airspeed went to zero when the pitot iced-over.

The mechanic who had helped me install a turn needle, venturi tube, and rate-of-climb gauge had explained how to use the gauges to recover from an unusual attitude. And, now I had to recover from one! I did, just in time to intercept a leg of the Buffalo LF radio range that led to the airport.

The tower operator put down his comic book when he saw me taxiing in to the FBO (the field had been closed, due to low weather). He had not seen me in time to flash a green light because I hadn't seen the airport until over the end of the runway. Now this was long before today's strict enforcement, and it wasn't even mandatory to have a two-way radio. I was summoned to the tower via a phone call to the FBO. The tower supervisor listened to my story—he had forgotten to put out a "special" weather advisory on the LF range frequency when the weather went sour. He let me off with these words of wisdom: "Son, when the weather ahead looks bad, why not turn around, or land where you are? Don't push ahead into worsening weather. You are up there where the weather is, you don't need me on the radio to tell you that conditions are too bad for you to come to this big airport."

The end result was a long lecture, and an hour of filling out Government papers. Then a hard slap on the wrist, and a final warning to "get an instrument rating, and put a receiver and transmitter in that little bird before you come back here again!" Then he tore up the prospective flight violation!

Boy, did I learn a lesson. I've been a wimp when it comes to bad weather ever since that episode. I don't fly when the weather isn't good enough for me—no matter how low the published minimums may go. I still remember that tall Buffalo radio station antenna going by my wingtip as I recovered from the partial-panel unusual attitude, just before latching onto the final approach course. I still recall the iced windshield and tiny hole that cabin heat had made at the bottom of the Plexiglas. I still wonder why anyone would even consider "partial panel" as an acceptable means of shooting an instrument approach to minimums. Every few years this episode returns to me as a nightmare.

And, nowadays, I wonder why the FAA thinks that big fines and loss-of-license can substitute for knowing. That guy at Buffalo really helped me, and set me straight for many more years. It could be that I'm still alive today, while many friends have perished, just because of an FAA employee's understanding.

Of course, Mother thought that I was "Ace Of The Base" for getting into Buffalo when even the airlines weren't flying. So she rode with me back to Pittsburgh. And nowadays she won't ride on the airlines because she watches television news religiously, and has been scared by the coverage of airline crashes—like the recent DC-10 crash at Sioux City, Iowa, after No. 2 engine blew up and ruined all of the control hydraulic systems.

But Mom doesn't look at the statistics. She would be safer aboard NorthWest or United, from Spokane to Tampa, than she would be on the automobile trip to or from either airline's terminal.

Unfortunately, she would not be as safe riding in the average GA airplane for that long cross-country trip. And it's not because the little airplane isn't capable of the trip, but mostly because the average GA pilot isn't anywhere near as safe as the average airline crew. Those guys train! They follow the rules! And, with a few rare exceptions, they don't do dumb things!

But I know many pilots who "bit the dust" because of something stupid. I remember one pilot who had built an award-winning acrobatic biplane. He was an outstanding pilot, mechanic, and homebuilder. He had all of the licenses, including ATP and had won awards with his acro biplane. But, he stalled out of a loop at very low altitude, with his wife aboard, while putting on a show for friends.

Or, a pair of company test pilots I used to work with. They were just doing a routine test flight on a Navajo. Routine, except that the left engine had been shutdown and feathered, and would not restart at the end of the tests. Nobody knows for sure what happened, except that they tried a single-engine landing approach, lowered the gear on base leg, then decided to go around. During the go-around the nose gear was observed to be in a trail position, and the main gear appeared to be down. Also, during the go-around, the left prop was ticking over very slowly, as though being driven by the starter motor.

With the gear mostly down, one engine dead, and the airplane losing altitude slowly, they made it almost five miles in the gentle descent before they hit pine trees and a power line.

What a way to go! They both knew that a Navajo, or any other recip twin could not fly on one engine with the gear down. Why not land with an "unsafe" on the gear lights? Why go around?

Test flying or not, this accident scenario just keeps happening on "routine" twin-engine emergency landings. The rules are simple enough: Set up a good approach, don't extend the gear until the landing is assured, don't attempt a go-around once the gear is down, or if you are below about 500 feet. Go ahead and land even if the gear does not show three green lights. Don't count on the gear retracting if you try a single-engine go-around.

Another fellow test pilot bought the farm one day doing Vmc tests at low altitude—too low an altitude for safety, even for a test pilot. Nobody, not even a company test pilot, should be doing Vmc tests way down low. How many of you have been guilty of performing "engine-out" training maneuvers way too low?

How many of us, just plain old pilots, or maybe CFI's with a student, have been guilty of slow-flight and "imminent" stall maneuvers below a safe spin recovery altitude? Do you like taking chances? Do you really think you can beat the odds?

Do you really perform a complete check of control surface movement as part of every pre-takeoff check? Another pair of test pilots didn't. They died in a flaming crash right after lift-off. The ailerons on their airplane, which was making its first flight out of the factory, were rigged backwards. These were highly experienced pilots—test pilots—but they apparently skipped an essential check. Their big recip twin lifted-off, rolled left, rolled right, then rolled left again right into the turf.

Can't happen to you, you say? What about that annual inspection where they had to replace some control cables? Did the mechanics really install the new cables correctly? How about that leftover sheet metal screw that's been rattling around under the floorboards for years? Is today the day that it'll work its way into an elevator cable pulley bracket, and lock-up all pitch control?

About five years ago I was riding copilot on a Twin Otter, following major overhaul. All pre-takeoff checks were normal, and we had checked control surface movements during the preflight inspection. We checked the trimtab movement also.

Takeoff went normally, but it needed some nose-down trim right after liftoff. But, nose down on the trim wheel made the nose come up more! The PIC was sharp—he quit trying right here. He landed immediately, straight ahead, while there was still runway remaining.

Post-flight analysis showed the trim travels were normal, but backwards! The new trim cables had been wound backwards on the elevator trim tab drum. We had checked for tab travel, but didn't check for proper direction of travel! We could blame it on dumb mechanics, maybe, but I think it was more to blame on even dumber pilots—me included.

This bit of control/trim travels doesn't just apply after picking up a factory-new airplane, or just after annual check. Suppose a lineboy installed a control-lock batten during a windstorm. Have you really checked that all controls move normally—not just the control wheel—but the ailerons, elevators, and, if you can see it, the rudder? The FAA lost one of their own airplanes several years ago when the pilot attempted takeoff with external control locks installed.

While we are at it on preflight checks—do you really check for water in the fuel system? There have been a lot of crashes recently from apparent contaminated fuel. That one little slug of water can ruin your whole flight. Sure, the preflight fuel-drain procedure may be tedious, and may ruin a lot of macadam or grass—but if you don't drain it, and check it, you might get a big surprise just after liftoff. Water in the gas will kill an injected engine just as surely as it will a carbureted engine! It will kill a turbine-type engine even quicker. If you habitually tie-down outside, or if you even park outside for one night, and it rains, figure on having water. Check it out!

Another area ripe for accidents is the unnecessary maneuver. For example, a long time ago, a Navy squadron-mate went off the starboard catapult on a left-over WWII carrier. I was sitting on the port catapult. He made an immediate right turn, to clear the bow of the ship so that I could launch into clear air. The turn was a little too tight. He stalled and splashed in. That loaded Cougar made like an aluminum submarine, and went right under.

He didn't really have to turn so soon and so tight. But, you know, I still see that kind of post-takeoff turn at the local airport. I've seen it done by everything from Cessna 150s to King Airs. What's the hurry? Get some altitude and airspeed before you try to maneuver.

And then there are the plain dumb stunts. Another military pilot I knew was the best of a group of new trainees reporting into a fighter squadron. He had completed his transition training into the Grumman F-11F "Tiger," a supersonic, afterburner-equipped hotrock. Even the instructor pilots were envious of his gunnery scores.

But, on the sly—without telling anyone, including his squadron commander—he purchased a used 85-horsepower racer. It was a slick little machine; fast as heck and with tiny wings. He almost did a loop in that thing one day, starting just a little above the local grass airport's runway. Witnesses described his loop as real tight going up and over the top, but he picked up a lot of speed coming straight down. It looked like he was going to make it. The nose kept coming up, but the airplane kept coming down. He almost completed the pullout.

Now he was a professional jet fighter pilot, but not a professional low-level, competition/airshow aerobatic pilot. That fatal episode caused a local Navy directive to be issued, restricting all of us from similar dumb stunts in civilian airplanes. But the point is that pilots should not need a government directive, Navy or FAA, to keep them away from dumb stunts.

Weather encounters also produce more than their share of dumb stunts. If you aren't the equivalent of a "professional" instrument pilot, then don't play games like flying an ILS approach to minimums. Boy, I still see a lot of that "amateur" weather flying these days at the local Podunk air terminal. We can hear the airplane noise up there in the early morning fog, but we can't identify the airplane until it taxies to the ramp. Some might say, "That's George, and he knows this area like the back of his hand. He can shoot the 12-mile VOR/DME approach just like it was an ILS." He can crash just like anyone else, too.

Another thing I see a lot of is pilots flying equipment that's not up to snuff. Some pilots keep flying airplanes that have potentially serious problems. How many times in the last year have you refused to fly a particular airplane—your own bird, or a rented one? When's the last time you taxied back to the maintenance hangar, before or after a flight, and informed the head mechanic that, "This airplane is grounded until you fix the problem?"

Sometimes even seemingly major items that could be caught go unnoticed. Like the pro pilot who caught a broken horizontal stabilizer spar during preflight inspection—it had been broken for a long time, and lots of other pilots had missed the discrepancy on the small rental airplane. Loads of other pilots and passengers had come real close to losing at the aviation roulette wheel.

I see things like the three guys in an Arrow who departed one night for a local flight. They were on night shift, and didn't bother to check the forecast. They got caught in pre-dawn fog—which had been predicted! With no instrument rating and no approach plates, they crash on the third attempt to make a visual night landing. Lots of other nearby airports were in the clear, including two with radar approach control. There's just no excuse for things like this.

As a finale, another personal incident. This one was close—I probably came within a couple of seconds of dying due to inattention. You gotta pay attention to what is important. Especially in the traffic pattern. My own "down-low/inattention" incident occurred in a military jet, at the end of a test flight. The test article was a new automatic throttle, and it wasn't responding on base leg. I put my head in the cockpit, resetting several circuit breakers, and checking a few gauges—on base leg, about to turn final. That was dumb! When I raised my head, the little Skyhawk was in at least a 45-degree bank, with the nose way down. This was a low-altitude unusual attitude, and I was only about 200 feet above the terrain! This has become another recurring nightmare for me.

But I see variations on this theme frequently, flying as passenger, or as CFI on a BFR. Things like landing check lists that are not completed on the downwind leg, prior to turning base. Or putting the gear down on base leg, when the pilot really is too busy (or should be busy flying the approach) to monitor that the gear really goes all the way down. Or messing with cowl flaps, fuel pumps, tank selector, seat belts, etc., on base leg.

To me, this is incredible. Complete that check list on the downwind leg, saving maybe the final flap setting. Anything else that's not completed and checked by the 180 degree position is plenty of reason to go around.

As near as I can see, dumb stunts are the meat of amateur GA's accident record. Please don't contribute any more dumb stunts to my already long list.

All's Not Automatic That's Automated

When NASA spoiled a military laser ray demonstration by lofting the wrong numbers to the Space Shuttle recently, critics were quick to question whether anything so complex as the Star Wars scheme could ever be made to fly in the real world.

The NASA wrong number incident was just one of many that have made automated flight seem less than ideal. In recent memory a Boeing 767 ran out of fuel because of errors laid to having metric rather than decimal measures on the gauges; another 767 had its engines put in idle by an overzealous computer; a DC-9 had double engine failure when the center-tank pumps weren't turned on after takeoff; and famed and ill-fated KAL Flight 007 wandered disastrously far off course due to what most analysts agree was probably an error in keyboard entry of navigational data.

All this has set task forces and study groups to work, trying to decide what's right and what's wrong with automation. And perhaps most important, they're trying to figure out where the good old-fashioned pilot fits in. As automation inevitably filters down from the heavy metal to the typical GA people-puller, the question becomes a personal and a vexing one. Like little children, when automation is good, it's very, very good. But when it's bad...

In a recent review of cockpit automation, an expert cites as flawed the widely accepted view that the role of the pilot is to be the observant den mother of a gaggle of automated instruments and controls. In this traditional scenario, the pilot sits quietly monitoring the flying instead of doing it. And there, says University of Miami professor Earl Wiener, is the problem.

"Clearly something is amiss," he writes. "The computer-based devices, which were supposed to eliminate human error, reduce workload, and simplify cockpit operations, have generally lived up to these expectations, but, almost as if exercising some perverse ingenuity of their own, they have created a host of new problems."

The problem, he notes, is that "humans are not reliable monitors. In the view of many, automation has taken the crews out of the loop to the extent that they may be unable to perform the supervisory and monitoring duties that we relegate to them."

Before the computers come marching in and we all succumb to their siren song, says Wiener, "A considerable dose of caution is recommended."

Flying into the Ground

If safety experts could find out why perfectly good pilots fly perfectly good airplanes into the ground, one of the great human factors mysteries of aviation would be solved.

The crashes in question are not cases of people spinning airplanes, or pulling the wings off, or otherwise losing control. What's at issue here are what the researchers call "controlled flight into terrain," or CFIT. It's a pilot coolly, calmly and carefully flying the machinery into an encounter of an unpleasant kind with very hard and very unforgiving ground.

In a search for some answers, researchers turned to the Aviation Safety Reporting System database, maintained by NASA. They found 258 reports of incidents where "except for an intervention, or by chance, the aircraft would have come in contact with terrain, bodies of water, or obstacles such as towers, tanks, smokestacks or buildings," or "situations which are believed to be conducive to an aircraft inadvertently coming into contact with terrain, bodies of water, or obstacles."

The 258 reports broke down as follows:

1. Problems arising from flight crew errors involving navigation, altitude control, or aircraft configuration—43 (16.6 percent);

2. Inappropriate ATC vectors or clearances, or ATC deviation from standard procedures—83 (32.2 percent);

3. Misinterpretation of charted altitude restrictions, loss of communications procedures, configuration of airspace—27 (10.5 percent);

4. Unlighted or unmarked towers, tanks, etc., or obstacles ineffectively lighted or marked—24 (9.3 percent);

5. Inadequate or unreliable navaids—52 (20.2 percent);

6. False or presumed inappropriate activation of Ground Proximity Warning System or Minimum Safe Altitude Warning devices—29 (11.2 percent).

Of the 43 flight crew error incidents, 30 were attributed to air carrier operations, 13 to general aviation. Of the general aviation encounters, a third were altitude errors on non-precision approaches, 25 percent were lateral deviations on approach, and another quarter were unsafe altitude while in VFR conditions. The rest were assorted problems including one rather spectacular IFR altitude bust of 24,000 feet!

The controller error category involved 36 general aviation incidents. A surprisingly large number (21 of the 36) were clearances below the minimum legal altitude, and most were reported by the controllers involved. Four more were the rather chilling "neglected while on radar vector" sort, which can rapidly become fatal in the vicinity of high terrain. The remaining categories involve less human factors, such as poor charting, bum navaids, etc.

When all the numbers are added up, it comes out to a lot of people in a lot of trouble. When the researchers took a close look, they found that human error produced 64 percent of the incidents. "A few of these produced errors which can only be described as blunders. In two

[this] set, the blunders prevailed despite the presence of other crew members and the clearance read-back to a controller.

"Human error," they conclude, "is the single greatest identifiable cause of CFIT incidents." Approximately two-thirds of the human errors in the study were attributed to controllers, principally radar vectoring below the minimum vectoring altitude.

The nature of the database, which involves voluntary reporting of incidents, is such that no valid conclusion can be drawn about the proportion of controller versus pilot errors in the real world. There is a strong incentive for controllers to report their errors via the Aviation Safety Reporting System, since it can protect their jobs if they are officially cited for the incident, so controller reports may be vastly over-represented in the database.

Unfortunately, there emerged no dominant pattern in pilot errors which might provide a key to understanding why people make the mistakes they do. "Errors by pilots were much more diverse," the researchers point out, suggesting that there is no one easy answer to the question of why people fly into the ground.

Nor is there one cure, other than increased vigilance, enhanced prevention efforts, and improved redundancy of both systems and procedures within the systems.

Index

age
    and heat shedding 47
    and mental abilities 44
    and regulations 43
    and visual capabilities 46
    relation to accident causes 43
alcohol
    accident statistics 100
    and disorientation 181
    and hypoxia 144
    effect on inner ear 181
    effect on judgment 181
    effects of, IFR 175
    effects on older pilots 45
    pilot attitude 184
    pilot impairment 179, 180
        effect of hangover 185
        effect of pilot experience
        182
allergy medications 195
altitude sickness 148
aspirin 187, 192
automation 215, 216

balance, sense of 155
Barany chair 160, 161
black hole 162
blood alcohol content 173, 175, 176
boredom
    and pilot failure 200
breathing
    effect of rate 145
    mechanics of 142
    rate 142

carbon dioxide
    and hypoxia 145
carbon monoxide
    and hypoxia 144
    as result of smoking 151
    from exhaust system 152

circadian rhythm 125
coffee
    and high blood pressure 197
    and pilot impairment 197
cognitive dissonance 202, 203
communications
    under stress 110
cones 48, 49, 51
contraceptive drugs 187, 188, 137

Daily Hassles Scale 109
day vision 49
drugs
    allergy medications 190
    and high blood pressure 188
    and seizures 187
    defined by FDA 189
    determining side effects 194
    effect on hearing 186
    effect on inner ear 192
    female considerations 187, 194
    prescription medications 186

ear block 84
ear plug
    and pilot stress 91
    comfort considerations 93
    custom fitting 94
    foam 95
    for children 83
    function 83
    molded 94
    Noise Reduction Rating 85
    selection 92
ear set 92
    comfort considerations 93
    one-side-only model 93
    shortcomings 94
eye movement research 76

failing aviator syndrome 199

fatigue
    air traffic controllers 134
    effect of altitude 137, 140
    effect of dehydration 137
    effect of stress 128
    long-term effects 127
    preventive measures 138
    recognition of 126
    symptoms 126
    two-pilot crews 131
fixation
    as result of fatigue 126

Hazardous Thought Patterns
    (HTPs) 27
headset
    comfort considerations 93
    for children 83
    noise attenuation 93
    Noise Reduction Rating 85
    one-side-only model 93
    proper adjustment 82, 93
    selection 92, 93
hearing loss 80, 86, 87, 89
    as occupational disease 84
    aviators' exposure to 85
    causes of 87
    cumulative nature of 85
    restoration techniques 100
    temporary 88, 99
hearing protection 80, 82, 85, 91-
    93, 96
hyperventilation
    sensitivity self-test 146
    symptoms 146
    symptoms similar to hypoxia
        146
hypoxia
    acclimatization 153
    and euphoria 153
    effect of smoking 151
    effect on night vision 145
    emergency procedures 150
    symptoms of 144, 151
    time of useful consciousness
        (TUC) 150

illusions
    and inner ear 156
    and instrument flying 154
    distance error 163
    effect of fatigue 169
    optical 155
    related to aircraft attitude 155
    related to fatigue, hypoxia 155
    related to speed 154, 158
    somatogyral (cause of motion
        sickness) 170
    suppression of 156
IM-SAFE 34
inner ear 156, 158
    and medical problems 165
    and motion sickness 170
    and turning flight 154
    mechanism of 155, 158
interpersonal relations
    and stress 109

judgment 8, 18, 21, 24, 28, 32, 34
    effect of attitude 33
    teaching 27

landing at wrong airport 201
Life Change Units 109

marijuana
    pilot impairment 196
Meniere's Disease 164
microphone
    dynamic 82, 93
    noise-canceling 82, 93
    procedure 82
motion sickness 169-171
    and earplugs 171
    preventive medication 170

night vision 49
    and carbon monoxide 54
    and cockpit design 58
    and exposure to sunlight 67
    and smoking 55
    and sunglasses 73
    and Vitamin A 50

night vision *(cont.)*
    autokinetic movement 50
    dark adaption 49
    effect of carbon monoxide 50
    effect of hypoxia 50
    effect of smoking 50
noise
    and accidents 96
    and communications 81
    and fatigue 90, 95
    and hearing impairment 79
    and high blood pressure 90
    and pilot fatigue 90
    and stress 90-91
    effect of long-term exposure 87
    effect of pure tones 80
    in cockpit 85, 90, 93, 97
    sources of 78
noise attenuation 92-93
noise level
    and microphone procedure 82
    in cockpit 80, 85-86, 88
noise protection
    for children 83
Noise Reduction Rating 85
nystagmus 141

oxygen
    and air pressure 143
    and breathing 142
    blood saturation 143
    FAA Regulations 148
    supplemental, equipment 149
    supplemental, limitations 143
    supplemental, use of 143

peer pressure 8, 18
perception (effect of fatigue) 139
pilot attitude 8, 30, 33
    and HTP 27
    and pilot experience 29
    effect on judgment 33
pilot error 27, 199, 218
    and judgment 111
    effect of stress 106, 107, 110-111

pilot failure 199-200, 207, 209
    early warning signs 199

REM (rapid eye movement) sleep
        135-137
    effect of alcohol and drugs 135
retina 48-49, 51, 66
    damage 67
rods 48-49

self-image 8
semicircular canals 157, 159
sleep
    habits 125, 129
    patterns 129, 131, 134-135
    proper amount 128-129, 133,
        136
    quality 135
sleep deprivation 122, 129, 133,
        136, 140-141
SNR (signal-to-noise ratio) 82-83
Social Readjustment Rating Scale
        109
spatial disorientation 154, 157,
        159, 165-169
    accident statistics 157
    demonstration and training 161
sterile cockpit 206, 209
stress 106, 109
    and speech recognition error
        111
    coping mechanisms 107, 109
    measuring effect of 109-110
    prevention, cure 121
    self-imposed, types 203
    sources of 199
sun screens 188, 193
sunglasses 50, 65-66
    and cataracts 67
    and night vision 72
    lens color, density 70
    polarized lenses 68-69
    selection of 69, 71, 73-75

time zones
    effect on fatigue 130-131

tinnitus 86-87, 89, 98
   control of 97
   reduction of 97-98
   use of maskers 90
transient ischemic attack (TIA)
   147

vertigo 156-161
   and medical problems 165
Vertigon 161

vision degradation (with age) 46
visual cues
   lack of, confusing 158, 160, 162
vitamins 188, 192

white noise 98
workload
   and pilot error 118
   individual threshold 121
   measuring 112